Toys From The Tales of Beatrix Potter

Toys From The Tales Of
BEATRIX POTTER

Margaret Hutchings

with sections on the baskets by

Eve Legg

and

the furniture and accessories by

Richard Hutchings

photography by

Eve Legg

Mills & Boon Ltd London

First published in Great Britain 1973 by
Mills & Boon Limited
17–19 Foley Street, London W1A 1DR

© Margaret Hutchings 1973
Reprinted 1975
Reprinted 1977
Reprinted 1979

Published in U.S.A. by F. Warne & Co. Inc.
Reprinted in F. Warne and Book Club editions 1974

ISBN 0 263 06102 7

Printed in Great Britain
by Thomson Litho Ltd., East Kilbride, Scotland.
and bound by
Hunter & Foulis Ltd., Edinburgh, Scotland.

Dedication

One of the best things about the preparation of this book has been the many opportunities it has given me to renew and enrich old and valued friendships and to make new ones.

I therefore dedicate it with affection and gratitude to all those who came forward to help me in so many different ways by lending me their own particular skill and talents.

To Eve Legg for supplying the section on Beatrix Potter's enchanting baskets and for spending her precious holiday crawling round the fields and woods surrounding my home in order to take the superb photographs which appear on these pages. They are *just* what I wanted!

To Richard, my eldest son, for immediately agreeing (in spite of many other commitments) to design the furniture and accessories for Part 3.

To Florence Dansey for working out the crochet designs (I can't crochet!).

To Valerie Duthoit for coming to the rescue!

To Eve Tenison Mosse and Gladys Haydon for trying out the patterns by making up duplicate toys.

To Kitty Burton for fetching and carrying and to Kathleen Lawson for so often cheering from the sidelines!

To Malvie for just being herself and for freeing me by doing the chores.

To Anne Wallis who typed and who cancelled an appointment with her doctor because it all made her feel so much better!

To my publishers for taking me back into the fold after such a long, albeit unavoidable, absence, and to my husband for putting up with it all.

Finally to Frederick Warne & Co. who have kindly permitted the use of the Beatrix Potter books, as well as being extremely friendly and helpful throughout the project.

Thank you all so *very* much.

Margaret Hutchings
South Weald
June 1972

Contents

PART THREE THE FURNITURE AND ACCESSORIES

Foreword

In this book Margaret Hutchings is following in the footsteps of Beatrix Potter, who soon after the publication of *The Tale of Peter Rabbit*, made a Peter Rabbit doll for one of the Warne children. 'I am cutting out calico patterns of Peter,' she told Norman Warne. 'I have not got it right yet, but the expression is going to be lovely, especially the whiskers (pulled out of a brush!).'

In her latest book Margaret Hutchings, by providing the necessary instructions and diagrams, is now making it possible for anyone who wishes, to make models of many of the favourite Beatrix Potter characters—and very delightful they are when finished as I have seen for myself.

Instructions and diagrams are also given for making some of the accessories such as Mrs. Tiggy-winkle's basket, Hunca Munca's cradle, and the coppy stools of Pigling Bland and Pig-wig.

Included in the book are a number of very attractive colour photographs showing how the various characters will look if placed in their natural settings.

Much care and thought has gone into the preparation of this book, which should provide interest and pleasure to all lovers of Beatrix Potter who find joy in creative work.

LESLIE LINDER

Author's Note

I first met the Beatrix Potter characters when five years old and through a haze of ether.

Having lost my appendix (on the kitchen table, for some reason best known to my parents!) I woke up to find 'a shape' that I took to be a nurse bending over me. This 'shape' told me at once that her name was Alexander, that mine was Pigling Bland and that she had a little book all about the two of us which she would read to me when I felt better. 'Alexander' and I corresponded for the rest of her life and the last we heard of her was that 'Alexander regrets she is too old and too stiff to come to Pigling Bland's wedding'!

That was the beginning and ever since, the 'Potter People', their furniture and accessories seem to have played a very large part in my life. 'Alexander' told me that when she first walked into our kitchen, to inspect *the* table (so exactly like the one Mrs. Tiggy-winkle used for ironing) she felt she had walked into that 'very stout, short person's' own kitchen. There it all was, black-leaded range, shining steel fender, flat irons, clothes-horse, rag rug, flagstones, hams hanging from the ceiling and all!

As a little girl I went visiting with my grandmother who carried a special cake or a pot of jam in Cousin Ribby's very own basket. I sat on Pig-wig's chair, drank from the pink-edged cups in *The Tailor of Gloucester* and played in Mr. McGregor's garden—or so it seemed, for so similar were all our belongings and surroundings.

Our cats were called Moppet and Mittens, our pigs Spot and Stumpy, our rabbits Peter and Benjamin (until we had to change one to Petronella!).

Now *I* am the grandmother, with a head full of memories and a shelf full of stories to read to Emma and Katie when they are old enough. Once again I have Ribby's basket—the perfect miniature replica made for me by Eve Legg. Timmy Tiptoes and Goody live in our garden, along with Peter, Benjamin and far too many Flopsy Bunnies. They chew the roses, destroy the pinks and massacre the seedlings but I love them just the same. Mr. Tod wanders across the grass two or three times a week, often stopping to stare at me working at my desk in the window—he seems in no hurry; Mrs. Tiggy-winkle comes occasionally, but not nearly often enough. Aunt Pettitoes and her brood live very near and so does Jemima Puddle-duck, whilst a stone's throw away Mr. Jeremy Fisher splashes happily in the streams and lakes. And now, as though all this peace and beauty were not enough, I have been given this wonderful opportunity to fulfil yet another lifelong ambition and turn my much-loved Potter people into toys. An awesome task indeed, but what a happy one! A task I approached almost with reverence and in fear of letting Beatrix Potter down.

Here then are the immortal little creatures for you to make for yourselves, and thanks to a good friend and my son, their baskets and chairs, their cradles and stools also! I would have liked Beatrix Potter to have seen them all—I hope she would have approved but above all I hope they will give you and your children and your children's children, pleasure.

M.H.

Introduction

The toys and models in this book have been carefully chosen from the many Beatrix Potter characters to cover a wide range and give variety to the worker.

For obvious reasons it was not possible to make them in the correct size and proportion one to another—particularly when such variable creatures as pigs and mice are included! In the film of the ballet *The Tales of Beatrix Potter*, all the animals were of a necessity the *same* size—because they were all portrayed by humans. Some consideration was given to making the toys all the same size in order to give them a certain uniformity, but the idea was finally discarded. The designs have therefore been worked out in groups or families, so that the members of each group are in the correct proportion one to another but the groups as a whole bear no relation to each other. The rabbits, squirrels, cats, frog, hedgehog and rats are all roughly life size. The pigs and duck much smaller and the mice rather larger than life.

It is essential to have Beatrix Potter's book about the animal you are making in front of you for reference. A list of the books from which the characters are taken appears on page 2 and reference is given to the relevant title at the beginning of each set of instructions (all page numbers refer to the current editions of the Beatrix Potter books). If you don't own the book yourself a neighbour may and your library certainly will, so borrow!

Always refer to the pictures in Beatrix Potter's books before those on these pages, otherwise a subtle change may gradually take place in the character you are shaping. One is reminded of the game where a message is whispered along a line of players, which usually ends up as something quite different from the way it started—so can a toy change its character if the original picture is not constantly used for reference.

None of the characters given here are intended as 'exhibition' pieces; the methods described are not necessarily 'right' or 'wrong' and should not be judged as such. They are designed solely to bring to life as nearly as possible the pictures in Beatrix Potter's books in order to create something for a child to love, not as a lesson in toy making. The methods used are those which were found quickest and simplest to achieve that end.

The colours have been matched as nearly as possible to the exquisite water colours illustrating the stories, but Miss Potter was delightfully inconsistent, changing the shades of dresses and coats from page to page and for no apparent reason. Messrs Warnes have been most understanding about this and allowed me a certain amount of licence. Spelling also has been taken from the little books—Mr. Jeremy Fisher wearing a 'macintosh' not a 'mackintosh'!

In the working diagrams, needles, pins, etc., have been drawn rather large in an effort to make the various processes really clear to the worker and, in some cases where it was thought a diagram would not illustrate a point sufficiently well, photographs have been substituted. Every effort has been made to set the various processes out as clearly as possible. Read the general instructions carefully before starting work and no problems should arise.

Instructions for making characters from the following Tales of Beatrix Potter appear in this book

The Tale of Peter Rabbit
The Tale of Squirrel Nutkin
The Tale of Benjamin Bunny
The Tale of Two Bad Mice
The Tale of Mrs. Tiggy-winkle
The Tale of Mr. Jeremy Fisher
The Tale of Tom Kitten
The Tale of Jemima Puddle-duck
The Tale of The Flopsy Bunnies
The Tale of Mrs. Tittlemouse
The Tale of Timmy Tiptoes
The Tale of Johnny Town-mouse
The Tale of Pigling Bland
The Tale of Samuel Whiskers
The Story of Miss Moppet
Appley Dapply's Nursery Rhymes

PART ONE
THE ANIMALS

General Instructions

READ THIS SECTION VERY CAREFULLY BEFORE STARTING WORK ON ANY OF THE ANIMAL CHARACTERS. Then when you have decided which toy to make, read through the instructions given for that particular toy, making sure you understand them and checking every cross-reference. If you don't own the Beatrix Potter book in question, borrow it from the library and read the story before making the characters concerned in it. Always keep it handy for reference whilst working. In this way, you will approach the work with a clear picture in your mind and creating the toy will not only be immensely satisfying but very much easier in every way.

FINDING SUITABLE MATERIALS

There are few things more infuriating than picking up a book and deciding to make something described in it, only to discover that you are quite unable to track down and obtain the necessary materials. The Needlewoman Shop, 146–8 Regent Street, London, W1R 6BA, do their best to keep stock of the felts, fur fabrics and joints used for the original models—*for personal shoppers*—and subject to supplies being available from the manufacturers.

If you prefer to look for your own fabrics, a 'treasure hunt' through a large department store is usually rewarding. For those near London, John Lewis of Oxford Street is probably the most promising venue, with a particularly good stock of cotton or similar prints in early spring and of fur fabrics in early autumn. It is best to hunt book in hand, matching the fabric to the pictures. All the Beatrix Potter books are so beautifully small that they will fit conveniently into your handbag, and the strange glances of the shop assistants as you peer, poke and pry among the rolls of material all add to the fun of the chase.

A little imagination is sometimes needed—Jeremy Fisher's macintosh, for instance, could present problems. Look among plastic accessories—a bath cap, make-up cape or shopping bag may be available in just the right colour. Fur fabric is not always available in reddish brown or grey for the squirrels—in this case buy white and dye it. If it comes up streaky, so much the better, but this hardly ever happens when you want it to! (N.B. Make sure your material and dye are suitable for each other.)

Finart wax crayons specially made for drawing permanently on to fabrics could be useful as a last resort if unable to find the exact 'print' you need in the shops. With them you can reproduce the necessary rose sprigs, checks or stripes on plain material. (N.B. Read the instructions very carefully first, making sure your crayons and material are made to be used together.)

It would be nothing short of sacrilege to use anything other than the correct materials for Beatrix Potter's enchanting creatures. Peter's coat must be *just* the right blue, Mrs. Tittlemouse's petticoats exactly the correct stripe, the kittens must be soft, and Mrs. Tiggy-winkle crisp and prickly. Rather wait a few days whilst sending away for what you need than spoil the finished effect by creating something which is just not right.

N.B. It is pre-supposed that all fur fabrics used for the toys will be at least 48 inches (1 metre 20 cm) wide and all cotton prints, etc., 36 inches (1 metre).

PREPARING THE PATTERNS

All the patterns are given full size at the end of the toy section. It is well worth taking time and trouble to prepare these accurately and in a form that can be used many times. When you have decided which toy you are going to make, trace the necessary pattern pieces on to thin cardboard (greaseproof paper from the kitchen is ideal for this purpose) and cut out each piece smoothly and carefully. Mark in the arrows, letters, numbers, 'openings', 'folds' and any other directions and label the pieces clearly (e.g. Tom Kitten, TROUSERS, 2 BLUE F). Punch a hole in each piece and thread them together with a pipe cleaner (Fig. 1). These prepared sets can be stored together in a special box and are always ready for use.

Labelling of parts
The materials necessary for cutting the parts are labelled on each pattern piece thus:

> F = felt
> FF = fur fabric

Any other materials are fully described, e.g. 'cotton', 'poplin', etc.

Piecing a pattern together

Because of the size of these pages it will be found necessary to piece on part of the squirrels' tails on pages 174–5 (rather appropriate in the case of Squirrel Nutkin who lost his tail in the story!). The pattern has been given the appearance of having been torn in two. When preparing your cardboard template, trace the main part of the tail including the broken line between the Xs then move the tracing paper so that this broken line rests on the corresponding line on the end piece and the Xs match, and finish tracing so that you have one complete tail piece. When transferring the patterns to cardboard, ignore the broken line which divided it.

CUTTING OUT

N.B. All turnings are already allowed on all the patterns

Cutting felt

Place the cardboard templates on the material trying them this way and that so as to use the felt in the most economical way. Draw round each one with a soft pencil (not a ball-point pen) and cut out exactly on the pencil line so that no marks are left to show on the finished toy.

Cutting fur fabric

Stroke the material to decide which way the pile runs, then turn it over and pencil a large arrow on the back indicating this direction. The arrows on the pattern pieces show which way the pile should stroke on the finished toy, e.g. downwards on bodies, upwards on ears. Place the card templates on the back of the material, their arrows following the arrow on the material and draw all round them with a soft pencil or tailor's chalk. (Ball-point pen may rub and stain the edges of the pile.) Use small, very sharp scissors for cutting, sliding them along under the pile in a short, snipping movement, cutting only the back of the fabric (Fig. 2A) never the pile (Fig. 2B). In this way the pile will be left to mask the seams on the finished toy, much improving its appearance.

Cutting pairs

Some parts are labelled 'cut 1 pair' as opposed to 'cut 2'. This is to remind you that the pattern piece needs to be reversed when cutting one of the parts or both the pieces will be facing in the same direction (e.g. Peter Rabbit's body on page 150).

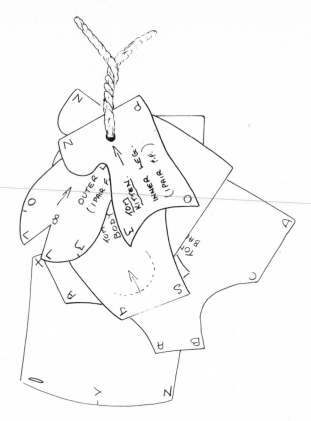

Fig. 1 A set of patterns prepared for storing

Fig. 2 Cutting fur fabric

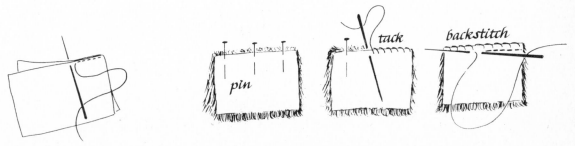

Fig. 3 Stab stitch   Fig. 4 Stitching fur fabric

Folds

Watch for 'fold' on some of the pieces. This method was found necessary in the case of some of the larger, evenly-shaped patterns in order to save space. It means just what it says—i.e. cut double, folded down the broken line. The best way to do this on thick material like felt or fur fabric, is to draw one half, then turn the cardboard template over at the broken 'fold' line and draw the second half. Alternatively, the half pattern can be traced twice on to the cardboard when making the template so that a complete pattern is made and used normally when cutting out. (Example of a fold—the squirrels' sleeves on page 193.)

Checking the pieces

Some of the animals have quite a lot of small parts, so to help you check that you have cut them all before starting to sew, the final number of pieces is given in each case under 'cutting out' (e.g. Peter Rabbit, page 29, No. 1). In some cases the pattern pieces for a single toy are taken from more than one character or part of the book. When this happens several sub-totals are given so that you can check the pieces as you go along. The final number is given at the end (e.g. Cousin Ribby, page 107, No. 1).

Storing the cut-out parts

A Polystyrene 'dish' from a supermarket (sold containing meat, etc.) is an ideal container for the cut-out pieces of one toy. Keeping them in this way, you have them all together and they are easy to sort and to 'get at'! As you stitch, stuff and join the various parts they can be put back in the container to await final assembly.

STITCHING

Stitching felt

Pin first then sew with a small, fine needle and Sylko or one of the Polyester threads exactly matching the felt. If working on the right side (e.g. round Jeremy Fisher's eye bulges) use a small, neat stab stitch or fine oversewing (e.g round Mrs. Tiggy-winkle's fingers), whichever is recommended in the text for the part in question. On the wrong side, either of these stitches may be used but stab stitch has the advantage of looking neater on the right side when the work is turned. Work very close to the edge of the felt leaving practically no turning (Fig. 3).

Stitching fur fabric

Work on the wrong side and always *pin* first, then *tack* by carefully oversewing, pushing the pile of the fabric through to the inside as you work (Fig. 4).

Any colour thread may be used for this tacking for although it is not removed (it adds extra strength to the work), being inside the finished toy it does not show. What better way to use up all those odds and ends on bobbins in the sewing machine and forgotten reels at the bottom of the workbox? After tacking, stitch either by machine or by hand using a firm, strong back stitch. (If one method is more suitable than the other for a certain toy, this is mentioned in the instructions.) Turnings of $\frac{1}{4}$ inch (a little less than 1 cm) have been allowed on all the patterns unless otherwise stated. It is a good idea to have your machine threaded up and handy so that you can tack a pile of pieces whilst sitting by the fire or in the garden, then machine them as they are ready. Some small parts such as inserting soles into feet (Peter Rabbit's legs, page 29, No. 5) are obviously easier to cope with by hand. Other parts such as ears inserted into seams whilst making up a head (Peter Rabbit, Fig. 19) are best partly machined then stitched by hand where several thicknesses of fur fabric are involved.

Stitching the clothes

It has been assumed that when making dresses, petticoats, etc., each worker will use the type of seam she prefers and neaten the inside raw edges round waists, armholes, etc., in her own way. No instructions have therefore been given for this.

Ladder stitch

This extremely useful stitch turns the edges of an opening 'into itself' and is by far the most satisfactory method to use for many toy-making processes. It consists of a small running stitch taken first on one side of an opening then on the other, which when pulled tightly, closes that opening invisibly (Fig. 5). Use it also for sewing on arms—a stitch alternately on the arm and body, working all round several times (Fig. 6); and for joining heads, tails, etc., to a body (Fig. 7). Fine thread will eventually break under the necessary pulling and is therefore useless for this stitch; the limbs will come off and the finished toy be unsatisfactory. Always use strong button thread in a long needle for ladder stitching fur fabric and double Sylko or similar in a long, slim needle for ladder stitching felt.

A long type of ladder stitch, stretching from under a 'chin' to a shoulder, chest or back is often useful for adding character to an animal by pulling its head forwards, backwards or to one side (e.g. the Flopsy Bunnies).

STUFFING

Turning the parts

A blunt stick or the wrong end of a pencil is often useful for turning heads, legs, etc., right side out after stitching, sometimes an awkward, fiddly job. After turning, push out all bulges and corners well before stuffing, with the help of a cocktail stick or the point of a pencil, but be careful not to pierce the material.

Packing the filling in place

Kapok was used for all the original models. A natural material, it has the advantage of adequately and firmly filling the various tiny bulges and corners so essential to the character of this type of toy, as well as being easy to handle and 'staying put' just where you want it. It is not however washable.

Work slowly and carefully when filling your toy, using only a very small amount of kapok at a time and pushing it into place with a stick of a suitable size. Cocktail sticks, wooden meat skewers, and dowelling of various sizes will all be found useful.

The cuddly, furry rabbits and squirrels can be reasonably soft but the 'models' such as the pigs, rats, mice, etc., must be of rock-like firmness, particularly those which contain any wire. In this case the best plan is to stuff until not one more scrap will go inside and then find room for a little more!

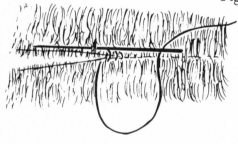

Fig. 5 Closing an opening with ladder stitch

Fig. 6 Ladder stitching a limb to body

Fig. 7 Joining a head to a body with ladder stitch

Using fur fabric cuttings

The snippings and cuttings left after cutting out a fur fabric toy may all be used to help fill up large body cavities. They are particularly useful in the case of a toy liable to tip forward, e.g. Cousin Ribby whose basket and umbrella can easily upset her balance. In these cases chop the cuttings fairly small and use them to stuff the tail and lower *back* part of the body. Fur fabric is heavier than kapok and used in this way is surprisingly efficient at helping to weight a toy in any of the directions you wish.

CROSS-REFERENCES

In a book of this type where much of the work is repetitive, a large number of cross-references cannot be avoided. To do so would add greatly to the size and price by printing identical instructions many times over. The easiest way to deal with this problem is to prepare a number of strips of paper and whilst reading through the instructions before starting work, slip one into each page referred to, perhaps pencilling a name or number on the end to help you see the correct place at a glance.

FINISHING

1 Go over all the seams and round the eyes with the eye of a large needle or the points of your scissors, pulling out any fur pile that is caught up in the stitching then give the toy a good brush.

2 Take a critical look at the aprons, dresses, etc. Are they immaculate in the true Beatrix Potter tradition, looking as though they have been freshly laundered by Mrs. Tiggy-winkle herself, or have they become rather 'tired' in the making? A little spray starch and a hot iron will work wonders in restoring the necessary crisp, pristine appearance. Mrs. Tiggy-winkle seems to have taken care of the laundry for most of her friends, so we mustn't let her down; after all, as she herself said, 'Oh, yes if you please'm, I'm an excellent clear starcher!'

Special Processes

Before starting work on any of the animals, read first the general instructions on pages 4–11, then the instructions for the toy you have decided to make, at the same time turning to and reading through any special processes referred to in the text and making sure you understand what is involved.

PREPARING WIRES

Some of the toys are strengthened by short lengths of wire inserted into necks (e.g. Jemima Puddle-duck, page 139) or legs and arms (e.g. Samuel Whiskers' legs, page 73). Ordinary galvanised wire obtained from any ironmonger is quite suitable and very inexpensive. Take your knitting needle gauge with you when you go to buy the wire and choose the thickness corresponding to a size 12 knitting needle. This is firm yet easy to cut and bend. Having cut off the length needed for the toy in question, bind the wire with ½-inch wide medical or electrical adhesive tape, making sure to cover the sharp ends (Fig. 8A and B). This will help to keep the wire in its place inside the toy as the kapok will cling to the adhesive tape. Binding the ends prevents the sharp points cutting through the toy as well as making for safety. Sometimes a little more padding than adhesive tape is necessary (e.g. Aunt Pettitoes' neck, page 62). In this case add an extra binding of narrow strips of rag (Fig. 8C), fastening off the ends by stitching (Fig. 8D) or sticking. In large toys such as Aunt Pettitoes a piece of cane or dowelling may be used to strengthen the neck instead of wire. This should be bound with rag in the same way but no adhesive tape is necessary.

MAKING WHISKERS

Many of the Beatrix Potter animals are of the whiskered variety and a little thought is needed before deciding the best material to use for each character. In the case of the soft cuddly toys such as the rabbits and cats whose span of life will almost certainly include a great deal of loving, hugging and taking to bed, you may prefer to use a strong grey or black button thread. This will of course stand up to any amount of wear and tear but has the disadvantage of drooping and crumpling. Horsehair (readily obtainable from a friendly farmer or pony club member) is ideal in many ways and stands crisply erect. It is, however, scratchy material to cuddle and will eventually bend and break. Always wash it well before use. Both button thread and lengths of horsehair should be inserted as in Fig. 9 so that they cannot be pulled out.

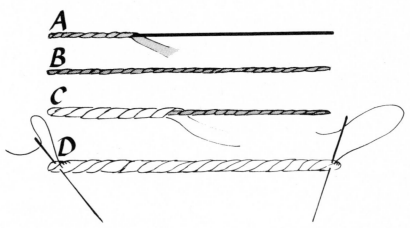

Fig. 8 Preparing wires

Bristles from a brush are absolutely ideal for making whiskers on models most of whose life will be spent on the nursery shelf as an ornament, for example, the rats and mice. If you intend to make any quantity of toys of this type, it is worthwhile buying a small cheap brush specially for the purpose. For the original models a 'refill' for a hearthbrush was purchased from Woolworths and the wooden top smashed with a hammer to release many useful bundles of doubled black bristles (Fig. 10). If only one or two toys are being made you will almost certainly be able to steal a bristle or two from one of your household's stock of brushes. These whiskers will be hairpin-shaped and should be inserted as shown by Fig. 11.

STARTING AND FINISHING OFF WHEN EMBROIDERING DETAILS

There are occasions such as when embroidering claws (e.g. the cats, Fig. 68), hairs and eyes (e.g. the rats and mice, Fig. 46) when difficulty may be

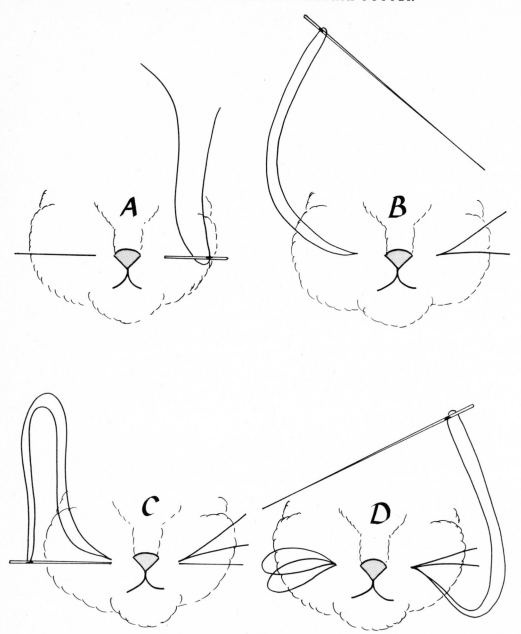

Fig. 9 Making whiskers from thread or horsehair

A Thread whisker double into a long needle. Insert needle into head at
  place where whiskers are required
B Pull whisker through leaving required length protruding on first side
C Push needle back again
D Pull needle through leaving loops of the required length on the second
  side

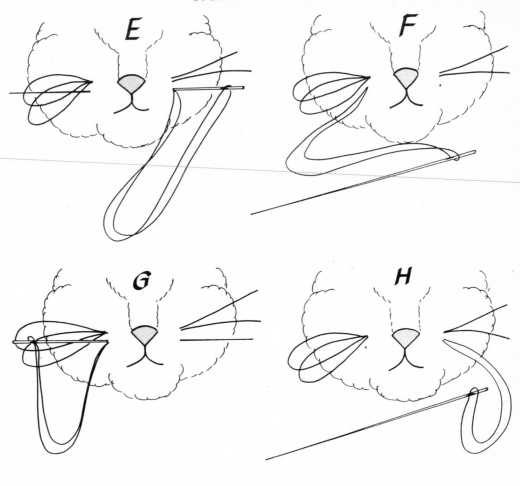

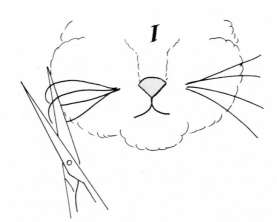

E Push needle back again—

F Leaving no loops

G Work backwards and forwards several times, leaving no loops, until the whiskers already made are absolutely secure and will not pull out

H Emerge finally on the side on which you started

I Cut off to correct length and cut through loops. You now have four whiskers each side. Repeat this process until you have the required number using double or single thread

experienced in deciding how to start and 'anchor' the thread firmly and how to finish off invisibly and securely. The best way to do this is shown by Fig. 12.

Fig. 10 Smash the top of a brush to release bundles of 'bristles'

NEEDLE MODELLING

Needle modelling is absolutely essential to bring out the full character and shape of many of the toys. It is a fascinating process rather like sculpture whereby dimples, fat cheeks, sunken eyes, etc., are introduced by a series of stitches taken backwards and forwards through the head or part of body in question and pulled tightly. Strong thread and a long, slim needle are very necessary and the picture of the animal you are making as well as the diagram in question should be carefully followed. Full instructions are given for each toy. However, every worker pulls a little more or less tightly than another and stuffs a little more or less fully, so don't be afraid to consult the pictures in the Beatrix Potter book in question and continue modelling in your own way until you are absolutely satisfied with your animal's features and characteristics. Without careful modelling the cats can so easily look like Teddy bears and Mrs. Tiggy-winkle like a Pekinese dog!

TINTING AND SHADING

To make the toys as near as possible to Beatrix Potter's pictures, a certain amount of tinting and shading is needed. There are various methods of doing this and before deciding which one to use and indeed whether in some cases to leave them plain, a little careful thought is necessary.

Leaving the toys plain
In the case of the rabbits which may be bedfellows for many years, you may

prefer to leave them plain. In the colour plates, Peter Rabbit, Benjamin Bunny, Flopsy, Mopsy, Cotton-tail and Mrs. Flopsy Bunny have been left in this way and I am grateful to Frederick Warne and Co. Ltd. for allowing me this little bit of licence.

Shading with dye

The Flopsy Bunnies in the colour plate opposite page 84, were lightly streaked by using a cold water dye applied with a paint brush. Although not guaranteed by the manufacturers to be absolutely fast if applied in this way, it seems to have stood up well to wear and tear and in any case to be very suitable for toys for older children which will not be sucked and wetted! Be sure your dye and material are suitable for each other. (It will be noticed that some of the Flopsy Bunnies have pink and some white ear linings and that both look equally well.)

Shading with wool

If not shaded, Squirrel Nutkin looks a little stark where the white, brown and beige pieces join. The lines are too clear and sudden. He could be shaded by any of the methods mentioned but the original (opposite page 277) was softened by taking a series of woollen stitches over the offending seams. When using this method work with a long needle and knitting or double darning wool that exactly matches the fur fabrics in question. In this case white and reddish brown. Squirrel Nutkin was also given a few brown stitches on the top end of the beige side of his tail—to break up and 'roughen' the smooth edge. This method of shading may also be useful for some of the cats, especially when used in conjunction with a second method (for example, Cousin Ribby's face, page 108, Fig. 70, where it supplements applied fur fabric 'patches').

Shading by patching

This method is useful where large blotches of contrasting colour are needed (for example, Tabitha Twitchit's head, Fig. 67 (page 104), and Moppet's back (page 117, Plate 7). It consists of simply cutting a patch of fur fabric in the necessary colour and to the required shape, pinning it in place and sewing it on with a kind of hemming stitch. If your fur fabric is one of the very nice, modern knitted-back varieties, no turnings are necessary as it will not fray at all, but if using a woven material, tuck in the raw edges as you work. In either case after applying, go round the edges of the patch with the points of your scissors, pulling out all the pile caught up in the stitching, then brush well to mingle the colours and soften the outline.

Shading with felt pen

Much experimenting on the original toys has shown that most felt pens are ideal for shading—the stripes and patches merely being drawn on as though

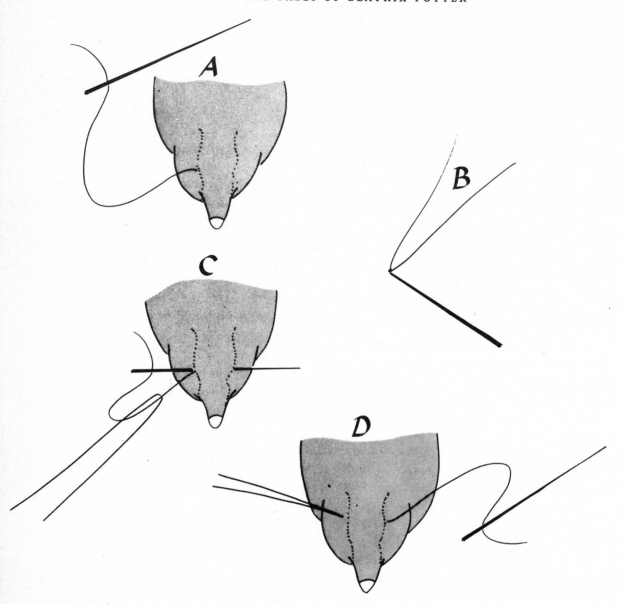

Fig. 11 Making whiskers from brush 'bristles'

A Thread a long needle with button thread which exactly matches the head of toy. 'Anchor' this thread firmly to head (see pages 20–1, fig. 12A–F) bringing the needle out finally where a whisker is required

B Put a tiny spot of colourless adhesive on the bend of a 'bristle'

C Pass needle and thread through bend of whisker and back into head

D Pull needle out at other side at the same time pulling bend of whisker well into head

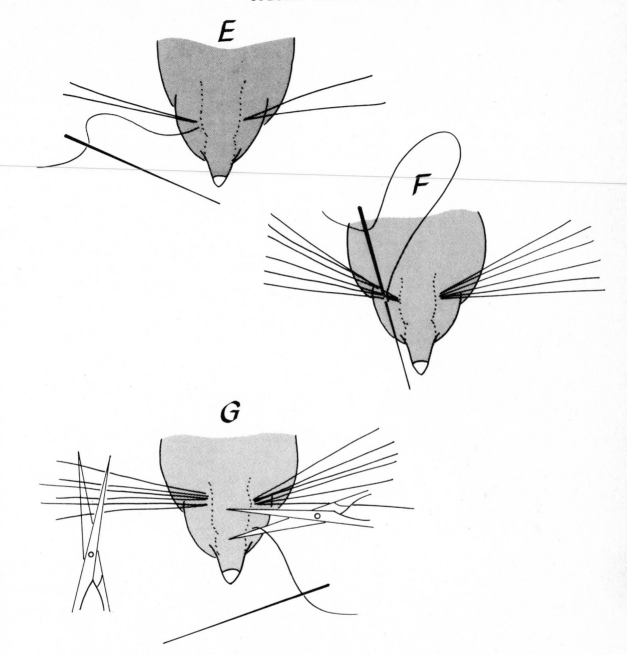

E Repeat B, C and D making a pair of whiskers on opposite side of face

F Repeat this process until you have sufficient whiskers. Then make a tiny, invisible stitch over each whisker, a short distance from where it enters the head, for added security

G Lose end of thread (see pages 20–1, fig. 12I–L) and cut off. Trim whiskers

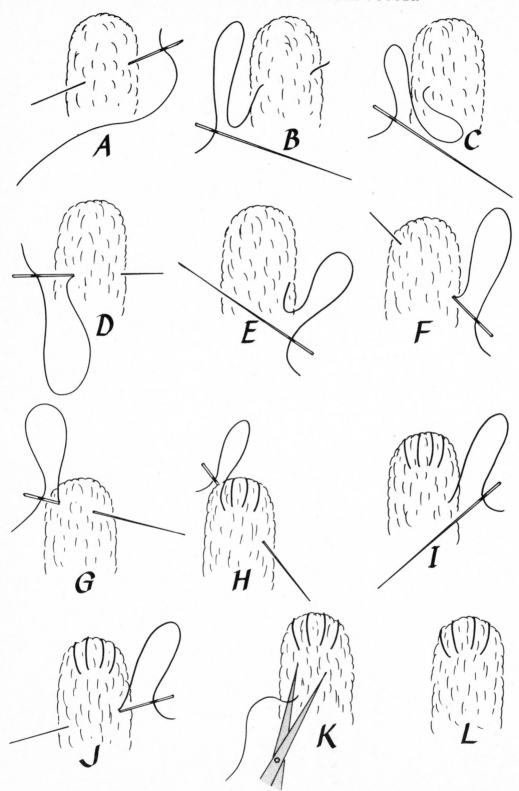

Fig. 12 Starting and finishing off when embroidering details—in this case cat's
claws

    A Use a long, slim needle: thread up the material to be used and push
        needle into limb at any position you wish

    B Pull needle and thread through carefully until only a tiny 'end'
        shows

    C Continue pulling until the end of thread just disappears inside the
        limb

    D Push needle back into limb into the same hole from which you have
        just pulled it out but bring it out in a new position

    E Pull needle out—leaving no stitch showing

    F Repeat D, bringing needle out in yet another position. Continue in
        this way until no amount of tugging will pull the thread out

    G Push the needle into limb by the same hole from which it has just
        emerged and bring it out at the place where you wish to embroider

    H Work the claws (or 'hairs' or eyes as the case may be)

    I Bring the needle out at any position on the limb

    J Repeat D as many times as is necessary to make thread absolutely
        secure

    K Cut thread close to limb

    L Leaving no end or mark showing

Fig. 13 Parts of a joint set

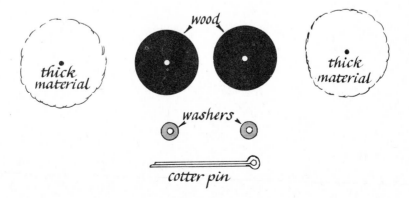

painting a picture, copying from Beatrix Potter's pictures. This method was used on Tom Kitten and Mittens (see opposite page 124). For the originals 'Koh-i-Dry' pens by Eagle were used but there are many others equally suitable on the market. Make sure the pens you use are non-toxic then try them on a scrap of fur fabric to get the right shades. (Koh-i-Dry brown comes up very gingery and is exactly right for the cats and kittens.) Try washing and drying your sample to make sure the colours remain fast and clear. Shading the toys in this way is the greatest fun and incredibly quick to do. The finished product is ideal for the older child but it is of course for you to decide whether you would use this method on a toy for someone still *very* young.

Shading with wax transfer crayons

The new wax transfer crayons used for drawing designs on plain materials and made up garments have been proved to show great possibilities in the field of fur fabric shading. Experiments were carried out with Finart crayons and they were found to be excellent for the purpose. If using this method read the instructions given for the crayons concerned very carefully and carry them out to the letter. In the main the design needed is drawn on a piece of paper then applied to the material in question with a hot iron. Therefore in toy making the shading is applied to the various parts of the toy after cutting out but before sewing up. Cut a paper pattern to match each piece, study the pictures carefully to see where you want the markings to come, draw them all on the paper pieces using the special wax crayons then transfer them to the fur fabric pieces by ironing and make up the toy as usual. N.B. Make sure when reading the instructions that your material and crayons are meant for each other and will 'marry' successfully and permanently!

Tinting with cochineal

Most of the pigs are greatly improved if tinted pink on snout, ears, cheeks, etc., as may be seen from the pictures in *The Tale of Pigling Bland*. Cochineal was used for the originals but water, coloured with red paint, may be used. Always thoroughly wet the parts to be tinted before beginning, as this helps the colour to run and merge on the felt in the most natural way possible. Apply very weak, watered down, colour sparingly with a small paint brush, brushing it well in. Leave to dry and if necessary, repeat the process.

Two important points to remember

1 Always start by using the colour very sparingly indeed—you can always add more but it is impossible to remove any gaudy red marks you may make by mistake. If this happens your toy will be ruined.

2 Take great care not to put the tint near the eyes—if it should run on to the

white of the eye, again your toy will be ruined and will take on a 'tipsy', blood-shot look.

Buying ready-shaded materials

There are, of course, a great many 'fun' fur fabrics on the market and it is possible that you may be able to find or indeed already possess a piece of material already shaded and exactly right for a certain animal. In this case you will save a lot of time and trouble—one word of warning, however. Make sure it *is* right. Surely no one can want to spoil the delightful Potter image by using anything other than the exact textures and colours which this great artist herself would have approved. If you have read the Leslie Linder and Margaret Lane books you will realise that she was, to put it mildly, 'particular' and none of us should dare to trespass!

JOINTING

Jointing is a knack which can best be compared with swimming or riding a bicycle. Suddenly, after much practice, one can do it. The necessary 'pull, stretch and turn' movement which gives a strong spring to the cotter pin and long life to the toy, once achieved and 'felt' will never be lost.

No instructions are given for jointing any particular toy. However, as many of them have heads or limbs very suitable for this process and some workers may wish to make toys with movable parts, methods of jointing are given on page 24 and may be applied to various characters. Benjamin Bunny shown opposite page 53 has jointed arms and legs, thus enabling him to sit down and move his arms. Parts of the toys which are particularly suited to jointing without major alterations to the patterns (such as severing heads from bodies) and the size of joint set needed for each one are as follows:

Peter Rabbit ⎫ Arms $1\frac{1}{4}$ inches
Benjamin Bunny ⎭ Legs $1\frac{1}{2}$ inches

Flopsy; Mopsy; Cotton-tail ⎫
Benjamin Bunny Grown-up ⎬ Arms $1\frac{1}{4}$ inches
Mrs. Flopsy Bunny ⎭

Squirrel Nutkin ⎫ Arms $1\frac{1}{4}$ inches
Timmy Tiptoes ⎬
Goody Tiptoes ⎭ Head $1\frac{1}{2}$ inches

Tabitha Twitchit ⎫ Arms $1\frac{1}{4}$ inches
Cousin Ribby ⎭ Head $1\frac{1}{2}$ inches

Tom Kitten ⎫
Moppet   ⎪ Arms ¾ inch
Mittens   ⎬ Head 1 inch
Miss Moppet⎭

In case of local difficulty, all these can be obtained from the address on page 4.

Each joint set consists of two board or wooden discs, two metal washers and a cotter pin. Before starting work, cut two circles of fur fabric, soft leather, felt or any thick material ¼–½ inch (1 cm) larger all round than the wooden discs (Fig. 13). These serve as 'masks' to soften the edges of the joints so that they cannot be felt from the outside.

Jointing a head

Run a gathering thread round open 'neck' of head. Thread the metal washer, wooden or board disc, then material circle on to the cotter pin, place upside down inside neck opening of firmly stuffed head. Pack stuffing very carefully all round the *edge* of disc so that no hardness can be felt on the outside (Fig. 14A). Be sure not to place any on *top* of the disc as this must be kept very flat. Pull up gathering thread and check that there are no empty hollows or dimples in the head. If there are, remove disc and fill up gaps, using small pieces of kapok and a slim stick. The head must be very firm. When you are quite satisfied, fasten off the gathering thread very securely, taking stitches across and round the pin but never between the split ends (Fig. 14B). Push the pin through the hole formed by gathers at top of *unstuffed* body (or through centre of top seam), thread on a material circle, then a wooden one, then a washer. Pull the body of the toy in all directions to make sure there are no folds or pleats of fur fabric between discs.

Fig. 14 Inserting a joint into a head

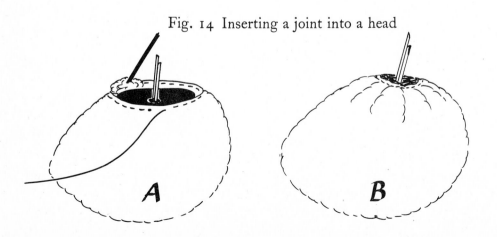

A   B

Turn the toy upside down, standing on its head on a table and with *small* snipe or round-nosed pliers ($\frac{1}{8}$-inch points), grasp one end of the pin *low down* and pulling upwards and outwards turn it away from you into the shape shown in Fig. 15A. Turn the toy round and pull and twist the other half of the pin away from you into a corresponding position. The bent cotter pin forms a spring and holds the head tightly in position. When you try to turn the head, it should be so tight that you can hardly move it. It will wear loose in play. If your joint is loose, undo it and start again even if it means unpicking the stitching and inserting a new pin. If you experience real difficulty, try making a 'sampler' by jointing two pieces of material together and keep experimenting until you get the right pull and twist movement. Fig. 15B shows an incorrectly turned pin which is useless; the head will very soon come off.

The very 'best fault' you can have in a joint set is a pin that is too long! This is much easier to grasp and turn and the surplus ends which protrude over

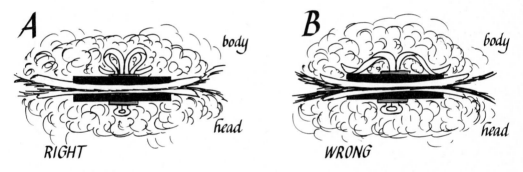

Fig. 15 Section showing right and wrong joints inside toy

the disc and would thus damage the toy can easily be cut off with nippers. Short pins are useless as you cannot grasp and turn them properly.

Jointing a limb
The arms and legs of the animals in this book which are suitable for jointing have a cut-away portion on the inner part to enable them to be sewn flat against the body. When jointing, therefore, that cut-away part must be filled up. Cut a circle of the fur fabric used for the limb in question, about $\frac{1}{2}$ inch (1 cm) larger all round than the wooden disc. Run a gathering thread all round the edge, place the wooden disc inside (Fig. 16A). Draw up and fasten in position with large stitches across the back (B). Stuff the limb tightly (C). Thread the metal washer and covered disc on to cotter pin (D) and place inside top cut-away portion, adding any necessary extra stuffing round outside of disc, not on top of it. Oversew disc in place all round outside edge, turning in the raw edges of

limb as you work (E). Then joint the limb to unstuffed body in the same way as given for head, pushing the pin through sides of body.

Points to remember

1 The limb should be completely flat on the inside where it will press against the body, but well rounded on the outside.
2 Make sure you place the limbs evenly on the body or your toy will be somewhat crippled.
3 It is easier to joint on first the head, then the arms and finally the legs. In this order, one part gets less in the way of the other and of your hands than it might otherwise do.

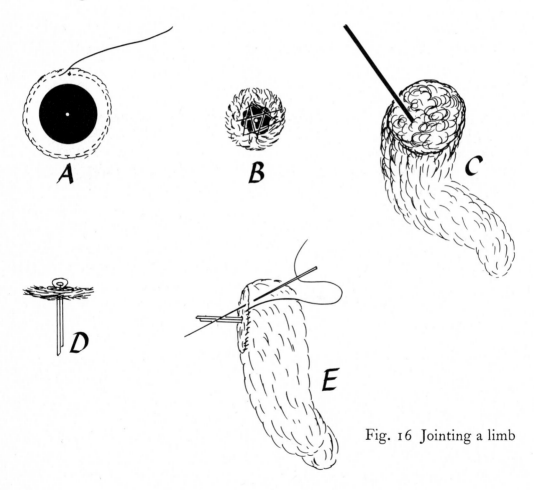

Fig. 16 Jointing a limb

The Rabbits

The Rabbit and Bunny families can be somewhat confusing to those who do not know them well. We read of them in *The Tale of Peter Rabbit*, *The Tale of Benjamin Bunny* and *The Tale of the Flopsy Bunnies*. The family tree on Fig. 17 will help you to sort them all out.

We do not meet poor Mr. Rabbit in the stories as he had previously had an unfortunate accident, having been 'put in a pie by Mrs. McGregor'! There is no mention of Old Mr. Benjamin Bunny's wife, so presumably he is a widower. Because Peter and Benjamin were cousins it seems probable that Mrs. Rabbit had been Miss Bunny before her marriage, although of course the connection may be that old Mrs. Bunny had previously been a Miss Rabbit!

Be that as it may, this lovable family lend themselves ideally to becoming cuddly toys and on the pages that follow instructions are given for making the second and third generations. All the rabbits are simple to make, being quite suitable for beginners to toy making and much of the work can be done on the sewing machine. It is however suggested that Peter Rabbit himself should be your first choice. In making him all the processes are covered, to help you fully understand the construction of a toy rabbit and when you start work on his various relations the general 'pattern' will be very much clearer.

The rabbits' fur coats can either be left plain or shaded in one of several ways (see tinting and shading on page 16). Their ears can be inserted at various angles —if you watch a rabbit you will see how their ears twitch sideways and forwards in ever-changing positions—it's almost uncanny. On the originals, fur fabric was used for ear linings on the large rabbits and felt on the small—you can, of course, use whichever you prefer.

PETER RABBIT

'*. . . but Peter, who was very naughty, ran straight away . . .*'
Refer to the cover of *The Tale of Peter Rabbit*, and cover and jacket of this book.

Fig. 17 The Rabbit/Bunny family tree

OLD Mr RABBIT (deceased) = Mrs RABBIT

← probably brother and sister → OLD Mr BENJAMIN BUNNY

PETER | COTTON TAIL | MOPSY | FLOPSY = BENJAMIN BUNNY

THE FLOPSY BUNNIES

A cuddly toy 16 inches (40 cm) high with removable coat and shoes.

Materials

¼ yard (23 cm) beige and ¼ yard (23 cm) white fur fabric.

18 × 24 inches (46 × 61 cm) blue felt (No. 99 Muscari) for jacket.

Three small brass blazer buttons for jacket.

Brown, fawn and white felt scraps for shoes and eyes.

Brown stranded embroidery cotton for nose.

Strong black thread for whiskers.

Kapok for stuffing. Finished toy weighs approximately 6 ounces (170 grammes).

Fig. 18 Folding base of Peter's ears   Fig. 20 Shape of rabbit's nose

Fig. 19 Inserting ear into head

Method

1 CUT OUT the pieces as given on pages 147–51 and 155 (37 pieces).

2 EARS. Place a beige and a white piece together, right sides facing, and stitch all round A–B–C. Turn right side out, pushing out points well. Oversew raw edge A–C. Fold in base A–C as shown by Fig. 18 and stitch securely in that position. Make the other ear in the same way and place on one side.

3 TAIL. Place the two pieces together, right sides facing, and stitch all round curved edge D–E–F. Turn right side out. Turn in straight edge D–F and oversew. Place on one side. (Stuff the tail a little if it seems too flat.)

4 ARMS. On an outer arm join the top dart 1–2. Place an inner white arm and beige outer arm together, right sides facing, and stitch all round G–I–H. Turn right side out. Make the other arm in the same way and place on one side.

5 LEGS. On a top outer leg join the two darts 3–4 and 5–6. Join this beige top piece to a white, lower, outer leg along J–K. Place this completed piece together with a white, inner leg, right sides facing and stitch N–J–3 and

L–K–M. Insert soles of feet, stitching all round N–L–N. Turn right side out. Make the other leg in the same way and place on one side.

6 BODY. * On both pieces slit inwards from O^1–P. Run a gathering thread from P–O^2. Pull up gathers so that O^2 rests on O^1 and stitch seam O–P. This gives fullness to the cheeks. * Take one side of body and the body gusset, place together, right sides facing and stitch Q–R–S, easing the under-chin piece Q–R in to fit. Join on the other body side in the same way but this time stitch round Q–R–S, then continue to T, joining the two body pieces together.

7 HEAD. Take an ear and looking at Fig. 19 stitch it firmly to the head piece at the position shown on pattern. Make sure you place the lining next to the outside of head, so that when Peter is turned right way out the lining will face outwards. Pin and check this position before stitching. Allow about $\frac{1}{2}$ inch (1 cm) of the base to protrude (into the head); this will help the ears to stand firmly erect later. Stitch the other ear to the other side of the head in the same way. Take the head gusset and stitch it to one side of head Q–O having the ear hanging downwards between the two pieces, i.e. on the inside of work—the right side of toy—and stitching right through base of ear when you come to it. (See page 9, 'Stitching fur fabric'.) Join the other side of head to the other side of head gusset in the same way, stitching Q–O then continuing to U, thus joining the back of the two body pieces together O–U. Turn right side out.

8 STUFFING AND ASSEMBLING. * Stuff the body, paying particular attention to the fat, puffy cheeks. Make sure there is no stuffing between the side of head and base of ear which projects inside. In this way the ear base will be pressed firmly against the side of head by the kapok filling the head and the ears will stand firmly erect, supported from inside. Look carefully at the picture on the cover of Peter's book while shaping the head in order to achieve the softly rounded forehead shown in the picture. Close opening. * Stuff legs and arms. Looking at the picture of Peter on the cover of his book, sew the two legs in place in a running position. To do this, place the open top flat against the body, pin in place then ladder stitch firmly all round (Fig. 6, page 10) one stitch on leg and one on body alternately, turning in the raw edge as you work. Sew the arms in place in the same way, the right one at a higher angle than the left as in picture. Sew on tail, sticking upwards in a saucy way.

9 EYES. Sew a brown pupil to each white eye as shown. Embroider a small highlight. Sew eyes one to each side of head, hemming neatly all round and experimenting by pinning first to make sure the position is just right for your particular rabbit. Take a few stitches right through the head from one front corner to the other and from one back corner to the other to sink the eyes slightly into the head. (See 'Needle modelling', page 16.)

10 NOSE. Embroider with brown stranded cotton as Fig. 20.

11 WHISKERS. Make as shown on pages 14–15, Fig. 9, using horsehair or stiff black thread.

12 SHOES. * Place a card sole between two of the felt pieces and oversew together all round edge (trimming a little off the card, if necessary, Fig. 22A on page 34). * Take a brown top piece and run a gathering thread round between the Vs, close to edge. Pull up gathers so that the Vs match Vs on soles. Oversew top to sole W–V–V–W. (See Fig. 22D but top piece will be a different shape.) Turn the shoe right side out. Make the other shoe in the same way, remembering to reverse the sole to make a pair. Slip them on to Peter's feet.

13 JACKET. '*It was a blue jacket with brass buttons, quite new.*'

* Take the sleeves and join underarm seams A–B. Insert sleeves into holes matching As, tacking, then machining close to edges. * Fold back collar as shown by broken line on pattern. Sew on three brass buttons as shown on pattern and make three corresponding button-holes on the other side. Put jacket on to Peter and do up the top button.

To make Peter Rabbit as pictured on page 11 of his book, make up a rabbit as given for his sisters Flopsy, Mopsy and Cotton-tail below but dress him in his blue jacket and shoes instead of their pink cloaks.

FLOPSY, MOPSY AND COTTON-TAIL

'. . . *who were good little bunnies, went down the lane to gather blackberries.*'

Refer to page 11 of *The Tale of Peter Rabbit* and colour plate opposite page 52 of this book.

Cuddly toys 16 inches (40 cm) high, with removable cloaks and baskets. Instructions for the baskets start on page 243.

Materials for each rabbit
   ¼ yard (23 cm) beige and ¼ yard (23 cm) white fur fabric for body.
   Brown and white felt scraps for eyes.
   Strong black thread for whiskers.
   * Pink felt (87 Bacchante) for cape, 5½ × 24 inches (14 × 61 cm) and an odd
       piece for collar (over from Timmy Tiptoes' jacket?).
   One small press-stud.
   Brown stranded cotton for nose.
   Kapok for stuffing. Finished toy weighs approximately 6 ounces (170
       grammes).

N.B. $\frac{1}{2}$ yard (46 cm) beige and $\frac{1}{2}$ yard (46 cm) white fur fabric makes three rabbits.

24 × 18 inches (61 × 46 cm) pink felt makes three capes if you join the collars neatly at fold in centre back.

Method

1 CUT OUT the pieces as given on pages 152–4 (7 pieces) also head gusset, tail, ears, inner arms, outer arms, eyes and pupils as given for Peter Rabbit on pages 147–51 and a piece of pink felt $5\frac{1}{2}$ × 24 inches (14 × 61 cm) for the cape (23 pieces in all).

2 EARS ⎫
3 TAIL ⎬ Work as given for Peter Rabbit, page 29, Nos. 2, 3 and 4.
4 ARMS ⎭

5 BODY. Work from * to * as given for Peter Rabbit, page 30, No. 6. Then take the underchin gusset and join to one body side Q–R, easing it in to fit. Take the body gusset and join the two pieces together R–W. Join this to the side of body to which you have already joined the underchin gusset S–X–R. Join this piece to the other body side S–X–R–Q. Join the back pieces together T–K.

6 SEAT. Take the seat gusset and join it to base of body all round T–S–W–S–T, easing to fit.

7 HEAD. Work as given for Peter Rabbit, page 30, No. 7.

8 STUFFING AND ASSEMBLING. Work from * to * as given for Peter, page 30, No. 8. Stuff the arms and pin the open ends flat against the sides of body, consulting the pictures in *The Tale of Peter Rabbit* for good positions. Sew arms in place, ladder stitching several times all round top. Sew on tail.

9 EYES ⎫
10 NOSE ⎬ Work as for Peter Rabbit, pages 30–1, Nos. 9, 10 and 11
11 WHISKERS ⎭ varying the position of pupil when making up the eyes.

12 CAPE (Fig. 21). Measure 4 inches (10 cm) in from the short end of main piece (front edge) and $1\frac{1}{4}$ inches (3 cm) up from one long side (bottom edge of cape). From this point cut an arm slit 3 inches (7.5 cm) long, parallel with front edge. Run a gathering thread along top edge. Pull up to fit short edge of collar. Fasten off gathers. Tack, then machine cape to collar on the wrong side, stitching close to the edge of felt. Sew press-stud to neck to fasten. Round off the two front corners.

Flopsy, Mopsy and Cotton-tail were all dressed alike in their pink capes when they went down the lane to gather blackberries, so make two more rabbits in the same way but vary the position of their arms and expression of their eyes. They each carried a different shaped basket (see pages 243–51).

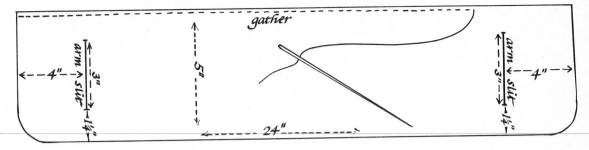

Fig. 21 Layout for cape (Flopsy, Mopsy, Cotton-tail)

BENJAMIN BUNNY

Benjamin was Peter Rabbit's cousin and so of course, very much like him. Instructions for making Benjamin's clothes are given below and they will fit Peter or Flopsy, Mopsy or Cotton-tail. If using the pattern for Peter, place the legs in a different position when attaching them. If using the pattern for the little girl rabbits, Benjamin's jacket and tam-o-shanter will fit but the clogs will not go on to the feet as these rabbits stand flat on the ground with no 'heels'. In the illustration opposite page 53, the pattern for Peter Rabbit was used but the limbs were jointed so that Benjamin could sit down. (See page 23 for jointing.)

Refer to the pictures in *The Tale of Benjamin Bunny*.

Materials for Benjamin's clothes

A piece of brown felt (Leather 36) 18 × 12 inches (46 × 30 cm) for jacket.
Two small brown buttons, for jacket.
$\frac{3}{4}$ ounce (20 grammes) 3- or 4-ply green wool (match colour from book) for tam-o-shanter.
A scrap of red wool for bobble.
Two knitting needles size 8.
Scraps of dark grey felt for clogs (cuttings from Pig-wig?, page 55).
Scraps of beige felt and pliable card for soles.
Thick, strong cardboard for heels.

Method

I JACKET: CUT OUT the pieces as for Peter Rabbit's jacket and sleeves, pages 147, 155 also two rectangles 1 × 2 inches (2·5 × 5 cm) for pocket flaps, using brown felt and cutting the jacket only to curved lines marked XXXX at top and bottom corners (5 pieces).
Work as given for Peter Rabbit, page 31, No. 13, from * to *. Stitch on the pocket flaps where shown on pattern by top edge only. Stitch the flaps turned upwards, then turn them downwards and press flat with a hot iron and damp

cloth. Round off the bottom two corners. Sew two small brown buttons
near top of front of jacket.

2   TAM-O-SHANTER: using size 8 knitting needles cast on 30 stitches.
Work 2 rows K.1 P.1 rib.

3rd row: (K.3 increase in next stitch) repeat to end of row, knitting the odd
  one or two stitches at end.

4th–6th row: Knit. Repeat 3rd–6th rows 6 times more.

30th–35th rows: Knit.

36th row: (K.3, K.2 tog.), repeat to end of row, knitting the odd one or two
  stitches at end.

37th–39th row: Knit. Repeat 37th–39th rows 6 times more.

63rd row: K.1, K.2 tog. all along row.

64th row: Knit. Repeat 63rd and 64th rows twice more.

Break off wool, thread end into needle and slip through the remaining
stitches. Pull out knitting needle, pull up stitches and fasten by stitching
several times through them. Sew up seam. Flatten and press tam-o-shanter
pulling it out lengthwise. Make a small red bobble and sew to centre.
Consult the pictures in *The Tale of Benjamin Bunny* for position on rabbit's
head.

'*Benjamin tried on the tam-o-shanter, but it was too big for him.*'

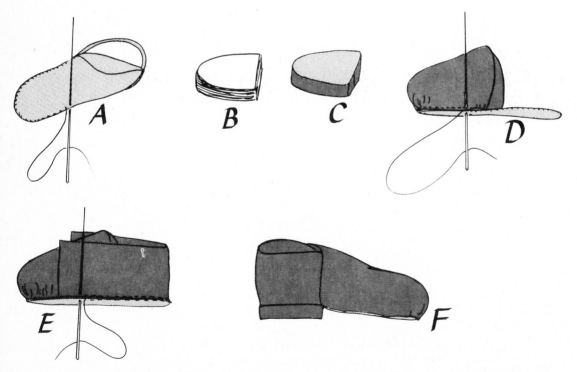

Fig. 22 Making Benjamin's clogs

3 CLOGS: CUT OUT the pieces as given on page 165 also the soles as given for Peter Rabbit, page 155 (24 pieces in all). Follow Fig. 22 opposite.

SOLES. (A) Work as given for Peter Rabbit, page 31, No. 12, from * to *.

HEELS. (B) Stick six of the cardboard pieces together making a thick heel. Stick a felt heel to the base. Stick a strip of grey felt all round the edge (C).

ASSEMBLING. Run a gathering thread round the front edge of upper V–V. Pull up gathers so that the Vs will match Vs on soles. Then on the wrong side stab stitch upper to sole W–V–V–W (D). Take the back upper piece and matching Xs stab stitch to sole on the wrong side. This will overlap the front upper piece for about 1 inch (2·5 cm) each side (E). Turn right way out (the front upper will now overlap the back) and push a tiny piece of cotton wool into the toe of clog to make it a firm shape. Stick heel in place (F). Make another clog in the same way, remembering to reverse the soles and heels so as to make a pair.

'*They left a great many odd little foot-marks all over the bed, especially little Benjamin who was wearing clogs.*'

BENJAMIN BUNNY GROWN UP

'*Benjamin used to borrow cabbages from Flopsy's brother . . .*'

Refer to colour plate opposite page 84 and to *The Tale of the Flopsy Bunnies*. Make exactly as for Benjamin Bunny, page 33 but omit tam-o-shanter and make the jacket in pink felt (Cyclamen 67) and omit the pocket.

Instructions for making his basket (as on the cover of *The Tale of the Flopsy Bunnies*) are on page 267.

MRS. FLOPSY BUNNY

'*When Benjamin Bunny grew up, he married his Cousin Flopsy. They had a large family and they were very improvident and cheerful.*'

Refer to *The Tale of the Flopsy Bunnies*, and colour plate opposite page 84 of this book.

A cuddly toy 16 inches (40 cm) high with removable pinafore.

Materials

As for Flopsy, Mopsy and Cotton-tail, page 31, except for item marked *.

A piece of pale blue poplin for pinafore 22 × 8½ inches (56 × 22 cm).

Method

Make up a rabbit exactly as given for Flopsy, Mopsy and Cotton-tail, page 32 working from numbers 1–11. When cutting out omit the cape and collar (21 pieces).

1 PINAFORE (Fig. 23): make a narrow hem down short edges of strip of material (back edges of pinafore). Cut two curved slits as shown among patterns on page 154, 3 inches (7·5 cm) from top edge and 3 inches (7·5 cm) from back edges of pinafore. Bind all round these slits using matching bias binding or a piece of the same material cut on the cross. These are the epaulettes. Run a gathering thread along top edge, pull up to fit neck and fasten off. Arrange gathers so that most of the fullness comes over the epaulettes, then bind the top edge (neck). Sew a small press-stud to fasten at centre back and turn up a narrow hem so that Flopsy's feet just show, then put the pinafore on to Mrs. Flopsy Bunny.

2 HER NET BAG: make from a sprout or vegetable net.

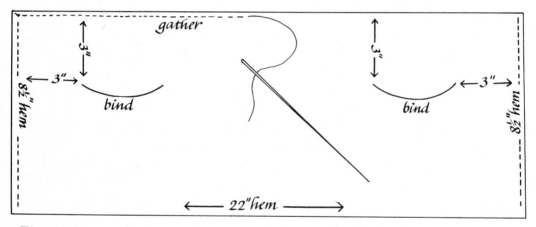

Fig. 23 Layout for Mrs. Flopsy Bunny's pinafore

THE FLOPSY BUNNIES

Beatrix Potter tells us '*I do not remember the separate names of their children; they were generally called the "Flopsy Bunnies".*'

Refer to the many pictures in *The Tale of the Flopsy Bunnies*, the colour plate opposite page 84 of this book and to Plates 1–6, pages 38–41.

As we have seen on Fig. 17, Flopsy and Benjamin had six children, who are pictured in every conceivable position, sometimes '*very soporific*' and sometimes playing round their parents. Six different designs follow, all about 8–10 inches (20–25 cm) long or high as the case may be. They may be made either as given for their older relations i.e. with fluffy stitched-in ear linings so that they are entirely cuddly, or they can become more of a model having stuck-in ear linings and tinted coats (see page 16, 'tinting and shading'). Suggested positions for eyes are given on the patterns.

FLOPSY BUNNY NO. 1 (Running)

Materials

¼ yard (23 cm) beige and ⅛ yard (12 cm) white fur fabric for body. (Sufficient for two bunnies if cut with care.)

Scraps of beige felt for soles of feet and pink or white for ear linings.

Scraps of brown and white felt for eyes.

Brown stranded cotton for nose.

Strong, black thread for whiskers.

Kapok for stuffing. Finished toys weigh approximately 3 ounces (85 grammes).

Method

1 CUT OUT the pieces as given on pages 156–8 (26 pieces).
2 EARS (Fig. 24): Fold long edges of ears A–B and C–B inwards and stick in place (A and B). Stick linings in place (C). Fold at base and stick or stitch either as E or F.

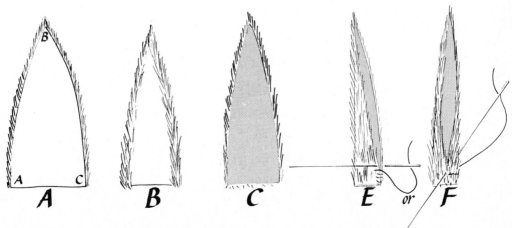

Fig. 24 Folding the Flopsy Bunnies' ears

Plate 1 Flopsy Bunny No. 1

Plate 2 Flopsy Bunny No. 2

Plate 3 Flopsy Bunny No. 3

Plate 4 Flopsy Bunny No. 4

Plate 5
Flopsy Bunny No. 5

Plate 6
Flopsy Bunny No. 6

3 TAIL	
4 ARMS	
5 LEGS	Work as for Peter Rabbit pages 29–31,
6 BODY	Nos. 3–11, but look at Plate I on page 38
7 HEAD	and when sewing on legs and arms, place
8 STUFFING AND ASSEMBLING	them so that the rabbit is in an attractive position on all fours. (Suggestions for
9 EYES	placing the limbs are shown on the pattern.)
10 NOSE	
11 WHISKERS	

12 MODELLING: pull head over to one side (look at picture) and using a long needle and strong thread, ladder stitch it firmly in this position.

FLOPSY BUNNY NO. 2 (Sitting propped up asleep)

'The little rabbits smiled sweetly in their sleep . . . they did not awake because the lettuces had been so soporific.'

Materials
As for Bunny No. 1 but no felt for eyes.

Method

1 CUT OUT pieces as given on page 159 (3 pieces) also head gusset, tail, ears, ear linings, soles of feet, outer and inner arms, lower outer leg, top of outer leg and inner leg as given for Bunny No. 1 on pages 156–8 (19 pieces), (22 pieces in all).

2 EARS. Work as given for Bunny No. 1, page 37.

3 TAIL	Work as for Peter Rabbit, pages 29–30, Nos. 3–8 but
4 ARMS	look at Plate 2, page 39, when sewing on arms and legs.
5 LEGS	Place the legs forwards side by side, one foot slightly
6 BODY	higher than the other so that your rabbit can sit propped
7 HEAD	up as though asleep with his head forward on his chest.
8 STUFFING AND ASSEMBLING	Sew the arms so that they meet in the centre of 'tummy' and catch in place there with a few strong stitches. Stitch the tail hanging downwards so that the rabbit sits on it.

9 EYES. Embroider a straight, brown stitch on each side of head to indicate a shut eye.

10 NOSE	Work as given for Peter Rabbit, page 31, Nos. 10–11.
11 WHISKERS	

12 MODELLING. With a long needle and strong thread stitch the chin to chest so that the head is really bowed.

FLOPSY BUNNY NO. 3 (Lying down asleep)

'The little Flopsy Bunnies slept delightfully in the warm sun.'

Materials

As for Bunny No. 1 but no felt for eyes.

Method

1 CUT OUT the pieces as given on pages 160–1 (4 pieces), also the ears, ear linings, head gusset, inner and outer arms, soles of feet and tail as given for Flopsy Bunny No. 1, pages 156–8 (13 pieces), (17 pieces in all).

2 EARS. Work as given for Bunny No. 1, page 37, No. 2.

3 TAIL. Work as given for Peter Rabbit, page 29, No. 3.

4 ARMS. On beige outer arm join top dart 1–2. Place this piece right sides together with a white inner arm and join G–Y and H–I. Now insert a felt sole into the end of arm, matching L with I and N with Y. Stitch all round LI–NY–LI. (In this case we are using the arm patterns for a hind leg because the shape is convenient for the position in which the finished rabbit lies.) This 'arm' is therefore now referred to as a 'leg'! Make another leg in the same way.

5 BODY. Work from * to * as given for Peter Rabbit, page 30, No. 6, then take the front gusset and join to one side of the body Q–R–S. Join this piece to the other side of body in the same way. Join the two body sides together T–K. Insert body gusset, stitching all round T–S–X–S–T.

6 HEAD. Work as given for Peter Rabbit, page 30, No. 7.

7 STUFFING AND ASSEMBLING. Work as given for Peter Rabbit, page 30, No. 8, from * to *. Stuff legs—look at Plate 3, page 40, and sew one to back of body curling forwards and the other to edge of underbody so that the sole of foot shows and the rabbit's hind legs appear to be curled round. Sew on tail.

8 EYES. Work as for Bunny No. 2, page 42, No. 9.

9 NOSE ⎫
10 WHISKERS⎭ Work as for Peter Rabbit, page 31, Nos. 10–11.

11 MODELLING. Stitch the rabbit's nose down between his front paws.

FLOPSY BUNNY NO. 4 (Bent over with arched back—eating)

'The Flopsy Bunnies simply stuffed lettuces.'

Materials

As for Flopsy Bunny No. 1 but no felt for soles of feet.

Method

1 CUT OUT the pieces as given on pages 162–3 (4 pieces) also inner and outer arms, pupils, eyes, tail, ears, ear linings and head gusset as given for Flopsy Bunny No. 1 on pages 156–8 (15 pieces) (19 pieces in all).

2 EARS. Work as given for Bunny No. 1, page 37, No 2.

3 TAIL ⎫
4 ARMS ⎬ Work as given for Peter Rabbit, page 29, Nos. 3–4.

5 BODY. Work as for Peter Rabbit, page 30, No 6, from * to *. Then take the body gusset and join the small dart 2–3, so that the 2s meet. Join this piece to one body side all round Q–R–X–S. Join the other body side to the other side of the gusset in the same way. Join the two sides of body together T–W. Now take the seat gusset and insert it, stitching all round T–S–2–S–T.

6 HEAD. Work as given for Peter Rabbit, page 30, No. 7.

7 STUFFING AND ASSEMBLING. Work as for Peter Rabbit, page 30, No. 8, from * to *. Stuff arms. Sew arms to sides of body (look at Plate 4) so that the 'paws' are on the ground, one each side of head. Sew tail high up on back, just below W (the rabbit has his body arched.)

8 EYES ⎫
9 NOSE ⎬ Work as given for Peter Rabbit, page 30–1, Nos. 9, 10, 11.
10 WHISKERS ⎭

FLOPSY BUNNY NO. 5 (Squatting)

Materials

As for Flopsy Bunny No. 1.

Method

1 CUT OUT the pieces as given for Flopsy Bunny No. 3 and add pupils and eyes as given for Flopsy Bunny No. 1, page 158 (21 pieces).

2 EARS. Work as given for Bunny No. 1, page 37, No. 2.

3 TAIL. Work as given for Peter Rabbit, page 29, No. 3.

4 ARMS ⎫
5 BODY ⎬ Work as given for Bunny No. 3, page 43, Nos. 4–5.

6 HEAD. Work as given for Peter Rabbit, page 30, No. 7.

7 STUFFING AND ASSEMBLING. Work as for Peter Rabbit, page 30, No. 8, from * to *. Stuff legs. Look at Plate 5. Sew one leg to each side at back of body so that the rabbit is squatting. Sew on tail.

8 EYES ⎫
9 NOSE ⎬ Work as given for Peter Rabbit, pages 30–1, Nos. 9, 10, 11.
10 WHISKERS ⎭

11 MODELLING. Bend the rabbit's head backwards and stitch to body.

FLOPSY BUNNY NO. 6 (Standing on hind legs)

Materials

As for Flopsy Bunny No. 1 but no felt for soles of feet.

Method

1 CUT OUT the pieces as given on page 164 (5 pieces) also the seat gusset as given for Flopsy Bunny No. 4 on page 162 and the ears, ear linings, eyes, pupils, tail, inner and outer arms and head gusset for Flopsy Bunny No. 1, pages 156–8 (16 pieces), (21 pieces in all).

2 EARS. Work as given for Flopsy Bunny No. 1, page 37, No. 2.

3 TAIL
4 ARMS
5 BODY
6 SEAT
7 HEAD
8 STUFFING AND ASSEMBLING
9 EYES
10 NOSE
11 WHISKERS

Work as given for Flopsy, Mopsy and Cotton-tail, page 32, Nos. 3–11, but when inserting seat gusset, W on body will match 2 on gusset so stitch all round T–S–W2–S–T. When inserting ears, place them so that they will hang down the back. Look at Plate 6, page 41.

If you wish to tint and shade your Flopsy Bunnies, consult page 16.

The Pigs

If you enjoy working with felt, the pigs are perhaps the most satisfying of all the toys to make. They are probably the easiest of all the felt toys (except for Jeremy Fisher), in spite of a certain amount of modelling which is necessary to shape their heads. If the instructions and diagrams are carefully followed there should be no difficulty experienced and a great deal of fun will come out of the work.

It is suggested that your first choice should be Pigling Bland himself. He is used as the basic example and having once made him, the instructions for the rest of his family will fall easily into place and prove much more simple to follow.

PIGLING BLAND

'Now Pigling Bland, son Pigling Bland, you must go to market. Take your brother Alexander by the hand. Mind your Sunday clothes and remember to blow your nose.'

Refer to the frontispiece of the book of the same name, as well as the colour plate opposite page 85 of this book.

A wired felt toy approximately 10 inches (25 cm) high.

Materials

    12 × 18 inches (30·5 × 46 cm) pink felt for the body (Petal 52). (24 × 18 inches (61 × 46 cm) will make Pigling Bland, Alexander and Spot, if the pieces are very carefully placed.)

Scraps of beige felt for ear linings, white for collar.

18 × 12 inches (46 × 30·5 cm) mauve felt for the coat (Mauve 72).

18 × 12 inches (46 × 30·5 cm) yellow felt for the trousers (Citron 41). (This will make two pairs.)

Scrap of blue/white striped cotton and four tiny pearl buttons for the waistcoat.

Scrap of red/white spot cotton material for the bundle.

Scrap of blue cotton material for the scarf.

*A wooden meat skewer for stick.

*A small piece of postcard for the pig licence.

Beige Sylko for bristles.

Black, white and red stranded cotton for eyes, nostrils and mouth.

Red water colour paint or cochineal for tinting cheeks.

A pipe cleaner and 14 inches (35 cm) of wire. Adhesive tape for covering.

Kapok for stuffing. Finished toy weighs approximately 4 ounces (113 grammes).

Method

1 CUT OUT the pieces as given on pages 166–9 (33 pieces).

2 HEAD. On the wrong side of both sides of head, work as given for Peter Rabbit's body, No. 6, page 30 from * to *. Join small dart 1–2 (remember to reverse one piece so as to make a pair). Still on the wrong side take the head gusset and join to one side of head A–O. Join the other side of head to the other side of gusset A–O, then continue stitching so as to join the two sides of head together O–B. Join the two sides of head together C–D. Turn right side out, easing top of head down through neck with the help of a small round-ended stuffing stick. Embroider the nostrils on snout as shown on pattern. Insert snout into head having the point X at the top between the two As and stab stitching all round on the right side. Place on one side.

3 BODY. On the wrong side join darts 3–4 which you have already cut out of two of the body pieces. Join the four body pieces together 3–H. The two with darts are the side pieces (the darts are the 'shoulders'), the two plain pieces are the front and back, so place them alternately when stitching together. Turn right side out. Place on one side.

4 LEGS (Fig. 25). Place the pieces together in pairs and stitch front seam J–K and back seam L–M (A). Turn right side out and insert a limb base into the end of both legs, stab stitching all round N–K–N–M–N (B). Place on one side.

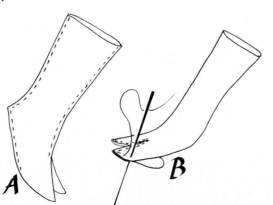

Fig. 25 Making Pigling Bland's legs

5 RIGHT ARM. On the wrong side join the top dart 5–6 on the outer piece. Place this piece together with the inner piece and on the wrong side join the front seam S–K and the back seam Q–R–M. Turn right side out and insert a limb base, stab stitching all round N–K–N–M–N on the right side. Place on one side.

6 LEFT ARM. Make in the same way as the right arm, remembering to reverse the pieces. Place on one side.

7 TAIL (Fig. 26). Take half a pipe cleaner (A). Fold a piece of the matching pink felt round it (B). Stab stitch the two sides of felt together close to the pipe cleaner (C). Trim off surplus felt (D).

8 EARS (Fig. 27). Stick an ear lining to two of the ear pieces (fronts), reversing one so that you have a pair (A). Using beige Sylko or one strand of embroidery cotton, take a series of stitches on the front (B) and back (C) to soften the outline of ear lining and indicate bristles. Place the fronts and backs of the ears together in pairs right sides together and stitch round E–F–G (D). Turn right side out, pushing points out carefully. Oversew E–G (E). Fold base as shown and oversew (F).

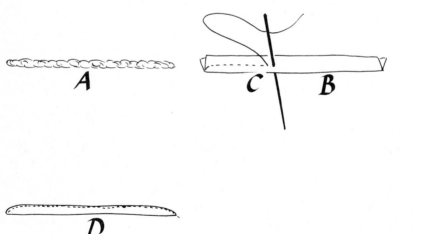

Fig. 26 Making Pigling Bland's tail

9 STUFFING AND MODELLING HEAD (Fig. 28). Stuff head very firmly indeed, paying particular attention to the snout and fat puffy cheeks, which need filling out really well so that the finished head is almost square. Push pointed scissors into head and cut a small hole for ear where indicated on pattern. (Make the hole the smallest size into which you can push the ear, so that the ear fits snugly.) Push the base of one ear into hole (point of ear

curling outwards) and stitch edge of hole on head to ear, working all round twice (A). Stitch inside edge of ear to head for about ½ inch (1 cm) upwards from slit (B). Insert other ear in the same way. Using six strands of black embroidery cotton, make a small black dot on each gusset seam ¾ inch (2 cm) down from ear (B) then work backwards and forwards from eye to

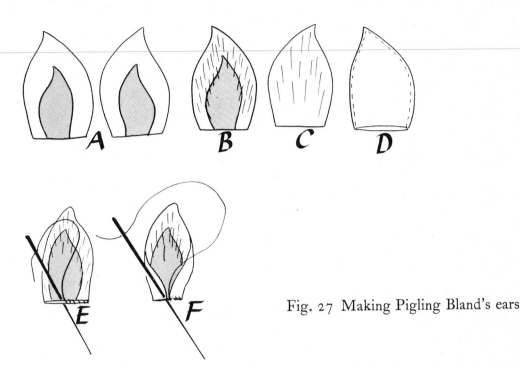

Fig. 27 Making Pigling Bland's ears

eye, through the snout, pulling the stitches tightly to sink eyes and raise snout (C). Take the needle through to mouth position (shown on pattern) and take a stitch each side of centre seam, parallel with the gusset seam. Stitch through head from one corner to the other to sink mouth (D). Using white stranded cotton embroider a small, white dot on the lower side of each eye, working backwards and forwards from side to side through snout (D). Using a long, slim needle and double Sylko which exactly matches the Pig's 'skin', take a series of invisible stitches right through the head from the edge of one ear to the edge of the other, pulling tightly so as to raise the face in front of ears. Work from the point where the ears are stitched to head gusset down to base of ear and on down the face for another ½ inch (just over 1 cm) (D). Now work up and down, bringing the needle out right under the cheek close to neck, and on top of cheek to make them really fat. Work forwards to about 1 inch (2·5 cm) from snout (F), then backwards and forwards, sideways, through cheek. Take a series of tight stitches across snout, about ½ inch (1 cm) from the tip, through to mouth corners, to 'angle' the snout

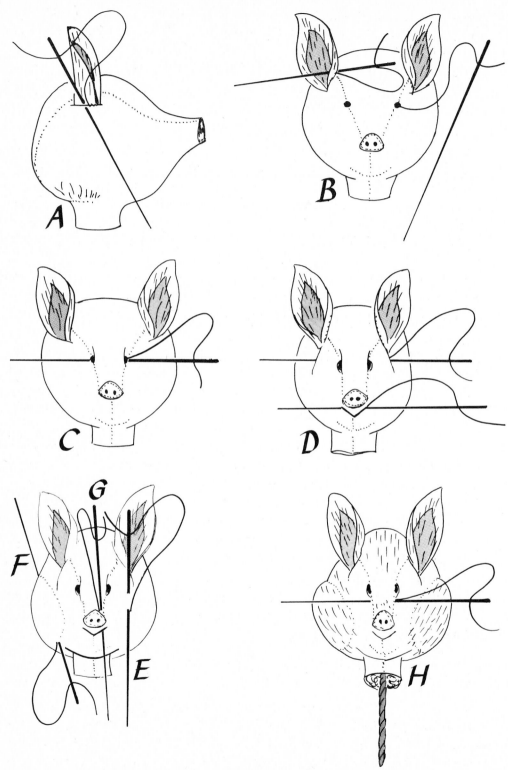

Fig. 28 Stuffing and modelling Pigling Bland's head

(G). Take a series of tight stitches from this point up to eyes, working from seam to seam through the snout to raise it (H). Look at your pig critically and if you feel he needs any more modelling, do it now.

Embroider bristles like those on ears, on cheeks, top and back of head (E and H). Finally, tint cheeks, snout, back and inside of ears, using weak, red, water colour. Allow to dry thoroughly before doing any more (preferably overnight). If necessary, add a little more colour.

10 ASSEMBLING. Prepare three pieces of wire as shown on page 13, Fig. 8A and B. Two 5 inches (12·5 cm) long for legs and one 4 inches (10 cm) long for neck. * Stuff the body. Push the neck wire up into head so that half is hidden (Fig. 28H). Pack more stuffing inside neck until it is rock firm. Push the other end of wire down into body. Pack more stuffing all round top of body and shoulders. Turn head slightly to the left and ladder stitch top of body to neck, working round and round several times and packing extra stuffing in as you work. Stuff the arms very firmly paying particular attention to the cloven hoofs and pushing tiny pieces of kapok right down into these points with a cocktail stick. * Stuff the hoofs on legs in the same way, then push a prepared wire down into each leg, reaching right down into the tip of one point of hoof (Fig. 25C). Continue stuffing legs, pushing tiny pieces inside with the point of a cocktail stick, so that the wires are completely embedded. Push points of scissors into two side panels of body as indicated on pattern, making a hole and a channel inside the body stuffing. Push the wire and about ½ inch (1 cm) of one leg up into body, making the hole just large enough to ease the leg through, so that it fits tightly. Ladder stitch body to top of leg, working round and round several times (Fig. 29). Insert other leg in the same way. Place the open ends of arms flat against the body 1 inch (2·5 cm) from neck on the top dart and looking at picture for positions, ladder stitch in place as shown by Fig. 6, page 10.

11 TROUSERS. Fold each piece in half at broken line on pattern and stitch small seams A–B and C–D. Join these two 'legs' together round centre seam E–C–E. Put trousers on to pig inside out and upside down and stitch all round leg (Fig. 30). Turn trousers up over body and stitch firmly all round waist, easing fullness in at sides. The bottoms of trouser legs thus have a full, 'tucked up' appearance.

12 SCARF. Cut a strip of pale blue material about 2 inches (5 cm) wide. Wrap round neck and tie like a cravat in front. Stitch firmly to front of body.

13 WAISTCOAT. Turn edges of waistcoat—indicated by broken lines on pattern—to wrong side (the tiniest possible turning). Machine round these edges. Overlap front edges A–B very slightly and machine. Sew four tiny pearl buttons down this centre seam. Pin in position on pig, so that the lower V covers top of trousers and the scarf is tucked inside top V. Stretch

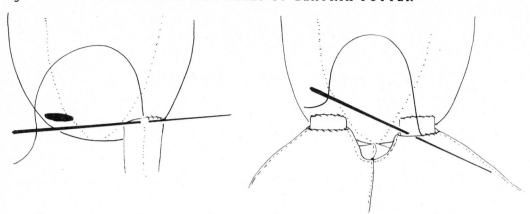

Fig. 29 Inserting Pigling Bland's legs   Fig. 30 Stitching trousers to legs

tightly over shoulders and round sides. Stitch firmly in place down sides and across shoulders, also at centre V and two front panels.

14 COLLAR. Cut a strip of white felt ¾ inch (2 cm) wide and 3 inches (7·5 cm) long. Stretch tightly round neck, covering sides of scarf and leaving a small gap at centre front. Stitch firmly to pig, working all round edge—look at picture.

15 COAT. Fold sleeves in half and join seams E–F. Turn right side out. On the coat join darts A–B. Slit up centre back C–D. Insert sleeves into holes matching Es. Put on to pig, turning the collar back as shown by broken line on pattern and stitching invisibly and firmly all the way down each front. Look at picture and stitch the arms to the body in positions shown.

16 INSERTING TAIL. Push the point of a slim pair of scissors well into body at the centre of slit in back of coat. Push the tail into hole, ladder stitch trousers to tail, working round twice. Slip end through slit in coat and twist into a curl. '*We curled their tails.*'

17 THE BUNDLE. Cut a 6-inch (15-cm) square of red and white spotted material, put a knob of stuffing in the centre. Lay the end of a wooden meat skewer or a smooth piece of twig well smeared with Copydex on the stuffing and make the square into a round bundle about the size of a walnut by tying the opposite corners together. The bundle should be well secured on the end of the stick. Add a few stitches for added firmness. Look at picture. Stitch the bundle to the left shoulder and the stick between the hoof points. '*Aunt Pettitoes gave to each a little bundle.*'

18 PIG LICENCE. Cut a rectangle of white postcard 1 × 1½ inches (2·5 × 4 cm). Fold in half lengthwise and print 'PIG LICENCE' on the outside. Place between the hoof points on the right hand and stitch in place. '*I have had no end of trouble in getting these papers from a policeman.*' If you feel the points on the 'foot' hoofs are too far apart, catch them together with a few neat stitches.

FLOPSY, Mopsy and Cotton-tail, who were good little bunnies, went down the lane to gather blackberries.

The Tale of Peter Rabbit

HE suggested that they should fill the pocket handkerchief with onions . . .

The Tale of Benjamin Bunny

ALEXANDER

'Pigling Bland and Alexander went to market.'

Refer to the frontispiece of *The Tale of Pigling Bland*, and to the colour plate opposite page 85 of this book.

A wired felt toy approximately 10 inches (25 cm) high.

Materials

Exactly as for Pigling Bland, page 46, but substitute green felt (Almond 2) for the coat and red/white striped material for the waistcoat. No white felt is needed.

Method

Make up exactly as given for Pigling Bland, pages 47–52, using the alternative colours but in Nos. 5 and 6 reverse the side on which you sew the darts and seams so that the left arm becomes the right and vice versa and in No. 10 turn the head to the right instead of the left. In No. 12 wrap the scarf across chest instead of folding as a cravat and omit No. 14, as Alexander does not wear a collar. Place the bundle and stick in a different position and omit No. 18, the Pig Licence.

Short guide: changes to be made in Nos. 5, 6, 10 and 12. Numbers 14 and 18 to be omitted.

PIGLING BLAND SITTING ON HIS COPPY STOOL

'Pigling . . . sitting on the edge of his coppy stool. . . . Pigling Bland sat by the fire . . .'

Refer to the many illustrations of Pigling Bland on a stool in *The Tale of Pigling Bland*, as well as the colour plate opposite page 276 of this book.

A felt toy with wired neck and weighted base for firm sitting.

Instructions for making the coppy stool appear on page 287.

Materials

As for the standing pig on page 46 except for the two starred items and only 4 inches (10 cm) of wire (instead of 14 inches). Also, a heavy stone about the size of a walnut.

Some strong cardboard.

Method

1 CUT OUT all the pieces given on pages 166–9 for the standing pig *except* the trousers and eight arm and leg pieces (23 pieces). Then cut two right inner and two right outer arms as given for standing pig on pages 167–8 (4

pieces) and all the pieces given for sitting pig on page 170 (8 pieces) making 35 pieces in all.

2 HEAD. Work as given for the standing pig, page 47, No. 2.

3 BODY. Work as given for the standing pig, page 47, No. 3 but join the body pieces together 3–X only, leaving the four lower parts open. Do not cut leg holes. This pig needs weighting at the base so that he will sit firmly on a stool much too small for him! * To achieve this, stick the two cardboard circles together so that you have a really strong piece. On top of the card stick a clean stone about the size of a walnut, first with Copydex (Fig. 31A) then with adhesive tape (B). Cut a rough circle of pink felt large enough to envelop the prepared base. Stick the underside of card circle to the centre with a scant smear of Copydex. Gather all round the edge, pull up gathers on top of stone and fasten off very securely (C) *. With the body right side out, tuck in the lower four points so that you have a double edge, slip the covered stone inside and pin the body to the covered card circle. Oversew body to weighted base (D), the flat, felt-covered card will allow the pig to sit securely. Place on one side.

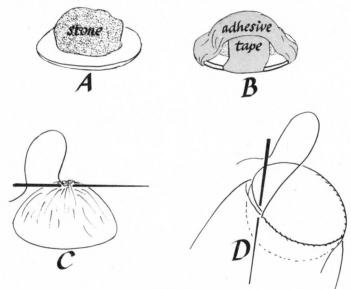

Fig. 31 Weighting the base of sitting pig

4 LEGS. Work as given for standing pig, page 47, No. 4, but using the different patterns.

5 ARMS. Make both arms as given for standing pig's right arm, page 48, No. 5, reversing one set of pieces when stitching to make a pair.

6 TAIL
7 EARS   } Work as given for standing pig,
8 STUFFING AND MODELLING HEAD } page 48, Nos. 7, 8 and 9.

9 ASSEMBLING. Prepare the wire as given on page 13, Fig. 8, for the neck. Work from * to * as given for the standing pig, page 51, No. 10, turning the head to whatever angle you wish. Sew on arms, placing the open ends flat against sides of body—the top arm seam at right angles to the shoulder dart on body about 1 inch (2·5 cm) from neck and ladder stitch all round as shown by Fig. 6 on page 10. The arms are stretched forward whilst Pigling warms his hands at the fire. Stuff the legs firmly, paying particular attention to the hoofs. Pin legs firmly in place—the back seams on the edge of flat base. The left leg hangs downwards and the right one is cocked in the air— test the pig sitting on the edge of a table and when you have the position you want, ladder stitch them in place.

10 TROUSERS 11 SCARF 12 WAISTCOAT 13 COLLAR 14 COAT 15 INSERTING TAIL	Work as given for standing pig pages 51–2, Nos. 11, 12, 13, 14, 15 and 16, using the alternative pattern for trousers (noting that the back seam continues E–X) and pushing a little kapok low down into the front part of the trousers to pad them out at the side and give the pig plump 'hams'. You will find the waistcoat a little broad as this pig has his arms closer together in the front than the standing pig—so merely tuck any surplus inside when stitching in place.

If you feel the points of the hoofs are too far apart, catch them together with a few stitches.

Sit Pigling on his coppy stool—instructions are on page 287.

PIG-WIG

'*A perfectly lovely little black Berkshire pig—she had twinkly little screwed up eyes, a double chin and a short, turned up nose.*'

Refer to picture of Pig-wig sitting on an oak chair on page 67 of *The Tale of Pigling Bland*, for the best view, as well as to the colour plate opposite page 276 of this book.

Instructions for making her chair appear on page 288 and her coppy stool on page 287.

Materials

9 × 12 inches (23 × 30 cm) dark grey felt for body (Mole 65).
Scraps of pink felt (over from Pigling Bland) for hoofs, limb bases and snout.
Scraps of black felt for ear linings.
A piece of blue/white cotton print for dress and drawers $\frac{3}{8}$ yard (33 cm).
Scraps of narrow white lace for trimming.
Black, white and light grey Sylko or embroidery cotton for bristles and nostrils.

14 inches (35 cm) wire and adhesive tape for stiffening.

Kapok for stuffing.

Finished toy weighs approximately 2 ounces (56 grammes).

Method

1 CUT OUT the pieces as given on pages 168 and 171 (36 pieces).
2 HEAD } Work as given for Pigling Bland, page 47, Nos. 2 and 3, but
3 BODY } embroider nostrils in black.
4 LEGS. Join a pink hoof piece to the end of each grey leg X–M by neatly oversewing on the wrong side. Remember to reverse the pieces to make two pairs, then work as given for Pigling Bland, page 47, No. 4.
5 ARMS. Join a hoof to each arm piece as given for the legs, then make both arms as given for Pigling Bland's right arm, page 48, No. 5, reversing the pieces to make a pair—but both the same shape.

Fig. 32 Pig-wig's ear

Fig. 33 Pig-wig's face   Fig. 34 Pig-wig's leg.

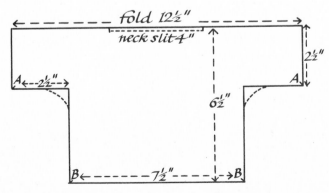

Fig. 35 Plan for Pig-wig's dress

6 EARS (Fig. 32). Work as given for Pigling Bland, page 48, No. 8, using black Sylko for the majority of the bristles but adding a few light grey and white stitches towards the tips to create a shine.

7 STUFFING AND MODELLING HEAD (Fig. 33). Work as given for Pigling Bland, page 48, No. 9, but this time add a lot of black bristles to create a black sheen on the grey felt. Shade the stitches towards the tip of the snout by using light grey and a little white Sylko. Make the eyes smaller than Pigling Bland's and add a white stitch both sides of the black pupil—look at picture.

8 ASSEMBLING. Work as given for Pigling Bland, page 51, No. 10, looking at the picture for position of head and arms. Sit Pig-wig on the edge of a table and bend and press legs until she sits really securely and will not topple when placed on her chair or stool. Work a few black and grey stitches over the joins between each arm and leg and the hoofs to soften the join and give a bristly appearance (Fig. 34).

9 DRAWERS. Fold each piece as shown on pattern and on the wrong side machine seams A–B. Join the two pieces together C–A–C. Turn right side out. Put on to pig, pull up high under arms and turning in top raw edge, stitch all round body, pleating in fullness. Tuck in raw leg edges and stitch drawers to pig's legs as close to body as possible, working all round and pleating in fullness.

10 DRESS. Cut a piece of blue/white cotton material as shown by the plan (Fig. 35), rounding off the underarm corners as indicated by broken lines. Fold along top line as shown on pattern and on the wrong side machine side seams A–B and turn up a narrow hem round bottom edge B–B–B. Turn right side out. Cut 4 inch (10 cm) head slit. Run a gathering thread round sleeves and neck, turning in raw edges as you work and leaving long ends. Do not fasten off. Put dress on to pig, pull up gathers and stitch firmly to wrists and neck, working all round. Make three tiny frills from narrow white lace by gathering along straight edge and stitch one round each wrist and one round the neck, covering edges of dress.

If you think the hoof points are too far apart, catch them together with a few neat stitches and make final adjustments to Pig-wig's position whilst sitting her on the edge of a table, so that she will be quite firm on her chair or her stool!

SPOT

'*Aunt Pettitoes . . . passed the handkerchief to Spot.*'

Refer to picture on page 19 of *The Tale of Pigling Bland*, as well as to the colour plate opposite page 85 of this book.

Materials

9 × 12 inches (23 × 30 cm) pink felt for body (Petal 52).

Scraps of fawn felt for ear linings.

$\frac{3}{8}$ yard (33 cm) pinky-mauve and white cotton print for dress and drawers.

Scrap of narrow white lace for trimming.

Fawn Sylko or embroidery cotton for bristles.

Black stranded cotton for eyes. Red for nostrils.

Kapok for stuffing. Finished toy weighs approximately 2 ounces (56 grammes).

14 inches (35 cm) wire and adhesive tape for stiffening.

5 × 5 inches (13 × 13 cm) fine white lawn for handkerchief.

Two small press-studs (000 gauge).

Method

1 CUT OUT the pieces as for Pig-wig on pages 168 and 171, but cut the arms and legs complete with hoofs as for all the other pigs and substitute the colours given above for those used for Pig-wig.

2 HEAD
3 BODY
4 LEGS } Work as given for Pigling Bland, pages 47–8, Nos. 2, 3, 4, 5 and 8.
5 ARMS
6 EARS

7 STUFFING AND MODELLING HEAD. Work as given for Pigling Bland, page 48, No. 9 but embroider two slits for eyes using black, stranded cotton (look at picture).

8 ASSEMBLING. Work as given for Pigling Bland, page 51, No. 10, looking at picture for position of arms and legs—the arms upwards, ready to hold the hankie and legs bent straight downwards.

9 DRAWERS } Work as given for Pig-wig, page 57, Nos. 9 and 10.
10 DRESS

11 HANDKERCHIEF. Make a narrow hem all round the edge of the piece of lawn.

12 HOW SPOT HOLDS THE HANKIE. Sew one half of a tiny press-stud under Spot's snout—between mouth and nose. Sew the other half to one tip of the limb base on the left arm. Sew one half of the second press-stud to one tip of the limb base on right arm and the other half to the edge of the sleeve on the left arm. You can then fix the left hoof to her face and the right hoof to the left arm and tuck the hankie over hoofs as in picture. If you are careful to sew the corresponding halves to each hoof—she can clasp her hands together when you want a change!

N.B. On page 28 of *Appley Dapply's Nursery Rhymes* there is a pig very like Spot sitting on a chair very like Pig-wig's! Make up Pig-wig in Spot's colours and you will have the pig in this picture.

AUNT PETTITOES

'Once upon a time there was an old pig called Aunt Pettitoes.'

Refer to the picture on page 14 of *The Tale of Pigling Bland,* as well as to the colour plate opposite page 85 of this book.

A 15-inch (38-cm) high flat-based toy with removable apron, cap and buckets.

Materials

12 × 18 inches (31 × 46 cm) pink felt (Petal 52) for the head and hands.
Scraps of deeper pink felt for ear linings.
¾ yard (69 cm) blue/white striped cotton material for dress.
9 × 9 inches (23 × 23 cm) scrim for apron.
11 × 11 inches (28 × 28 cm) blue/white flowered cotton material for mob cap.
9 inches (23 cm) very narrow elastic.
About ½ yard (46 cm) old sheeting, curtain lining, etc. for foundation.
Kapok for filling head and hands and approximately ½ lb (230 grammes) cheaper filling for body.
24 inches (61 cm) beige tape for apron strings.
Black and white stranded cotton for eyes and mouth.
Two shades of beige, and light brown Sylko or embroidery cotton for bristles.
Two small press-studs for hands.
Two ¼-pint cream cartons ⎫
Two 4½-inch (11·5-cm) wires ⎬ for buckets.
Aluminium paint ⎭
5 inches (13 cm) wood for neck stiffening.

Method

1 CUT OUT dress as shown by Fig. 36 and the pieces as given on pages 172–3 (17 pieces).
2 EARS. Work as for Pigling Bland, page 48, No. 8 but add many more bristles and use a darker shade of Sylko on and towards linings and a paler shade towards the edges (Fig. 37).
3 HEAD. Work as given for Pigling Bland, page 47, No. 2, using black stranded cotton for the nostrils. Then work as given for Pigling Bland, page

48, No. 9, noting that there is extra fullness on this pattern so that the cheeks are fatter than ever and that the mouth (see pattern) is larger and smiling. You will need a very long needle, and pliers to pull it through, for much of the modelling. Make the eyes with the whites above the pupils instead of below (Fig. 38) and her ears pointing *inwards*. Aunt Pettitoes is an old pig and has a double chin. When all the other modelling is finished, make the chin by stitching tightly through front of head from top of one dart to the top of the other (Fig. 38). Make her bristles darker towards the snout and add a few slim, brown wrinkles (look at picture). Prepare a 5-inch (13-cm) piece of wood or doubled wire as shown by Fig. 8D, page 13, to strengthen neck. Push well up into head, leaving the bottom half protruding. Add any extra necessary stuffing.

4 ARMS (Fig. 39). Place two of the pink felt hand pieces together and on the wrong side join H–K and L–M. Turn right side out. Insert hoof base, stab stitching all round N–K–N–M–N as for Pigling Bland (Fig. 25B, page 47). Stuff firmly. Make the other hand in the same way. Cut two pieces of odd cotton material 3 × 4 inches (7·5 × 10 cm). Fold in half so that you have a piece 3 × 2 inches (7·5 × 5 cm). Machine long edge. Turn right side out. Tuck in raw edges at one end and machine. Machine across arm again, about ½ inch (1·5 cm) further down, making a hinge. Stuff this arm piece firmly except for the last ½ inch (1·5 cm). Push hand up into it, front seam of hand to seam on arm. Pin, then stitch cotton arm to hand, working all round. The completed limb should be about 5 inches (13 cm) long from end to end. Sew a tiny press-stud inside the hoof tips so that when fastened, Aunt Pettitoes can hold the buckets.

5 BODY (Fig. 40). * Cut a circle of very strong cardboard the size of a saucer for the base. If the card is not so strong that it will not whip or bend, cut another and stick the two together. Cut a double circle of cotton material, about 1½ times as large as your board. Gather all round the edge, place board in centre, pull up gathers and fasten off securely so that the base has a smooth, taut outside; the gathers will be hidden inside. Cut a double piece of cotton material 12 inches (30 cm) wide and long enough to fit round edge of base circle plus a seam allowance. Fold the piece in half and on the wrong side machine ends together. Still on the wrong side pin this tube all round base, leaving about ½ inch (1·5 cm) turning and having base also on wrong side. Oversew firmly, using strong double thread (Fig. 41). Turn right way out and using any cheap, odd stuffing, fill body firmly for 7½ inches (19 cm). Run a strong gathering thread all round body at this point, pull up to form the 'waist', leaving an open centre hole about 2½ inches (6·5 cm) across. Fasten off thread. * Fill the waist gap with stuffing. Run a strong gathering thread round top of body, turning in raw edges about ½ inch (1·5 cm). Stuff top of body firmly.

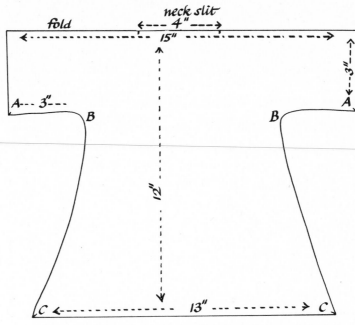

Fig. 36 Plan for Aunt Pettitoes' dress

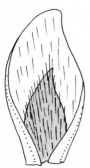

Fig. 37 Aunt Pettitoes' ears

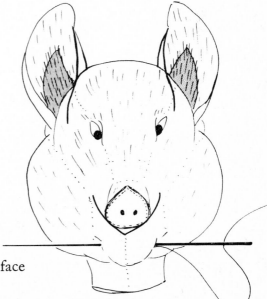

Fig. 38 Aunt Pettitoes' face

6 ASSEMBLING. Push padded wood protruding from head down into body. Push any necessary extra stuffing round it so that everything is very firm, pull up gathers on body top and stitch several times round neck and through the rag covering the wood. The finished body should be about 9½ inches (24 cm) high—entire pig about 15 inches (38 cm). Stitch arms by hinge firmly, one each side of pig—hoofs pointing forward, tops about 1 inch (2·5 cm) down from neck.

7 DRESS. On the wrong side, machine side seams A–B–C. Turn right side out and cut neck slit. Run a gathering thread round neck slit and sleeves, turning in raw edges–leave long ends and do not fasten off. Try on to pig (the head should be quite difficult to push through slit). Leave pig on one side for the present, complete with dress.

8 APRON. With a blue felt pen draw crossed lines on the scrim to make the apron look like that in the picture. Turn back a narrow hem round all four edges and stitch invisibly by hand. Sew a 12-inch (30-cm) beige apron string to each side of top. Put on to pig, crossing the strings at back and bringing forward and tying at centre front of apron. Test length of dress while apron is on and pin up hem (just touching the ground). Remove apron and dress. Stitch hem. Put dress back on pig, pull up gathers and stitch neatly all round neck and wrists. Put apron back again.

Fig. 39 Aunt Pettitoes' arm

Fig. 40 Aunt Pettitoes' body

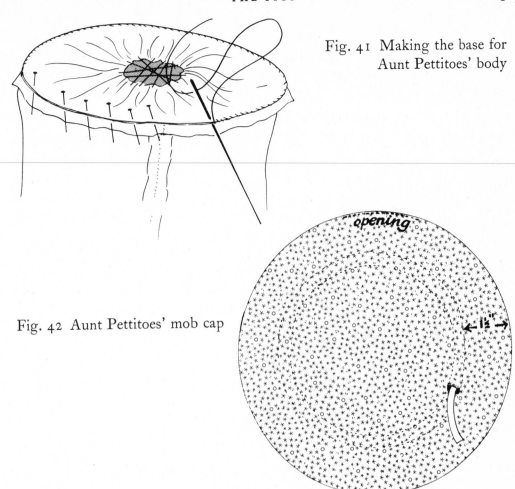

Fig. 41 Making the base for Aunt Pettitoes' body

Fig. 42 Aunt Pettitoes' mob cap

9 MOB-CAP (Fig. 42). Place a large dinner plate approximately 10 inches (25 cm) diameter on a double piece of blue/white flowered material, right sides inside and pencil all round. Machine all round on pencil line, leaving a small opening. Turn right side out, pushing out into a perfect circle. Invisibly oversew opening. Press. Pencil a rough circle, approximately 1½ inches (4 cm), in from the edge. Machine round this circle. Machine another circle about ½ inch (1·5 cm) away from the first—towards the inside. Cut a small cross-wise slit between these two rows of machining in *one* of the pieces of material only. Button-hole round slit to prevent fraying. Insert 9 inches (23 cm) of very narrow elastic into this hem. Join ends neatly and ease them into the slit so that they are lost. Put on pig's head behind ears.

10 BUCKETS. With a piece of hot wire (either heated in the fire or by being held in the flame of a lighted match), bore a hole at each side of the top of the cream cartons. Curve each piece of wire for handles by bending it round the carton. With pliers turn each end up and slip into the holes on

cartons from inside to outside. Lightly sandpaper the cartons to remove any grease and make a good surface for the paint. Paint all over inside and out with aluminium paint. Hang up to dry then give a second coat. When dry put the buckets in Aunt Pettitoes' hands and do up the press-studs so that she will hold them.

The Squirrels

Squirrel Nutkin and his grey cousins are very similar to the rabbits in construction, except that their heads and bodies are separate so can be easily adapted for jointing (see page 23). They take a little longer than the rabbits to make because of their tiny fingers and toes and need careful balancing when stuffing owing to their large tails.

It is advisable to make Squirrel Nutkin first, as the instructions given for him are basic for Timmy and Goody also. If difficulty is experienced in obtaining fur fabrics in suitable colours, buy white and dye it. In this case make sure to ask of what fibre the material is made when you buy it (nylon, wool, acrilan, etc.) so that you can choose a suitable dye.

SQUIRREL NUTKIN

'A little red squirrel and his name was Nutkin.'

Refer to the many pictures in *The Tale of Squirrel Nutkin*, as well as to the colour plate opposite page 277 of this book.

A cuddly toy approximately $12\frac{1}{2}$ inches (31·5 cm) high.

Instructions for making his raft are on page 289, his basket on page 278.

The head of this toy is made separately from the body to allow for various positions should you wish to make several squirrels, or to adapt it for jointing.

Materials

Reddish brown fur fabric for main parts of body ($\frac{1}{2}$ yard /48 cm) will make two squirrels).

Oddment of white fur fabric for body gusset (remnants from rabbits?).

Oddments of beige fur fabric for one side of tail and ear linings (remnants from rabbits?).

Scraps of matching brown, dark brown, black and white felt for eyes, hands and claws.

Brown stranded embroidery cotton for nose.

Black brush bristles for whiskers.

Twenty pipe cleaners for stiffening fingers.

Kapok for stuffing. Finished toy weighs approximately 9 ounces (255 grammes).

Method

1 CUT OUT the pieces as given on pages 174–9 (piecing together the tail pattern by matching the Xs when tracing this piece (see top of page 6) (32 pieces). The finished squirrel is much improved if the leg portions on body gusset (as marked by broken line on pattern) are cut in beige fur fabric and joined to the main white part. If doing this, cut each piece a little longer at broken line to allow for the join and in this case you will of course have 34 pieces. Cut out 20 claws as given for Mrs. Tiggy-winkle on page 213 but using black felt (54 pieces).

2 HANDS ⎫ Make exactly as given for Mrs. Tiggy-winkle, page 128, Nos.
3 CLAWS ⎰ 7 and 8 and Fig. 79.

4 ARMS. On the wrong side join small darts 1–2 on the outer arms. Place each inner arm on top of an outer arm, right sides together, and on the wrong side join seams A–B and C–D. Turn right side out. * Run a gathering thread round the wrist end of each arm, turning in raw edge as you work. Insert the prepared hands, pushing them well in so that Ds on arms rest on centre backs of hands. Pull up gathers to fit and stitch each arm firmly to a hand, working several times round and taking a few stitches right through wrist. Bend pipe cleaners to contour of arm and stuff firmly so that they are completely embedded. * Place on one side.

5 EARS. Smear Copydex sparingly on the wrong sides of ears and stick each beige piece to a brown, pressing firmly together, especially round edges to prevent the material fraying. Roll the base inwards from each side and stitch in place as given for Samuel Whiskers, Fig. 45 on page 76.

6 TAIL. Place the pieces together, right sides inside, and stitch all round E–F–E. Turn right side out and machine down centre broken line G–H. Stuff fairly firmly and place on one side.

7 HEAD. Join head gusset to one side of head I–J then join on the other side of head, stitching all round K–I–J. Turn right side out and stuff, pushing the nose out into a point and filling out sides very well to make back of head rather square and indicate fat cheeks. Place on one side.

8 BODY. If using two colours for body gusset, join the legs to main part first. Then place the two pieces together right sides inside and on the wrong side join them L–M. On the wrong side join this prepared gusset to one body piece L–N–O–P, then join the other body piece to other side of gusset L–N–O–P. Join the two body pieces together R–S and T–U. Insert base,

stitching Q–R–Q and V–M–V. Turn right side out. Insert the remaining two prepared hand pieces (which become feet!) into the ends of legs as described under 'Arms' No. 4 opposite, working from * to *. Gather up top of body U–L–U, turning in raw edge and fasten off firmly, thus closing opening. Finish stuffing body, paying particular attention to bent top of leg N–O. If the shape of this does not please you when finished, do a little needle modelling to keep the stuffing in place, working right through body and body gusset as shown by broken line on pattern thus creating a sort of 'haunch'. Close opening.

9 ASSEMBLING. * Make two slits on head for ears, looking through Nutkin's book to find the best position. (On the original they were inserted where shown by broken lines on pattern, so that they formed an almost straight line with back of head.) Push pointed scissors down into slits to make a channel inside head, then push lower part of ears into these holes and ladder stitch edge of slit to ear, working round and round several times. If you find it necessary, using a long needle and strong thread, take a stitch or two through head from the inside of one ear to the inside of the other and pull tightly to secure side of ear flat against head. * Place open end of head over gathered top of body and pin all round, adjusting it to the position you want (tilted upwards, downwards, turned sideways, etc.). Ladder stitch firmly in place, working several times round. † Ladder stitch arms in place after first pinning and adjusting to the position you want and working as shown by Fig. 6 on page 10. Looking at pictures, bend the top of tail over and taking very long ladder stitches, secure it firmly in this position—beige cut-away side on top. Place the cut-away section flat against base of squirrel as shown by broken lines on pattern and turning in raw edge. Ladder stitch firmly in place, working all round the three sides of brown side of base of tail. Ladder stitch base of body to inside beige edge of tail as marked by XXXX on pattern. † Catch tail to centre of back a little higher up, using ladder stitch and very strong thread.

10 EYES. Looking at the pictures in Nutkin's book to find a good position (page 39 shows the eyes clearly) pin, then neatly hem the two beige eye patches in place. Work all round the edge with the eye end of a large needle pulling out any pile caught up in the stitching and merge one colour into the other to give as soft and natural an effect as possible. Looking at pictures, neatly sew a brown pupil to each white eye then sew completed eye to head. Using a long needle and strong thread, take a few stitches through head from each end of eye patch to the same position on the other side to slightly sink it into the head.

11 NOSE. If your fur fabric has a very long pile, trim a little away round the nose area then using thick, dark brown, stranded cotton work a small stitch each side of head, working over each one, two or three times so that these

nostril markings show clearly. Pull and pinch the nose upwards to give it the perky effect shown in the book. If necessary, take a few invisible stitches through the tip, working from side to side and up and down and pulling the thread very tightly to secure the desired 'tip tilt'.

12 WHISKERS. Using black brush bristles and looking at the pictures for position, sew three or four whiskers to each side of nose (see page 18, Fig. 11). Should you wish to shade the toy refer to page 16. The squirrel shown on plate opposite page 277 was shaded by woollen stitches taken over the seams to soften the colour changes.

Squirrel Nutkin does not wear clothes but you could make him a nut to hold as given for Timmy Tiptoes, page 69, or a fishing line and raft (instructions, page 289). You can easily make Nutkin's brother Twinkleberry and some of his cousins by varying the positions of head and arms on the pattern and adding a tiny sack of nuts. If you wish to make the little rush basket in which they all carried the new-laid egg you will find the instructions on page 278.

TIMMY TIPTOES

'*Once upon a time there was a little, fat, comfortable grey squirrel, called Timmy Tiptoes.*'

Refer to the many pictures in *The Tale of Timmy Tiptoes*, as well as to the colour plate opposite page 244 of this book.

A cuddly toy with removable jacket and nut, approximately $12\frac{1}{2}$ inches ($31\cdot5$ cm) high.

This squirrel is made exactly like Squirrel Nutkin but entirely in grey.

Materials

$\frac{1}{2}$ yard (48 cm) grey fur fabric for body.

Scraps of felt in grey for hands, pink for ear linings, fawn for nut, pale fawn for top of nut, black and white for eyes, dark grey for claws.

*12 × 18 inches ($30\cdot5 \times 45\cdot5$ cm) pink felt (Bacchante 87) for jacket.

*One small hook and eye to fasten jacket.

Two small press-studs to hold nut.

Twenty pipe cleaners for stiffening hands.

Kapok for stuffing. Finished toy weighs approximately 9 ounces (255 grammes).

Method

1 CUT OUT the pieces as given for Squirrel Nutkin, pages 174–9 except the eye patches and ears (26 pieces), using grey fur fabric for all the body

pieces and grey felt for hands, also two pink felt and two grey fur fabric ears as given for Samuel Whiskers on page 185 (4 pieces), 20 claws in dark grey felt as given for Mrs. Tiggy-winkle on page 213 and the jacket, sleeves and nut on pages 192–3 (7 pieces) (57 pieces in all).

2 HANDS ⎫
3 CLAWS ⎬ Work as given for Squirrel Nutkin, page 66, Nos. 2, 3 and 4.
4 ARMS ⎭

5 EARS. Stick a pink felt lining to a grey fur fabric ear, roll the base inwards as given for Samuel Whiskers, Fig. 45 on page 76. Shade inside with black felt pen.

6 TAIL ⎫
7 HEAD ⎪ Work as given for Squirrel Nutkin, pages 66–8, Nos. 6, 7, 8,
8 BODY ⎪ 9, 10, 11, 12, remembering that all the pieces are grey and
9 ASSEMBLING ⎬ that there are no eye patches on Timmy Tiptoes. Consult
10 EYES ⎪ his book for eye positions. Do not sew the tail too high up
11 NOSE ⎪ on body because Timmy wears a jacket.
12 WHISKERS ⎭

13 JACKET. On the wrong side neatly oversew the two back darts A–B, then push the needle through to the right side and oversew the remainder of dart B–C. The reason for this is so that when the collar is turned over, the stitches will not show. On the wrong side join sleeve seams D–E. Turn right side out and on the wrong side insert sleeves into arm holes, matching Ds and stitching all round. Press back collar along broken line on pattern and sew a small hook and eye at E. Put on to squirrel and fasten hook and eye. Tuck the back up a little and smooth down between tail and body.

14 NUT. On the wrong side oversew the three pieces together G–H. Turn right side out and stuff firmly, shaping it well as you work. Neatly stitch the round top piece in place. Stitch one half of a very small press-stud to either side of nut, towards the lower end and another of the same size one half to the palm of each hand. The nut can then be fixed to the hands or the hands can be fastened together.

GOODY TIPTOES

'. . . he had a little squirrel wife called Goody.'

Refer to the many pictures in *The Tale of Timmy Tiptoes* and for head position to that on page 44, as well as to the colour plate opposite page 244 of this book.

A cuddly toy with removable dress, apron, nut and sack, approximately 12½ inches (31·5 cm) high.

Materials

Exactly as for Timmy Tiptoes, page 68, except for those marked * (2 items).

½ yard (48 cm) pink/white flowered material for dress.

8 × 6 inches (20·5 × 15·5 cm) white cotton material, and 24 inches (61 cm) of ½-inch (1-cm) wide white tape for apron.

8 × 7 inches (20·5 × 18 cm) scrim for sack.

Three tiny press-studs, one larger press-stud, one 'carpet' press-stud and one small hook and eye for fastening.

Method

1 CUT OUT the pieces as given for Squirrel Nutkin, pages 174–9, except the eye patches and ears (26 pieces) using grey fur fabric for all the body pieces and grey felt for hands, also two pink felt and two grey fur fabric ears as given for Samuel Whiskers on page 185 (4 pieces). 20 claws in dark grey felt as given for Mrs. Tiggy-winkle on page 213 and the dress bodice, sleeves and nut patterns, pages 192–4 (7 pieces), (57 pieces in all).

2 HANDS
3 CLAWS } Work as given for Squirrel Nutkin, page 66, Nos. 2, 3 and 4.
4 ARMS

5 EARS. Work as given for Timmy Tiptoes, page 69, No. 5.

6 TAIL
7 HEAD } Work as given for Squirrel Nutkin, page 66, Nos. 6, 7 and 8.
8 BODY

9 ASSEMBLING. Work as given for Squirrel Nutkin, page 67, No. 9 from * to *. Then close opening on head and looking at page 44 of *The Tale of Timmy Tiptoes*, sew head firmly to top of body, tilted upwards, to make Goody quite different from Timmy. Then continue working as No. 9 for Squirrel Nutkin from † to †. Do not sew tail high up to centre of back because of Goody's dress.

10 EYES
11 NOSE } Work as given for Squirrel Nutkin, pages 67–8, Nos. 10, 11 and 12, but consult pictures in *The Tale of Timmy Tiptoes* for
12 WHISKERS position of eyes.

13 DRESS. Cut a strip of the pink/white material 32 × 7 inches (81 × 18 cm) for skirt. Gather along one long edge, pull up gathers to fit base of bodice B–F–B. Stitch skirt to bodice. Turn back a narrow hem all down centre back edges of bodice and skirt, A–B–bottom of skirt. (The dress needs a centre back opening because of tail.) Join sleeve seams D–E and insert a sleeve into each armhole matching Ds. Run a gathering thread round top neck edge. Put dress on to squirrel, pull up gathers to fit neck and fasten off. Pin up bottom hem so the dress touches the ground. Remove dress. Stitch bottom hem. Turn back a narrow hem round both sleeves and bind neck gathers

with the narrowest possible binding cut on the bias from matching material. Fasten dress at back with two tiny press-studs, one at top and one 1 inch (2·5 cm) lower down and a tiny hook and eye at waist. Leave skirt open. Put dress on to squirrel. Sew one half of a large 'carpet' press-stud to centre of back so that it protrudes between the lowest press-stud on dress and the hook and eye at waist. Sew the other half to the corresponding position on tail. This can then be fastened and unfastened so that Goody can be dressed and undressed! Tuck the back of skirt between tail and body.

14 APRON. Make as given for Mrs. Tiggy-winkle, page 131, No. 19, working from * to * but using the larger piece of material as given in list above. Tie on to Goody after 'un-snapping' tail.

15 NUT. Make as given for Timmy Tiptoes, page 69, No. 14. Sew one half of a press-stud to the nut and one to Goody's right hand for her to hold it with.

16 THE SACK. Fold the piece of scrim in half so that the piece is 4 inches (10 cm) wide and 7 inches (18 cm) long. On the wrong side machine the long and one short side to form sack. Turn back a narrow hem round top. Turn right side out. Sew one half of a fairly strong press-stud to top of sack and the other half to the palm of Goody's left hand so that she can hold it. The original was half filled with real cob nuts.

The Rats and Mice

The characters in this section are all made on the same basic principle and are dressed felt models rather than cuddly toys. The mice are made larger than life for obvious reasons. The hairy appearance of their skin is achieved by working a series of small stitches in one strand of cotton or Sylko of various shades, closely together. It is fascinating work, to be done at your leisure—not hurried over. Striking effects can be slowly built up by constantly looking at the pictures in the books concerned and choosing your colours and stitch density accordingly. These animals do not have removable clothes and you may find the basic body shapes under the garments rather strange. Each one has been designed to be built up by stages to look like the picture being copied, so don't be alarmed when the first few parts appear ungainly and incorrect. Carry out the instructions and all will be well in the end!

It is recommended that you make Samuel Whiskers first as his head is basic to all the other rats and mice. You will notice as you work through this section the three distinct shapes of hands drawn by Beatrix Potter—star-shaped as in Hunca Munca, pointed as in The Old Woman who Lived in a Shoe and fingered as in Mrs. Tittlemouse.

SAMUEL WHISKERS

'*Opposite . . . as far away as he could sit was an enormous rat.*'

Refer to the cover of *The Tale of Samuel Whiskers*, as well as to the colour plate opposite page 245 of this book.

A sitting felt model approximately 8 inches (20 cm) high.

Materials

Odd scraps of old sheeting or similar for body foundation.

Odd scraps of any colour felt for legs (this will not show).

Scraps of fawn felt (String 32) for head. (N.B. A piece 9 × 12 inches (23 × 30 cm) will make both this toy and Anna Maria.)

Scraps of pink felt (Petal 52) for hands, tail, nose and ear linings (over from pigs?).

18 × 12 inches (46 × 30 cm) green felt (Lime 1) and two tiny green buttons for coat.

Scraps of yellow felt (Citron 41) and five tiny pearl buttons for waistcoat (over from pigs' trousers?).

Odd pieces of chamois leather (or deeper yellow felt) for trousers.

Scraps of brown or very pale fawn or white felt, some thick cardboard and a postcard for shoes.

Two or three shades of brown and white stranded embroidery cotton for hairs and eyes.

Four or five pipe cleaners for stiffening tail and fingers.

A strip of thin foam rubber for padding tail.

Black bristles (from brush) for whiskers.

15 inches (38 cm) wire for stiffening legs.

Kapok for stuffing head, arms and legs. Cheaper stuffing (if preferred) for body. Finished toy weighs approximately 7 ounces (200 grammes).

Two tiny press-studs (000 gauge).

Method

1 CUT OUT the pieces as given on pages 184–7 (51 pieces). Keep the two circles of green felt which you cut from the armholes of the coat and place them with the other pieces (53 pieces).

2 BODY. Machine the three pieces together A–C–B on the wrong side, leaving opening as shown. Turn right side out and stuff firmly. Close opening. The body is used with a seam down centre front so that the rat will have a fat tummy and flat back. Mark tummy with a pencil for identification later.

3 LEGS. These will not show on finished model so any odd pieces of felt will do—they are merely a foundation for trousers. On the outer legs join the top darts 1–2, remembering to reverse one piece so as to make a pair. Place each outer leg on an inner leg and join seams F–G and D–E. Turn right side out. Take two pieces of wire 7½ inches (19 cm), prepared as on page 13, Fig. 8A and B. Bend approximately 1½ inches (4 cm) upwards for foot. Slip the wire into the felt leg and bend it to the same contour, then bend the top end inwards. (This piece will eventually push into body side.) Stuff the leg firmly using small pieces of kapok and embedding the wire so that it cannot be felt from the outside (Fig. 43).

4 ATTACHING LEGS. Push pointed scissors into body side on the lower end of the two front panels where marked by X on pattern. Push top of leg wires into holes and arrange the body with legs extending forwards (look at

pictures). Pin open tops to body and ladder stitch leg to body, working several times round top of leg and pushing in more stuffing as you work (see Fig. 6, page 10). Place on one side.

5 TROUSERS. On the wrong side, machine the three pieces together C–B. Fold each trouser leg in half (reversing one so as to make a pair) and machine seams H–I. Turn right side out. On the two front panels only of main trouser piece, cut out holes as shown by broken lines on pattern. Insert trouser legs into holes matching Hs and having these points on the *inside* of leg towards centre front seam of body, the high bulge marked by broken lines on pattern on the top outside of leg and the cut-away part marked XXXX on pattern on the lower inside. Pin, then oversew all round. Turn right side out. Pull trousers on to body, pulling up as high as possible and making sure that the points B on trousers exactly match the points B on body. Stitch firmly in place all round waist. Place on one side.

Fig. 43 Samuel Whiskers' leg

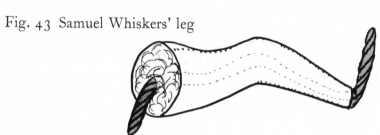

6 SHOES (Fig. 44). Take a card base, smear a little Copydex round front edge (A). Stick a 'top of shoe' to the base, taking a tiny turning at the back round broken line on pattern, pleating edge to fit (B). Stick a 'back of shoe' in place in the same way (C). Stick a white felt base in place (D). Stick five cardboard heel pieces together to make a thick wedge. Stick a white felt heel to these pieces and cover the short, straight edge with white felt (E). Stick a strip of brown felt all round curved edge (G). Stick heel to base of shoe (H). Take a card sole and cut a piece of white felt slightly larger. Gather all round the edge and lay sole in the centre (I). Pull up gathers and fasten off by criss-crossing thread over card sole on the wrong side (J). Stick sole to base of shoe (K). Push a little Copydex on a cocktail stick down into toe of shoe and press top to base to make this part flat. Bend toe up a little. Stick back of shoe to top at sides. Run a gathering thread round top of shoe and stuff firmly (L). Place on one side. Make the other shoe in the same way, reversing the pieces to make a pair.

7 ATTACHING SHOES. Roll back trouser legs. Push a shoe on to each foot wire (toes turning inwards). Pack more stuffing round ankles. Pull up gathers on shoes and stitch firmly to bottom of felt leg. Roll down trouser legs. Smear a little Copydex all round *inside* of bottom of trouser legs and stick to shoes—to avoid any gaps.

8 HEAD. † * Take one head piece and on the wrong side join the dart 3–4. Slit from O² to P. Run a gathering thread from O¹ to P. Pull up gathers so that O¹ rests on O² and joins seam O–P. * This gives fullness to the side, back of head. Repeat from * to * on the other side of head, reversing the

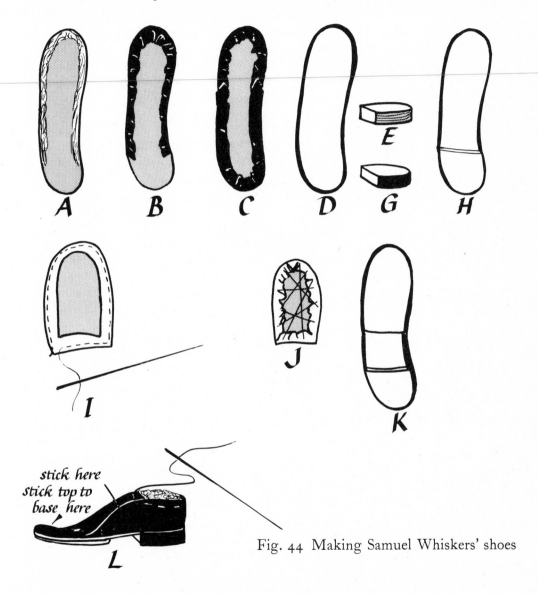

Fig. 44 Making Samuel Whiskers' shoes

second piece to make a pair. Join one side of head to head gusset J–K. Then join other side of head to other side of gusset in the same way. † Join two sides of head together J–3–L. Turn right side out, pushing out point of nose well. Stuff very firmly with kapok, filling out bulge made by darts and the larger one made by gathers, so that they are really fat. Place on one side.

9 EARS * (Fig. 45). On the fawn pieces, embroider a series of straight stitches

in two shades of brown Sylko or cotton to represent hairs, covering the top two-thirds only (A). These are the backs of the ears. Stick a pink piece to the wrong side of each of these for linings (B) *. Roll the two edges inwards and stitch in place. Shade the inside part of ears with brown and black felt pens (C).

10 FINISHING OFF HEAD. Make two slits on the edges of head gusset, on top of head where shown by broken lines on pattern. Push the points of your scissors into slits and well down into head to make a channel for base of ears. Push one ear well into each slit so that they are completely embedded up to end of fold. Ladder stitch in place, working several times round each ear. Sew a tiny circle of pink felt (matching ear linings) gathered up to form a knob to the tip of nose (Fig. 46). Embroider eyes on gusset seams, having the top ends approximately $\frac{3}{4}$ inch (2 cm) away from ears, using two strands of embroidery cotton and following shape on Fig. 46. Take a few stitches through head from eye to eye and pull tightly to sink eyes very slightly (Fig. 46A). (One stitch from one top corner to the other, one from one bottom corner to the other and one from one *inside* corner to the other gives a good shape—leave the *outer* corners.) Take a few similar stitches through point where mouth will be, to draw this in a little (Fig. 46B). Looking at Fig. 46 embroider hairs to match those on ears—upwards from front, over head and down the back. Looking at Fig. 50 of Anna Maria (page 79) and using six strands of embroidery cotton indicate the mouth by a stitch on each side of head. Do not add whiskers yet.

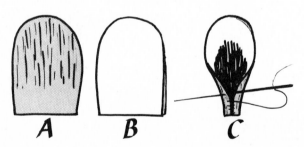

Fig. 45 Samuel Whiskers' ears

11 ATTACHING HEAD TO BODY. Stuff neck very firmly. Place head on top of body, covering points A and ladder stitch several times all round, one stitch on neck and one on body alternately, pulling head downwards at front as you work (look at picture).

12 WAISTCOAT. Overlap the two fronts M–N and machine stitch on the right

side. Sew five tiny buttons down centre front. Put on the rat, crossing tabs Q–R at back of neck and stitching them in place. Pull waistcoat tightly towards back and stitch R–S.

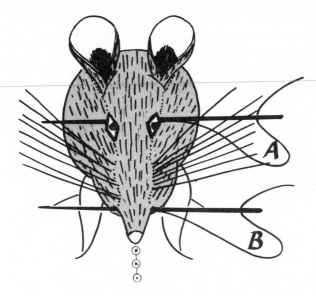

Fig. 46 Samuel Whiskers' head

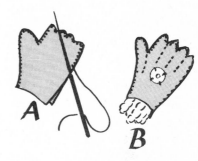

Fig. 47 Samuel Whiskers' hand

13 COAT. On the wrong side join the two shaping darts 5–6. Place collar lining on the *right* side where indicated by broken line on coat pattern and matching Ts and Us on lining with those on coat. Stitch lining to coat T–T. Turn lining over to wrong side and press. Invisibly catch lining to inside of coat T–U. Join sleeve seams V–W and turn right side out. Stitch sleeves into holes in coat matching Vs. Split centre back of coat up to X and sew a tiny green button to each side of slit. Place on one side.

14 HANDS (Fig. 47). * Place the hand pieces together in pairs and oversew all round (A). Push a short piece of pipe cleaner into each finger in turn and stab stitch between each one. Stuff hand with a little kapok * and sew one half of a tiny press-stud to each palm.

15 ASSEMBLING HANDS, COAT AND BODY. Slip a hand into each coat sleeve—thumbs towards the inside and matching thumb with sleeve seam. Invisibly stitch sleeve to hand, working all round. Stuff sleeve with kapok and keep this in place by oversewing the two green felt circles which you originally cut from these holes, back into place. Put coat on to rat and arrange carefully, pinning in place and rolling collar back round neck (look at picture). Stitch coat firmly to body at base of collar each side of front and at centre back slit. Sew one half of a tiny press-stud to each knee, placing the opposite half to that on each hand on the appropriate knee. Snap a hand to each knee as in picture. (You can change this position and snap the hands together in a clapping attitude.)

16 TAIL * (Fig. 48). This needs to be pliable so that it can be bent to any position, yet have a soft rather nasty appearance. It is therefore stiffened with pipe cleaners and padded with foam rubber. Take two pipe cleaners and join them together by twisting so that you have a piece 11 inches (28 cm) long (A). Cut a strip of thin foam rubber the same length as the pipe cleaners, tapering from just wide enough to stretch round them to almost $\frac{3}{4}$ inch (2 cm) at other end. Wrap this round the cleaners by binding with cotton, starting and fastening off ends by stitching (B). Cut a similarly tapered piece of pink felt (to match hands) and oversew in place (C) covering foam rubber. * Draw black section markings all along tail using a ball-point pen. Make a hole in lowest part of back of rat by pushing pointed scissors through trousers into stuffing. Push about $\frac{1}{2}$ inch (1·5 cm) of fat end of tail into the hole (with the stitched side underneath) and ladder stitch firmly in place. Curl tail round towards front.

17 WHISKERS. Attach about six whiskers each side of face as given on page 18, Fig. 11, looking at picture for positions.

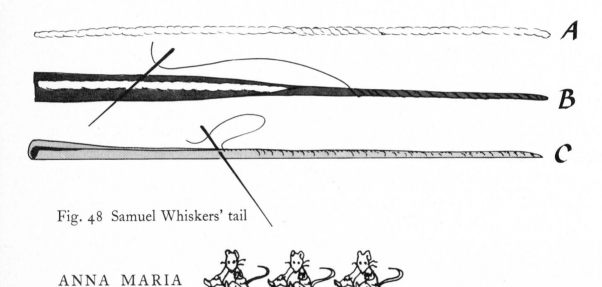

Fig. 48 Samuel Whiskers' tail

ANNA MARIA

'. . . *an old woman rat.*'

Refer to the many pictures in *The Tale of Samuel Whiskers*, as well as to the colour plate opposite page 245 of this book.

A felt toy approximately 9 inches (23 cm) high.

Instructions for making her wheelbarrow are on page 289.

Materials

Fawn felt for head and body (String 32). A piece 9 × 12 inches (23 × 30·5 cm) will make this toy and Samuel Whiskers.

Scraps of pink felt (Petal 52) for ear linings, hands, nose and tail (over from
    pigs?).

¼ yard (23 cm) pale blue poplin for dress.

A piece of white cotton material 5½ × 6½ inches (14 × 15·5 cm) for apron.

20 inches (51 cm) of ½-inch (1-cm) wide white tape for apron strings.

Scraps of blue felt (over from Peter Rabbit's jacket), fawn felt and card for
    shoes.

Twelve pipe cleaners for stiffening arms and tail.

Two or three shades of brown and white stranded cotton for hairs and eyes.

A strip of foam rubber for padding tail.

Black brush bristles for whiskers.

A little kapok for stuffing head and hands—any sort of filling for body.

A stone about the size of a walnut for weighting. Finished toy weighs
    approximately 6 ounces (170 grammes).

Fig. 49 Making Anna Maria's 'shoulders'

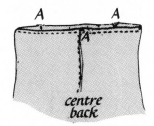

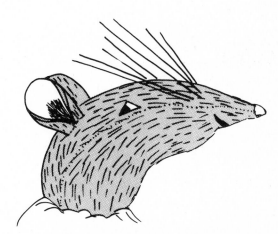

Fig. 50 Anna Maria's head

Method

  1 CUT OUT the pieces as given on pages 188–9 (18 pieces). Also the hands as
     given for Samuel Whiskers on page 186 (22 pieces).

  2 BODY. Machine the three pieces together A–B. Then fold the completed
     piece so that one of the seams comes at centre back and machine straight
     across the top for shoulders (Fig. 49). Turn right side out. Stuff firmly.
     Place on one side.

  3 WEIGHTING. The body needs to be weighted in order that Anna Maria will
     eventually stand firmly in various positions. Work from * to * as given for

Pigling Bland, page 54, No. 3, Fig. 31, using fawn felt instead of pink. Ease the covered stone into the base of body and oversew all round B–B–B to edge of felt covered card circle. Place on one side.

4 HEAD
5 EARS
6 FINISHING
    OFF HEAD

Work exactly as given for Samuel Whiskers, pages 75–6, Nos. 8, 9 and 10, noting that this head is slightly smaller and more pointed. Copy eye shape from Fig. 50 pulling them in at two bottom corners only. Turn in the opening L–K, making a long, smooth line from O–J (as this rat does not have a neck) and ladder stitch opening.

7 ATTACHING HEAD. Ladder stitch head firmly to top of body, placing so that rat looks straight forward. Work round and round several times using strong thread.

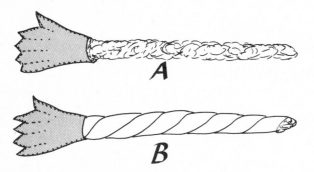

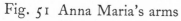

Fig. 51 Anna Maria's arms

8 HANDS AND ARMS. Work from * to * as given for Samuel Whiskers, page 77, No. 14, but use a full-length pipe cleaner in each finger. Twist these together as shown by Fig. 51A then bind them with a strip of rag sticking the ends of rag in place. Bend the top 1 inch (2·5 cm) at right angles and stitch to top of back of rat (thumbs towards centre). Stick an odd scrap of felt across the bound wire and stitches to completely cover these parts—as indicated by broken lines on Fig. 51C.

9 SHOES (Fig. 52). Take a card sole and smear a little Copydex round shaped edge of underside (A). Taking a very narrow turning, stick a blue felt top piece to it (B). Stick a felt sole to base to neaten (C). When dry, stuff blue felt front tightly (D). Smear Copydex over the piece of sole left showing (D) and stick to base of body as shown by E and F. Place on one side.

10 TAIL. Make and attach this exactly as given for Samuel Whiskers, page 78, No. 16, Fig. 48, but have it 1 inch (2·5 cm) shorter.

11 DRESS. Using pale blue poplin cut out the top as shown by the plan on Fig. 53 and also a piece 7½ × 20 inches (19 × 51 cm) for the skirt. Fold the top

piece as shown on plan and on the wrong side machine side seams A–B–C. On the skirt, join the two short 7½ inch (19 cm) ends. Run a gathering thread round one edge. Pull up gathers to fit base of top piece C–C–C. Pin skirt to top, having seam at centre front where it will eventually be hidden by the apron. Machine the two pieces together all round waist. Turn dress right way out. Try on to rat, pin up hem so that the feet just show. Remove dress, hand stitch hem. Press. Run a gathering thread round neck slit, turning in the raw edge as you work. Put dress back on to rat, pull up gathers to fit neck and stitch in place. Tuck in the raw edges of sleeves so that only the tips of hands show and invisibly stitch to hand, working all round and pleating sleeve to fit.

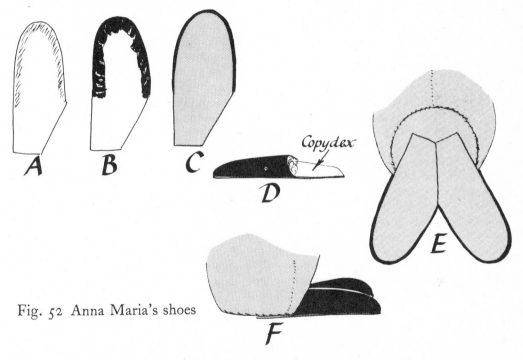

Fig. 52 Anna Maria's shoes

12 APRON. Machine the narrowest possible hem down the sides and turn up a ½-inch (1·5-cm) hem along bottom edge. Turn the top edge over on to the right side and gather along this edge. Pull up gathers to make top of apron 3 inches (7·5 cm) wide and fasten off. Pin the tape across front of top edge so that it covers the raw edge and gathers, leaving an equal length each side for the strings. Machine tape in position across both of its edges. Put on rat, tying a bow at back.

13 WHISKERS. Work as for Samuel Whiskers No. 17, page 78.

Anna Maria may be bent into many positions—she will stand firmly even though bending forward to hold her wheelbarrow. Instructions for making this are on page 289.

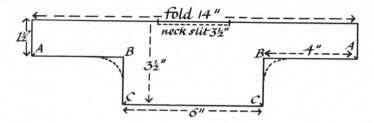

Fig. 53 Plan for top of Anna Maria's dress

THE OLD WOMAN WHO LIVED IN A SHOE

'I think if she lived in a little shoe-house—That little old woman was surely a mouse!'

Refer to the illustration on page 24 of *Appley Dapply's Nursery Rhymes*, as well as to the colour plate opposite page 224 of this book.

A sitting felt model approximately 6 inches (15 cm) high.

Instructions for making her chair are on page 290.

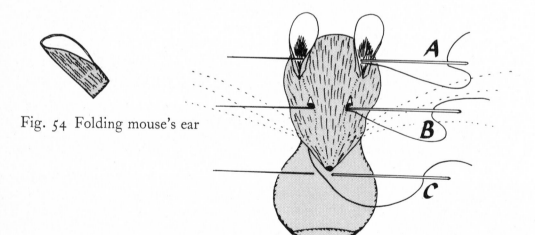

Fig. 54 Folding mouse's ear

Fig. 55 First stages of The Old Woman who Lived in a Shoe

Materials

9 × 12 inches (23 × 30.5 cm) fawn felt (String 32) for head and body.
Scraps of pink felt (Petal 52) for ear linings and tail.
Two or three shades of brown, very pale beige and white stranded embroidery cotton or Sylko for hairs and eyes.
Four pipe cleaners for stiffening tail and arms.

A strip of thin foam rubber for padding tail.

$\frac{1}{4}$ yard (23 cm) pink/white check gingham for dress (look at picture).

Scraps of crisp white cotton material for cap and apron.

12 inches (30·5 cm) of $\frac{1}{2}$-inch (1·5-cm) wide white tape for apron strings.

$\frac{1}{2}$ yard (48 cm) white broderie anglaise 2 inches (5 cm) wide for drawers.

A few yards each of pale blue and white 3-ply wool for shawl.

Scraps of red and white felt for shoes and stockings.

Fine green mending yarn (Chadwicks 460) and two large safety pins for 'knitting'.

Black brush bristles for whiskers.

A small pebble for weighting.

A little kapok for stuffing. Finished toy weighs approximately 2 ounces (56 grammes).

Method

1 CUT OUT the pieces as given on page 180 (26 pieces). Also a piece of white material $2\frac{1}{4} \times 8\frac{1}{2}$ inches (6 × 21·5 cm) for apron, two circles of similar material 5 inches (13 cm) diameter for cap, a strip of gingham 3 × 36 inches (7·5 × 91·5 cm) for skirt and two pieces each 5 × $2\frac{1}{2}$ inches (13 × 6·5 cm) for bodice (32 pieces in all).

2 BODY. Place the two pieces together and on the right side oversew the two side seams A–B. Prepare base as given for Pigling Bland, page 54, No. 3 working from * to * using fawn felt and a smaller pebble. Insert base into wide end of body, flat side outside and oversew body to base, working all round B–B–B. Stuff body very firmly, leaving top end open and place on one side.

3 EARS. Work as given for Samuel Whiskers, page 75, No. 9 from * to *. Fold ears in half and oversew bottom edge and $\frac{1}{4}$ inch (0·5 cm) upwards (Fig. 54). Place on one side.

4 HEAD. Work as given for Samuel Whiskers, page 75, No. 8 from † to †. Insert underchin gusset stitching J–C on both sides. Join small seam C–L. Turn right side out, easing top of head down through neck with a blunt stuffing stick. Push out point of nose well. Stuff head very firmly, filling out the bulges made by darts and gathers to give a good shape. With pointed scissors cut two slits for ears as indicated on head pattern. Push about $\frac{1}{4}$ inch (0·5 cm) of ends of ears into slits and ladder stitch edge of slit to ears, working round several times. With a long, slim needle and strong thread take a few stitches through head from the inside of one ear to the inside of the other, pulling the stitches tightly to attach inside of ears to sides of head (Fig. 55A). Shade inside of ears with brown and black felt pens. Embroider eyes, using two strands of dark brown and white cotton—placing them 1 inch (2·5 cm) down from ears, having inside corners on seam lines and

copying shape from Fig. 55. Take a few stitches through head from the inside corner of one side to the same position on the other, pulling tightly to sink eyes slightly (Fig. 55B). Using medium brown cotton embroider the slightest suspicion of a nose at tip. Using one strand of cotton in two or three shades of brown and very light fawn, embroider hairs from tip of nose to just behind ears all round face, making a concentration of pale fawn stitches towards the nose. (The cap will eventually cover back of head.) Do not insert whiskers yet.

5 ASSEMBLING HEAD AND BODY. Add more stuffing to the neck and push it into open end of body (body seams at sides). Ladder stitch body to head using strong thread and working several times round. Pull head well down and forwards by taking a few long ladder stitches from high up under chin to well down on front of body and pulling tightly (Fig. 55C).

6 LEGS. Machine the four red shoe pieces to the four white stocking pieces as close to edge as possible, then place these four pieces together in pairs, right sides facing and secure with a pin. Machine them together A–B–A as close to edge as possible, easing the toe gently down through leg with a blunt stick. (This is a fiddly job but makes for a better finish than if the pieces were oversewn together on the right side, thus not necessitating turning.) * Stuff legs. Place open ends against lower edge of front of body with approximately ½ inch (1·5 cm) between them and ladder stitch in place, working all round top of leg (Fig. 56A). Pull legs downwards by taking a few long ladder stitches from underneath tops to the base (Fig. 56B). Place on one side. (Don't be alarmed at the strange appearance of the mouse at this stage— you are really making a foundation for the clothes.)

7 DRAWERS. Gather along top edge of broderie anglaise, pull up to fit mouse and stitch in place all round waist. Place on one side.

8 TAIL. Make this exactly as given for Samuel Whiskers, page 78, No. 16 working from * to * but making this tail 8½ inches (20·5 cm) long and as slim as possible. Push the points of your scissors into centre back of base of body, making a small hole. Push tail into this hole and ladder stitch in place. Thread end of tail out through a hole in broderie anglaise. Catch the front and back edges of lace together at centre of base, pulling the front edge down between the legs, then catch the two side edges together in the same place. Catch the tips of red shoes together so that the toes are turned in (Fig. 56C).

9 ARMS. Place the four pink pieces together in pairs, pin then machine them together close to the edge A–B–A. Turn right side out. Twist two pipe cleaners together, push each end into an arm. Stuff arms, having pipe cleaners in centre of kapok (Fig. 57A). Keep stuffing in place with a few stitches across open ends of arm (Fig. 57B).

10 SLEEVES. Fold pieces in half lengthwise and taking a narrow turning,

WHEN Benjamin Bunny grew up,
he married his Cousin Flopsy. They
had a large family. . .

The Tale of The Flopsy Bunnies

Aunt Pettitoes and Spot seeing
Pigling Bland and Alexander
off to market.

The Tale of Pigling Bland

machine seams E–F. Leaving sleeves inside out, ease narrow ends over tips of hands, matching seams, and back stitch in place (Fig. 57D). Pull sleeves right way out, up over arms and leaving them a little loose and full, stitch top to pipe cleaners (Fig. 57C). Sew exposed portion of pipe cleaners very firmly to back of mouse $\frac{1}{2}$ inch (1·5 cm) down from neck join.

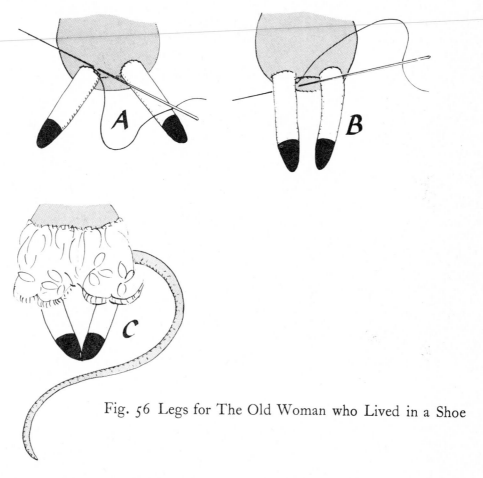

Fig. 56 Legs for The Old Woman who Lived in a Shoe

11 SKIRT OF DRESS. The length 36 inches (92 cm) pre-supposes that your gingham is very fine and soft; if not, 30 inches (76 cm) or less will probably be sufficient. The skirt needs to be very full and crisp. Machine short ends together to form a ring. Machine the narrowest possible hem round bottom edge. Press. Run a gathering thread round the top as close to edge as practicable. Pull up gathers tightly, put on to mouse and using the long ends of gathering thread, stitch firmly in place all round waist making sure the skirt covers the panties and that the tiny red shoes just show.

12 BODICE. This does not show on finished mouse and is merely two strips of gingham, one over each shoulder, overlapped at front and back. Press back

$\frac{1}{4}$ inch (0·5 cm) turning, down the long edges of the two pieces—do not stitch. Lay one strip over one shoulder. Oversew the edges together under arm. Tuck surplus length inside and stitch to mouse at waist, just covering raw edge at top of skirt. Stitch the other piece in place in the same way, overlapping the first piece at front and back.

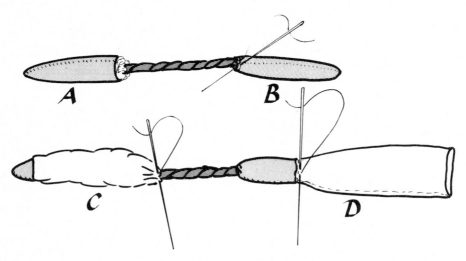

Fig. 57 Making arms and sleeves for The Old Woman who Lived in a Shoe

13 MOB CAP. Cut two circles of white cotton material 5 inches (12·5 cm) diameter. Pin the two circles together to prevent slipping and on the wrong side machine all round the edge, leaving a small opening. Turn right side out. Turn in raw edges of opening and invisibly close it. Press. Run a gathering thread all round, a little over $\frac{1}{2}$ inch (1·5 cm) from edge. Pull up gathers to fit head, easing most of the fullness towards the front and having a straight piece at the back (where the shawl will cover neck). Looking at picture, stitch cap in place all round head—on the line of the gathering thread.

14 SHAWL. Using 3-ply blue wool and size 13 needles, cast on 32 stitches. K.1 row. Continue in garter stitch, knitting 2 stitches together at the beginning of each row until 10 stitches remain. Cast off. Using white wool, work a row of double crochet round the curved edge, leaving the straight cast-on edge plain. Pull round the mouse's shoulders, stitching points together and to body at centre front.

15 WHISKERS. Insert three whiskers each side of face as given on page 18, Fig. 11. See broken lines on Fig. 55 for size and position.

16 APRON. Cut a strip of white cotton material $8\frac{1}{2} \times 2\frac{1}{4}$ inches (22 × 5·5 cm). Machine the narrowest possible hem along short sides and bottom edge.

Press. Run a gathering thread along top edge about $\frac{1}{4}$ inch (0·5 cm) in. Pull up gathers until top edge is 3 inches (7·5 cm) long. Fasten off. Tack the tape doubled over top raw edge to form a binding, leaving an even length each side for strings. Fold these strings in half lengthwise and continue tacking, also turning in raw ends. Machine across end, along edge of string, across top of apron, along edge of second string and across second end. Tie on to mouse.

17 THE KNITTING. Using size 13 or 14 needles and fine darning wool, cast on 6 stitches. Work 17 rows in K.1 P.1 rib. Break off wool, leaving a long end. Wind this end into a tiny ball about 12 inches (30 cm) from knitting. Fix ball to prevent it unwinding by stitching several times through it with matching wool. Darn in starting end. Look at picture. Bend arms sharply forwards, so that hands almost meet in centre at waist. Using strong cutting nippers, cut off pin part of two large safety pins and discard the rest. Push points of pins through hands for knitting needles. Slip three stitches of the prepared knitting on to each pin, securing by running a needle threaded with matching wool through them and stitching to hands. For extra safety put spots of colourless nail varnish on each stitch.

18 ARRANGE the mouse's tail, skirts, etc., and sit her on her chair, the instructions for which are on page 290.

HUNCA MUNCA

'*Hunca Munca has got the cradle and some of Lucinda's clothes.*'

Refer to the illustration on page 48 of *The Tale of Two Bad Mice*, as well as to the colour plate opposite page 225 of this book.

A sitting felt model approximately 7 inches (18 cm) high (made a little larger than life) holding a thimble toy baby (instructions, page 90).

Instructions for making the chair and the cradle are on pages 251 and 291 and for the bedclothes and sleeping babies, pages 93–4.

Materials

9 × 12 inches (23 × 30·5 cm) fawn felt (String 32) for head and body.
Scraps of pink felt (Petal 52) for arms, ear linings and tail.
Two or three shades of brown, beige and white stranded cotton or Sylko for hairs and eyes.
Six pipe cleaners for stiffening arms, legs and tail.
Scraps of black and white felt for shoes and stockings.
Scraps of white cotton material for pantalettes.
$\frac{1}{4}$ yard (23 cm) pale blue poplin (or similar) for dress.

Scraps of lace for dress and pantalettes.

Brush bristles for whiskers.

A small pebble for weighting.

A little kapok for stuffing. Finished toy weighs approximately $2\frac{1}{2}$ ounces (70 grammes).

Method

1 CUT OUT the pieces as given on page 181 (14 pieces), also the head, head gusset, underchin gusset, ears, body and base as given on page 180 for The Old Woman who Lived in a Shoe (26 pieces in all).

2 BODY. Work as given for The Old Woman who Lived in a Shoe, page 83, No. 2, but after stuffing body, oversew top edge A–A.

3 EARS. Work as given for Samuel Whiskers, page 75, No. 9, Fig. 45.

4 HEAD. Work as given for The Old Woman who Lived in a Shoe, page 83, No. 4 but after stuffing turn the protruding neck inside and ladder stitch opening so that the underside is quite flat. This mouse has no neck. Copy the shape of eyes from the picture—they are large and dark with tiny white highlights. Make the hairs rather dark and work them all over the head as she does not wear a cap.

5 JOINING HEAD TO BODY. Using strong thread, ladder stitch head to body, placing the point K on head to centre of top oversewn edge A–A of body and working along back and then along front, taking long ladder stitches well down on front of body, so as to pull the head downwards.

6 LEGS. Work as given for The Old Woman who Lived in a Shoe, page 84, No. 6 as far as * (making the shoes black instead of red). Cut three pipe cleaners in half; twist these pieces together in threes, making two thick pieces. Push one of these pieces well down into each leg then stuff all round it. Place open ends flat against front of base of body with about $\frac{1}{4}$ inch (0·5 cm) between them and ladder stitch each leg to body, working all round top of leg as shown by Fig. 56A (page 85), noting that these legs will be a little closer together than those in the figure.

7 TAIL. Make as given for Samuel Whiskers, page 78, No. 16, working from * to * but making the tail $8\frac{1}{2}$ inches (21·5 cm) long and as slim as you possibly can. Push the points of your scissors into centre back of base of body, making a small hole. Push tail into hole and ladder stitch firmly in place.

8 PANTALETTES. Fold each piece in half as shown by 'fold' on pattern and on the wrong side machine leg seams X–Y. Join the two pieces together W–V–Y–V–W, leaving a small opening V–Y at the back for the tail. Turn up a narrow hem round bottom of each leg Z–X–Z and sew a narrow piece of lace round each one. Turn right side out. Run a gathering thread round the base of each leg, also round top edge, turning in this raw edge as you

work. Leave thread hanging and do not pull up gathers. Bend the legs at knees and ankles and slip pantalettes on to the mouse, pushing the tail through the hole at base of centre back seam. Pull up gathers round top to fit mouse's body and stitch pantalettes to body all round waist. Pull up gathers at base of legs and stitch to mouse's legs, working all round each ankle and leaving about $\frac{1}{2}$ inch (1·5 cm) of white stocking showing between lace and shoe.

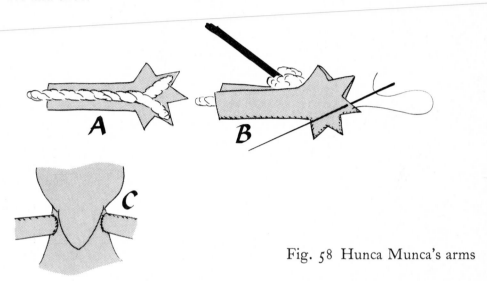

Fig. 58 Hunca Munca's arms

9 ARMS. Cut two pipe cleaners in half and twist the pieces together except for a short section at one end. Lay this piece on one of the felt arm pieces as in Fig. 58A so that the two ends extend into two of the fingers. Place another felt piece on top and oversew the two together all round, pushing small pieces of stuffing into each finger as you work (B). Stuff the arm firmly with the pipe cleaners embedded in the centre and as you work, push the cleaners well down all the time. Trim off the protruding ends of pipe cleaners. Place the open end of each arm flat against the side seam of body about $\frac{1}{4}$ inch (0·5 cm) down from head and ladder stitch in place (C).

10 DRESS. Cut a strip of pale blue poplin $4\frac{1}{2}$ inches (11·5 cm) wide and 22 inches (56 cm) long for the skirt. On the wrong side join the short ends to make a ring. Turn up a narrow hem all round bottom edge. Stitch a piece of white lace all round the bottom so that the edge of lace is level with edge of dress, i.e. so that it does not protrude below blue material. Run a gathering thread round top edge of skirt about $\frac{1}{4}$ inch (0·5 cm) from edge. Put on to mouse, pull up gathers to fit waist and stitch to body, working all round. Cut a piece of matching blue material $6\frac{1}{2} \times 4$ inches (16·5 × 10 cm) for the bodice (Fig. 59). Fold in half lengthwise and on the wrong side machine underarm seams R–S and S–R. Turn right side out. Run a gathering thread

round sleeve edges T–R–T, turning in raw edges as you work. Do not pull up gathers or fasten off, and leave threads hanging. Cut a neck slit at centre of fold, just small enough to squeeze the head through. (About 3 inches (7·5 cm) long.) Run a gathering thread all round this neck slit, turning in raw edge as you work. Do not pull up gathers or fasten off—leave thread hanging. Put bodice on to mouse, easing the head carefully through slit. Pull up both sets of sleeve gathers to fit wrists and stitch to arm so that only the hand shows. Pull up neck gathers and using a long, slim needle stitch to mouse's neck, working all round. Tuck raw edge in at waist and stitch to mouse so that it just covers raw gathered edge at top of skirt. Cut two pieces of lace 7 inches (17·5 cm) long. Run a gathering thread along straight edge. Pull up gathers slightly and stitch a piece over each shoulder, from centre front to centre back of waist—sloping outwards to form a 'fichu'.

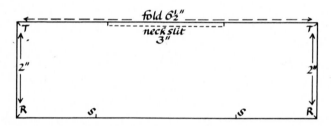

Fig. 59 Plan for bodice of Hunca Munca's dress

11 WHISKERS. Insert two or three whiskers each side of face as given on page 18, Fig. 11, and a short pair each side, high up on head in front of ears. (Look at picture.) Settle Hunca Munca in her chair (instructions, page 291).

12 THE BLANKET. Cut a piece of cream flannel or similar material approximately 3 × 4 inches (7·5 × 10 cm). Work a row of blanket stitch all round the edge using pink stranded cotton or fine wool and lay it on Hunca Munca's lap, ready to hold her baby.

HUNCA MUNCA'S BABY

This is a thimble toy, so that he can be removed from Hunca Munca's lap and played with on your finger.

Refer to the picture on page 48 of *The Tale of Two Bad Mice*, as well as to the colour plate opposite page 225 of this book.

Materials

Scraps of fawn and pink felt (over from Hunca Munca) for head, ears, hands and tail.

Beige, brown and white stranded cotton for hairs and eyes.

Scrap of white stockinette for nightie (discarded socks or T-shirt).

One pipe cleaner for stiffening tail.

An old plastic thimble for finger grip.

Method

1 CUT OUT the nightie, hands, head, head gusset and ears, as given on page 182 (10 pieces).

2 HEAD. On the wrong side join head gusset to one side of head A–B. Join on other side of head to other side of gusset B–A then join the two head pieces together A–C. Turn right side out and stuff. Gather round open neck B–C–B, pull up tightly and fasten off. Stick the pink ear linings to fawn ears. Roll the base inwards and stitch as you did for Hunca Munca. Push pointed scissors into each side of head gusset at top of head and push ears well in. Ladder stitch in place. Shade inside of ears with a brown felt pen. Looking at picture and at Fig. 60A, embroider eyes and nostrils using brown and white stranded cotton. Embroider a few beige and brown hairs.

3 FINGER GRIP. Find an old plastic thimble which has holes worn through the top or pierce two holes with a hot needle. Stitch thimble firmly to base of head, using strong thread and a long, slim needle and working through holes in thimble (Fig. 60A).

4 NIGHTIE. Fold the piece in half across top as shown on pattern and on the wrong side back stitch, then oversew side seams D–E. Turn up a narrow hem round bottom edge E–E–E; leave inside out and place on one side.

5 TAIL. Work as for Samuel Whiskers, page 78, No. 16, working from * to * but make it only 4½ inches (11·5 cm) long and as slim as possible. Sew tail to underarm seam of nightie (Fig. 60B) and turn right side out. Gather round edge of each sleeve, turning in raw edges as you work. Slip a hand into each sleeve so that the tiny armpiece is completely hidden. Pull up gathers to fit and stitch sleeve firmly to wrist so that just the tiny star-shaped hands show (Fig. 60C).

6 ASSEMBLING. Make a very small hole at centre of top of nightie as shown on pattern—just large enough to ease the base of the thimble through when the hole is stretched. Push thimble downwards through hole and ladder stitch nightie to base of head, turning in raw edge as you work. Add a few tiny whiskers if you wish, working with strong thread as shown by Fig. 9, page 14.

7 MANIPULATING. The thimble inside nightie acts as a finger grip to hold the toy firmly in place and must therefore fit tightly. Stick small pieces of

medical adhesive tape round inside of thimble until it really fits the person
who is to play with Hunca Munca's baby.

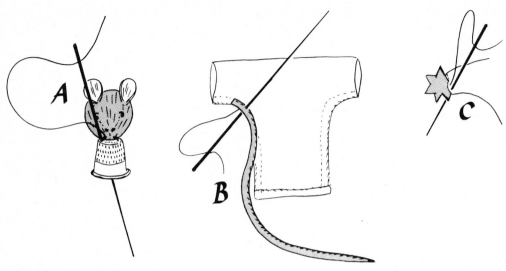

Fig. 60 Hunca Munca's baby

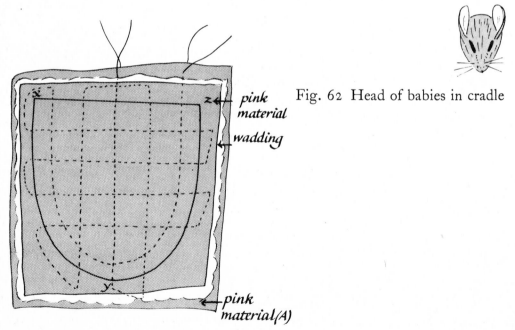

pink
material

wadding

pink
material (A)

Fig. 62 Head of babies in cradle

Fig. 61 Quilting the eiderdown

BED CLOTHES FOR HUNCA MUNCA'S CRADLE

Refer to the picture on page 48 of *The Tale of Two Bad Mice*, as well as to the colour plate opposite page 225 of this book.

Mattress

1 Cut out the pieces on pattern, page 182 (2 pieces) using any suitable material. The original was white poplin.
2 Machine the two pieces together on the wrong side, all round the outside edge except for opening. Turn right side out. Stuff with kapok and close opening. Using strong button thread 'tie' through the mattress in positions shown by X on pattern to keep stuffing in place. Put mattress into cot.

Pillow

1 Cut a piece of white cotton material $3\frac{1}{4} \times 5\frac{1}{2}$ inches (8×14 cm).
2 Fold in half widthwise and machine on the wrong side round two sides. Turn right side out, stuff rather full and close open side. Put into cot.

Eiderdown

A simple piece of quilted material does not give the warm, 'puffy' effect in the picture, so work in this way:

1 Using pencil, draw the eiderdown shape on a slightly larger piece of suitable pink material. Pencil in markings for quilting. Tack this piece, pencilled side up, to a piece of wadding or similar padding and on the back of the wadding tack another piece of the pink material (Fig. 61).
2 Machine over all your pencilled quilting markings, working backwards and forwards, turning machine on edges *outside* the eiderdown shape (Fig. 61). Do not machine round outline shape. This is the top of your eiderdown— the right side being the lower piece of material without the pencil marks (A on Fig. 61).
3 Tack a further piece of material to *right* side of this piece and machine all round curved edge X–Y–Z of outline shape, following your pencil mark.
4 Cut away all thicknesses of material and wadding to within about $\frac{1}{4}$ inch (0·5 cm) of the curved edge and turn eiderdown right way out. You now have a quilted piece of material on top and plain underneath, forming a bag.
5 Stuff the eiderdown with kapok and turn in and neatly oversew top straight edge X–Z.
6 Using matching pink cotton, stitch firmly right through the eiderdown at each point where the lines of quilting cross, pull tightly and fasten off. This gives the puffy effect. Place on cradle.

THE SLEEPING BABIES

Make four thimble toys exactly as given for Hunca Munca's baby on page 90 but do not stuff the heads so full and pinch and squash them to a more pointed shape. Embroider brown slits for the closed eyes (Fig. 62). Pack the babies tightly into the cradle, as in the picture.

They can, of course, be taken out and used as thimble toys with the baby on Hunca Munca's lap. You will completely fill one hand having four sleeping babies and one wide awake.

MRS. TITTLEMOUSE

'*Once upon a time there was a wood-mouse and her name was Mrs. Tittlemouse. She lived in a bank under a hedge.*'

Refer to the many pictures in *The Tale of Mrs. Tittlemouse*, as well as to the colour plate opposite page 232 of this book.

A flat based felt model approximately 6 inches (15 cm) high.

Instructions for making her basket are on page 262.

Materials
    Scraps of fawn felt (String 32) for head.
    Scraps of pink felt (Petal 52) for ear linings.
    Scraps of yellow felt for shoes.

Fig. 63 Petticoat 'base' for Mrs. Tittlemouse

Two or three shades of brown, very pale beige and white stranded embroidery cotton or Sylko for hairs and eyes.

Twelve pipe cleaners for stiffening tail and arms.

A strip of thin foam rubber for padding tail.

$\frac{1}{8}$ yard (11 cm) blue/white striped cotton material for petticoat base.

$\frac{1}{4}$ yard (23 cm) pink/white striped cotton material for dress.

$\frac{1}{2}$ yard (46 cm) deep pink ribbon for apron strings.

Scrap of fine white lawn or similar for pinafore.

A tiny press-stud for fastening.

A circle of firm cardboard approximately $2\frac{3}{4}$ inches (7 cm) diameter for base
(small tumbler?).

Black brush bristles for whiskers.

4 inches (10 cm) wire, adhesive tape and rag for body and neck foundation.

Kapok for stuffing. Finished toy weighs approximately 2 ounces (56
grammes).

Method

1 CUT OUT the head, head gusset, ears and underchin gusset as given for The
Old Woman who Lived in a Shoe, page 180 (8 pieces). The arms as given
for Hunca Munca, page 181 (4 pieces), the bodice of dress and feet, page
181 (5 pieces), (17 pieces in all).

2 EARS
3 HEAD } Work as given for The Old Woman who Lived in a Shoe, page
83, Nos. 3 and 4, copying the shape and position of eyes from the
pictures in Mrs. Tittlemouse's book. (For the original page 24 was
used.) Embroider hairs all over head as she does not wear a cap and
sew a tiny circle of pink felt over tip of nose. Place on one side.

4 PETTICOAT BASE. Work as given for Aunt Pettitoes, page 60, No. 5
(body) having the card circle $2\frac{3}{4}$ inches (7 cm) diameter and the strip of
material (which should be blue/white vertical stripes) $4\frac{1}{2}$ inches (11·5 cm)
wide. This is a much smaller and lighter toy so a single thickness of material
and thinner card will be quite adequate. Fill with kapok and pull up
gathers, leaving a centre hole of only about $\frac{1}{2}$ inch (1 cm) diameter. The
finished base (which is also the petticoat) should stand about $3\frac{1}{4}$ inches
(8·5 cm) high (Fig. 63). There is no top of body as with Aunt Pettitoes so
work only from * to *.

5 FEET. Stick the foot pieces together in pairs, then stick these to base of
petticoat so that they just peep out at the front (arrange seam at centre back).

6 TAIL. Make this exactly as given for Samuel Whiskers, page 78, No. 16,
working from * to * but making this tail $8\frac{1}{2}$ inches (21·5 cm) long and as
slim as possible. Push the points of your scissors into base of centre back of
petticoat, making a small hole. Push tail into this hole and ladder stitch in
place.

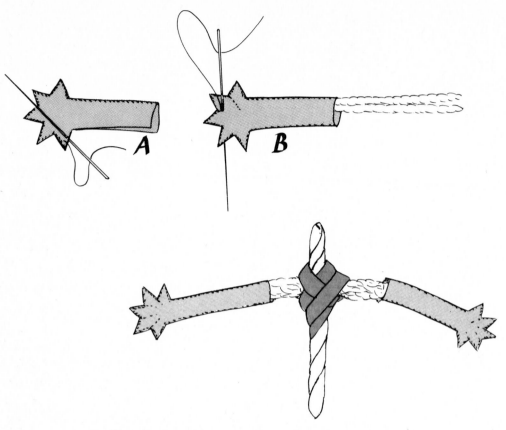

Fig. 64 Making arms for Mrs. Tittlemouse

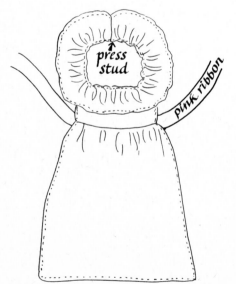

Fig. 65 Mrs. Tittlemouse's pinafore

7 ARMS. Place the pieces together in pairs and oversew very neatly together all round except for the short, straight ends (Fig. 64A). Push a pipe cleaner down into first finger and stab stitch between that finger and the next. Push another pipe cleaner into the second finger, stab stitch between that and the next (B). Continue in this way until all five fingers have a pipe cleaner stiffener inside. Push a little stuffing into arm to make it quite firm. Make the other arm in the same way. Place on one side.

8 NECK AND BODY FOUNDATION. Prepare 4 inches (11 cm) of wire with adhesive tape and rag (see page 13, Fig. 8D). Curl ends of pipe cleaners in arms round this wire about $1\frac{1}{2}$ inches (4 cm) from top and keep in place by criss-crossing adhesive tape firmly round wire and cleaners (Fig. 64). Push top of wire up into head of mouse. Gather round neck. Pull up gathers and stitch neck firmly to rag bound wire.

9 BODICE OF DRESS. Fold the piece in half as shown on pattern and on the wrong side machine under-arm seams A–B. Turn right side out. Bend arms downwards and slip lower end of foundation wire and arms into neck slit, bending and bringing arms through sleeves and out at ends and passing the body wire out of base of bodice between B and B. Gather round the edge of each sleeve, turning in raw edges as you work, pull up gathers to fit wrists of mouse and stitch sleeves to hands working all round. Stitch neck slit of bodice to head, ladder stitching all round and turning in raw edge as you work. Stuff bodice and sleeves. Push lower end of body wire down into hole in centre of petticoat base. Ladder stitch base of bodice to petticoat, working all round.

10 SKIRT OF DRESS. Cut a strip of the pink/white striped material (stripes across the short way) 20 × 5 inches (51 × 13 cm). Join short ends. Machine a narrow hem round bottom edge. Turn in raw edge at top and run a gathering thread all round. Slip skirt on to mouse, pull up gathers to fit, arrange seam at centre back and ladder stitch skirt to base of bodice.

11 WHISKERS. Stitch three or four whiskers each side of nose as shown on page 18, Fig. 11.

12 PINAFORE. This does not show clearly in the pictures as Mrs. Tittlemouse often wears it tucked up with her dress, so follow Fig. 65 for shape. Cut three pieces of fine white lawn or similar, $3\frac{3}{4}$ × $4\frac{1}{4}$ inches (9 × 11 cm) for main part, 2 × 2 inches (5 × 5 cm) for bib and $8\frac{1}{2}$ × $1\frac{1}{2}$ inches (21·5 × 4 cm) for frill. (Good parts of an old hankie are very suitable for this.) Machine the narrowest possible hem round two long and one short side of the main part. Gather along the other short side. Pull up these gathers, so that the top of pinafore is a little narrower than the bib, i.e. about $1\frac{3}{4}$ inches (4·5 cm). Fasten off. Place bib piece on top of right side of main part, both edges level and machine the two pieces together across gathers. Press the bib upwards, fold in half and press down towards back of apron. Tuck in the raw edge and

slip stitch across back of gathers. (The bib is now narrow and double.) Turn in the raw edges at sides and oversew neatly. Machine a narrow hem all round frill. Run a gathering thread along one long side. Pull up gathers so that frill fits round the mouse's neck. Fasten off threads. Find centre point of top of bib and centre point of gathers on frill. Pin frill to top edge of bib and stitch in place. Sew a small press-stud to ends of frill and a piece of pink ribbon to each side of waist. Put on to mouse and either tuck it up with Mrs. Tittlemouse's dress or leave both skirt and dress down—copying whichever picture you prefer in her book.

Arrange Mrs. Tittlemouse in her typical busy, bustling attitude by bending her forwards from the waist. She can hold her basket in one hand—her tail in the other!

Instructions for basket are on page 262.

JOHNNY TOWN-MOUSE

'Johnny Town-mouse was born in a cupboard.'

Refer to the picture on page 36 of *The Tale of Johnny Town-mouse*, as well as to the colour plate opposite page 233 of this book.

A felt toy approximately $6\frac{1}{2}$ inches (16·5 cm) high.

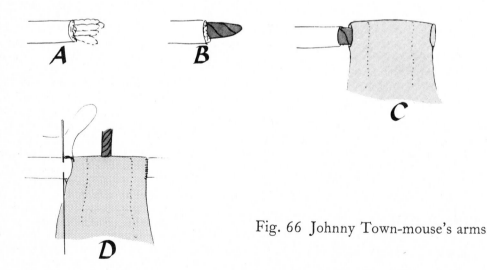

Fig. 66 Johnny Town-mouse's arms

Materials

12 × 9 inches (30 × 23 cm) fawn felt for head and body (String 32).

Scraps of pink felt for hands, feet, tail, ear linings and nose (Petal 52).

12 × 9 inches (30 × 23 cm) blue felt for coat (Muscari 99).

Scraps of white felt for waistcoat, collar and dicky.

Scrap of white ribbon or tape ½ inch (1 cm) wide for tie.

Three tiny pearl buttons.

Two or three shades of brown and beige stranded embroidery cotton for hairs and white for eyes.

Twelve pipe cleaners for stiffening fingers and tail.

Narrow strip of thin foam rubber for padding tail.

Black brush bristles for whiskers.

Thin card for stiffening feet.

Strong cardboard and a small pebble for base of body.

2½ inches (6·5 cm) wire for stiffening neck.

Kapok for stuffing. Finished toy weighs approximately 2 ounces (56 grammes).

Method

1 CUT OUT the pieces on pages 190–1 (17 pieces). Also the arms as given for Hunca Munca on page 181 (4 pieces) and the head, head gusset, under-chin gusset and ears as given for The Old Woman who Lived in a Shoe on page 180 (8 pieces), (29 pieces in all).

2 EARS
3 HEAD
Work as given for The Old Woman who Lived in a Shoe, page 83, Nos. 3 and 4, copying the shape and position of eyes from the pictures in Johnny Town-mouse's book. Embroider hairs all over head as he does not wear a cap and sew a tiny circle of pink felt over tip of nose. Place on one side.

4 BODY
5 WEIGHTING
Work as given for Anna Maria, page 79, Nos. 2 and 3, folding the body for shoulders so that the front piece comes at centre front and the seam joining the two back pieces at centre back, thus making a protruding seat at back and top of leg at each side of front.

6 TAIL. Make this exactly as given for Samuel Whiskers, page 78, No. 16, working from * to * but making this tail 7½ inches (19 cm) long. Push the points of your scissors into centre back of base of body, making a small hole—push tail into this hole and ladder stitch in place.

7 FEET. Stick the pieces together, each card stiffener between two felt pieces. Cut down between toes as shown on pattern. Trim each toe to a sharp little point using small scissors. Stick the feet to base of body by the heels only, so that they protrude well to the front.

8 ARMS. Make as given for Mrs. Tittlemouse, page 97, No. 7. Cut off pipe cleaners leaving only about ½ inch (1 cm) protruding (Fig. 66A). Bind these tightly with adhesive tape (B). Push the points of your scissors into top of sides of body, making a small hole. Push the bound wires into these

holes (C). Arrange arms so that the hands are in the correct position and ladder stitch top of arms to body (D). Squeeze and pinch fingers into an attractive shape and bend arms downwards.

9 ASSEMBLING HEAD AND BODY. Prepare $2\frac{1}{2}$ inches (6·5 cm) wire as shown on page 13, Fig. 8A and B. Make a small hole in centre top of body and push one end of wire down into it (Fig. 66D). Make a similar hole in base of head and push the other end of wire into this so that the head rests on the shoulders. Ladder stitch head to body, working all round several times.

10 DICKY SHIRT-FRONT. Place on to mouse with the curved edge C–D tightly pulled up under chin. Stitch firmly to shoulders and round lower edge.

11 COLLAR. Place round neck. Pull tightly and stitch Es together under chin.

12 TIE. Slip a piece of narrow white ribbon or tape under collar and tie in a neat flat bow at centre front. Trim off ends.

13 WAISTCOAT. Join front edges F–G overlapping them as little as possible. Sew three tiny pearl buttons, evenly spaced, down this join. Put on to mouse, stretching tightly backwards and stitching down outside edges H–I.

14 COAT. On the wrong side join sleeve seams J–L. Turn right side out. On the wrong side join side seams of coat J–K. Insert sleeves into armholes, matching Js. Press back collar as shown by broken line. Put on to mouse arranging carefully and securing with a few invisible stitches at fronts. Slit up centre back for 2 inches (5 cm) to make coat tails and stitch coat to body at top of these slits.

15 WHISKERS. Stitch three or four whiskers each side of nose as shown on page 18, Fig. 11.

The Cats and Kittens

This little family needs more care than any of the other toys—it is so easy to make them look like Teddy Bears! Before starting, read the section on 'Tinting and Shading', page 16, very carefully indeed and decide which method to use. Follow the instructions for shaping and modelling the head and you should produce a good, typical cat face. However, a little more or less taken on a turning, a little less stuffing, slacker or tighter modelling may make just that difference and your particular cat look not quite right. If this happens, take a critical look at it and see if one or more of the following adjustments will help:

1 Stick a tiny piece of fur fabric to the head in front of and at outer corner of each ear to square up face. (Pin first to get the effect.)
2 Are the eyes too high (a common fault)? Too close? Too far apart?
3 Is the position and shape of mouth good? (It can make the cat look tiger-fierce or very bad-tempered if too large and droopy!)
4 Try tip-tilting the nose by pushing and holding it upwards. If this improves the expression (it will give a younger, kittenish appearance) keep it in place by taking strong modelling stitches from top of bridge of nose to deep under chin (through head) and pulling these very tight. This will turn the nose up a little.
5 Try squashing the head flatter from top to bottom, thus pushing the cheeks out sideways.

Above all, don't be afraid to keep experimenting until your cat really pleases you.

A little licence (by kind permission of Messrs Warnes) has been taken over the colours of the cats' fur coats and eyes—it having been found almost impossible to reproduce Miss Potter's delicate shadings exactly.

It is suggested that you make Tabitha Twitchit first, as in so doing you will cover all the processes necessary for the rest of her family.

TABITHA TWITCHIT

'... Mrs. Tabitha Twitchit expected friends to tea ...'

Refer to the many pictures in *The Tale of Tom Kitten*, as well as to the colour plate opposite page 124 of this book.

A cuddly toy 16 inches (41 cm) high with removable skirt, jacket and apron.

Materials

⅓ yard (30 cm) white fur fabric for body.

A few scraps of black fur fabric for tail and markings.

Scraps of pink, white, black and green felt for ear linings, nose, paws, foot pads and eyes.

Black stranded cotton for mouth and claw markings.

Black brush bristles for whiskers.

Kapok for stuffing. Finished cat weighs approximately 8 ounces (230 grammes).

¾ yard (70 cm) lavender-coloured cotton material for skirt and jacket.

Odd pieces of white organza, georgette or similar for frills and fichu.

A piece of fine white cotton material for apron, 6 × 11 inches (15 × 28 cm).

About 40 inches (1 metre) white tape 1 inch (2·5 cm) wide for frill round apron.

¾ yard (70 cm) lavender-coloured ribbon ½ inch (1 cm) wide for apron strings.

A small gilt button for brooch.

Four small press-studs to fasten jacket.

12 inches (31 cm) elastic for waist of skirt.

Method

1 CUT OUT the pieces as given on pages 195–204 (38 pieces).

2 EARS. On both ears turn the two long edges inwards as far as broken line on pattern and stick in place. Stick pink felt linings in place. (As shown for the rabbits by Fig. 24A, B and C, page 37.) Place on one side.

3 HEAD. This is the most important part of the toy—don't try to hurry over it. It pays to 'make haste slowly', so that you bring out the full character of the mother cat. Stitch by hand, as it is important that each seam and dart is absolutely accurate. On the underchin gusset join small darts 1–2. On both head pieces join darts 3–4. Join underchin gusset to one head piece, carefully matching A–1–B. Join the head gusset to these pieces A–C–D–E, then join on other side of head B–3–1–A–C–D–E. Turn right side out. Stuff head firmly paying particular attention to the bulges at junction of

nose and mouth (C–A–C and 1–A–1 on pattern), making sure that these are very full and firm as they give the cat its characteristic shape. Fill the cheeks out *sideways*, thus flattening the head a little. Leave the neck hole open. Clip a little pile from round the nose and mouth and most of it from down the bridge of nose. Pin, then invisibly sew the pink felt nose in place, matching As and embroider mouth, using six strands of black embroidery cotton (Fig. 67A).

With a long needle and strong white thread, take a series of stitches from one side of bridge of nose to the other, working from the top of nose upwards for about 1 inch (2·5 cm) and pulling the stitches tightly to raise the bridge in a typical cat shape (A and B). Take a series of stitches from top of cheek through face to deep under neck end and pull tightly to puff out cheeks (B). Look at the pictures of Tabitha and cut two or three pieces of black fur fabric to correspond to the markings on her head. * Pin these in place, making sure the pile runs in the same direction as that on the white fur fabric of the head. Stitch in place, using strong thread and a sort of hemming stitch. If the black fur fabric has a knitted backing there is no need to tuck in the raw edges, but if it is woven, tuck them in as you work— or tack them back first. Go all round the edge of each black patch with the points of your scissors or the eye end of a large needle, pulling out any pile caught up in the stitching then brush the head to mingle the black and white fur and soften the edges, also to remove any loose black pile * (C).

Pin the ears in place, long sides to the outside and curling the shorter sides forwards at top of head. Take great care to place them in the best possible position by looking at the pictures of Tabitha in Tom Kitten's book, then using a long needle and strong thread, stitch them firmly in place. The best way to do this is to take a long stitch on the head behind ear, then one through ear to the front and a stitch on the head in front of ear, a stitch through ear to the back and another stitch on head behind ear and so on, working twice across the base of each ear (C).

4 EYES. Neatly stab stitch each white eye to an odd piece of black felt, working all round (D). Cut away the black felt, leaving just a very narrow black edge to eye. Stick or stitch on pupils (E). Beatrix Potter's delicate water colours show Tabitha's eyes without any colour but a toy looks rather anaemic made like this so stick the tiny curved green 'iris' pieces one each side of each pupil (Fig. 67F). * Sew eyes to head, placing them along top of cheeks— hem invisibly all round. Pull out fur fabric caught in the stitching. Take a few stitches through front of face from the front corner of one eye to the same place on the other, pulling tightly to sink and shape eye socket. Do not make whiskers yet. *

5 ARMS. On the outer arms join top darts 5–6. Place each outer arm on top of an inner arm, right sides facing and on the wrong side stitch I–H and

Fig. 67 Making and modelling Tabitha's head

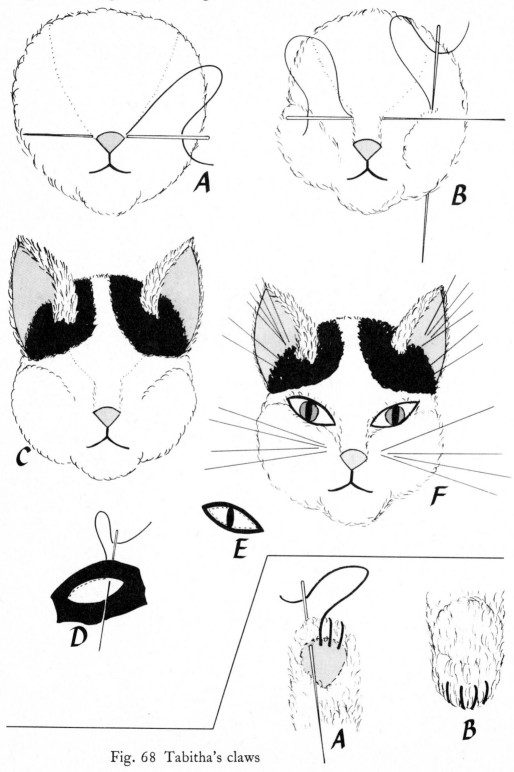

Fig. 68 Tabitha's claws

F–G. Open out the gaps between F and I and insert the pink felt paws, pinning in place and matching Fs and Is. Tack by oversewing, then back stitch firmly F–I–F. Turn arms right side out and stuff firmly. Using six strands of black embroidery cotton, work four large stitches from each felt paw over the tips of arms to represent the four divisions between claws (Fig. 68A and B). See Fig. 12, page 20, for starting and finishing. Place on one side.

6 TAIL. Place the two pieces together, right sides facing and on the wrong side stitch together all round except for the short, straight end. Turn right side out. Stuff, leaving end open. Look at picture and cut a piece of white fur fabric to make the large marking on tail. Stitch this in place as described for the head markings No. 3 between * and *.

7 BODY. Place the two body gusset pieces together, right sides facing, and on the wrong side stitch J–K. Join this piece to both body pieces O–N–M–J. Join the two body pieces together P–Q and R–S. Insert the seat gusset, matching letters and stitching all round O–P–O–K–O. Gather round top edge S–J–S, pull up and fasten off. Stuff body and sew up opening R–Q. Place the foot pads on seat gusset, matching Os and invisibly stitch in place. Work four black stitches on feet just as you did on the arms. We cannot see Tabitha's body in the pictures as it is covered by her dress, but she probably has a large black patch somewhere. If you want to make her look really nice when undressed, sew a large patch of black fur fabric to one side in the same way as described for the head markings, No. 3 * to *. With a long needle and strong thread, take a few stitches through each side of body from the out-side to body gusset, working along broken lines and line of crosses on body pattern and pulling them tightly to model and indicate hind legs and haunches.

8 ASSEMBLING. Place open end of head over top, gathered part of body and ladder stitch firmly in place. Take a few long stitches to pull head slightly over to one side at an attractive angle. Sew tail to back of body at P. Pin arms to sides of body, placing open ends flat at position shown on pattern and arranging them at whatever angle you wish. Ladder stitch several times round the tops.

9 WHISKERS. Make these in the three positions shown on Fig. 67F, working by the method shown in Fig. 11, page 18.

Tabitha wears a lavender colour Victorian type skirt and jacket and a frilly white apron.

10 THE SKIRT. Cut a strip of the lavender cotton material 9 × 32 inches (23 × 81 cm). Join the short ends to make centre back seam. Make a narrow hem all round one edge (the top) and insert elastic to fit the cat's waist. Try on to cat and pin up bottom hem so that the skirt just touches the ground.

Take skirt off, slip stitch hem invisibly by hand. Press and put on cat.

11 THE JACKET. * Fold sleeves in half and stitch seams A–B reversing one to make a pair. On the jacket piece stitch shoulder seams C–D. Insert sleeves into armholes, matching As and gathering superfluous fullness on sleeves to the top forming a puff. Bind the neck edge. Try on to cat and turn and pin front edges back so that they just overlap. Pin up sleeve edges to elbow length. Remove jacket and invisibly stitch these four hems, by hand. * Place the two peplum pieces together, right sides facing, and pin to avoid slipping. Machine all round E–F–E. Turn right side out, push out corners, flatten, press. Pin one side of peplum to base of main part of jacket, right sides facing, and matching E–G–E. Machine round E–G–E. On the wrong side of jacket turn in top edge of peplum E–G–E covering raw edge at base of main part and slip stitch in place.

12 THE FRILLS AND FICHU. Cut two strips of fine white material such as organza or georgette $20 \times 2\frac{1}{4}$ inches (51×6 cm) for the sleeves and one strip 16×5 inches (41×13 cm) for a fichu for the neck.

Join the short ends of the sleeve frills and machine a narrow hem all round one edge. Run a gathering thread round the other edge, pull up gathers to fit edges of sleeves and sew a frill invisibly just inside each sleeve so that they will hang down over elbows. Neaten inside with a piece of tape or binding.

Take the fichu piece and machine a narrow hem down both long sides. Look at pictures and drape the piece round the jacket neck, tacking it here and there and easing in fullness, tucking in ends and stitching at front. Sew a small gilt button in place for a brooch and sew four small press-studs to front to fasten. Put jacket on to cat.

13 APRON. Tack a narrow turning back all round curved edge. Gather along one edge of tape for frill, pull up gathers to fit curved edge of apron and tack to back so that the frill just shows. Machine close to edge of apron and again a little further in, thus attaching frill and covering raw edge of turning. Gather along top of apron. Pull up gathers to 5 inches (13 cm) and fasten off. Bind top of apron with the lavender ribbon, covering gathers and leaving an equal length each side for strings. Put apron on to Tabitha, tying a bow at the back.

N.B. If you would like to add petticoats as a finishing touch to this character, see Cousin Ribby, page 109, No. 10.

You can arrange Tabitha in any of the positions shown in the book. As you will see by the picture, the original was given a small pink felt tongue and is shown licking her paw after her son Thomas had scratched her. The paw can be fastened up to the chin by means of a press-stud, so that it can be undone to allow for play and undressing.

COUSIN RIBBY

'The visitor was a neighbour, Mrs. Ribby; she had called to borrow some yeast.'

Refer to the picture on page 15 of *The Tale of Samuel Whiskers*, as well as to the colour plate opposite page 124 of this book.

A cuddly toy 16 inches (41 cm) high with removable petticoat, dress, apron, shawl, cap, bonnet and umbrella.

Instructions for her basket are on page 257.

Materials

¼ yard (23 cm) beige fur fabric for main parts of body.

¼ yard (23 cm) white fur fabric for arms, front gusset and markings on hind legs and face.

Small scraps of brown fur fabric for ears and other dark markings.

Brown wool for shading head and tail.

Scraps of pink, white, black and green felt for ear linings, nose, foot pads, paws and eyes.

Black stranded cotton for mouth and claw markings.

Black brush bristles for whiskers.

Kapok for stuffing. Finished toy weighs approximately 8 ounces (230 grammes).

Three or four small pebbles or marbles for weighting.

¾ yard (69 cm) pink rose-patterned material for dress.

⅓ yard (30 cm) striped cotton material for petticoat (optional).

⅓ yard (30 cm) blue-green taffeta or similar for apron and umbrella.

½ ounce (15 grammes) pale blue double knitting wool for shawl.

½ ounce (15 grammes) pink wool for woolly cap.

Scraps of white wool for edging shawl and cap.

¼ yard (23 cm) lavender cotton material for bonnet.

Oddment of milliner's or pelmet buckram for stiffening bonnet.

1½ yards (1 metre 35 cm) lavender ribbon ½ inch (1 cm) wide for bonnet strings and trimmings.

1½ yards (1 metre 35 cm) very narrow elastic for waist of petticoat and edge of sleeves.

Four small press-studs for fastening dress.

A small gilt clasp or button for brooch.

Method

1 CUT OUT (A) the nose, paws, foot pads, underchin gusset, body gusset, outer arms and inner arms, as given for Tabitha Twitchit on pages 199, 202–4 using the same colours (12 pieces).

(B) The tail, head gusset and seat gusset as given for Tabitha Twitchit on pages 195, 202 but using beige fur fabric (4 pieces).

(C) The body and head as given for Tabitha Twitchit on pages 198, 204 using beige fur fabric for the main parts but joining on white for the front of face and hind legs (below lines of XXXX). When cutting these pieces remember to allow a little extra on beige and white parts for seaming (8 pieces).

(D) The apron as given for Tabitha Twitchit on page 197 using bluey/green taffeta (1 piece).

(E) The sleeves as given for Tabitha Twitchit on page 201, the bodice (page 206) and a matching strip 32 × 9 inches (81 × 23 cm) for the skirt of dress (4 pieces), all in rose-patterned cotton material.

(F) The ears, eyes and bonnet (patterns page 205) (12 pieces).

You should now have 41 pieces in all. This cutting out process sounds complicated, merely because duplicate patterns for another toy but in different colours are needed. It is not as difficult as it appears—work slowly and calmly!

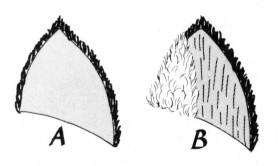

A   B   Fig. 69 Ribby's ears

Fig. 70 Ribby's face

2 EARS (Fig. 69). Stick each pink felt lining to a brown back (A). Stick a tiny piece of white fur fabric to each ear as shown. Using brown felt pen, add a few shadings (B). Place on one side.

3 HEAD. On the two main parts piece together the white and beige pieces at line of XXXX. Then work exactly as given for Tabitha Twitchit, page 102, No. 3 but instead of stitching the large black patches in place, look at the pictures of Cousin Ribby and at Fig. 70 and sew on two or three narrow strips of brown fur fabric from top of head to varying lengths down back of head. Add long stitches in brown wool for extra shadings on the face, still looking at the pictures for the best positions.

4 EYES. Stick the small black and white dots firmly in place on the green eye pieces. Work as given for Tabitha Twitchit, page 103, No. 4 from * to *.

5 ARMS. On the inner arm pieces join the curved dart marked by XXX to make the finished arms curved inwards, then work as for Tabitha Twitchit, page 103, No. 5.

6 TAIL. Work as for Tabitha Twitchit, page 105, No. 6 but instead of making a large black marking, look at the pictures of Ribby and sew two or three brown, crescent-shaped markings to the underside, softening them with a few brown wool stitches.

Ribby has a lot of weight in front (her arms, basket and umbrella) and is inclined to tip forwards. This can be easily remedied by wrapping one or two clean pebbles or marbles in soft material and pushing them down into the tail among the stuffing. This extra weight will ensure she stands very firmly.

7 BODY. On the two main parts, piece together the white hind leg and the beige body at the line marked XXX then work as given for Tabitha Twitchit, page 105, No. 7, omitting large black patch but adding as many or as few streaky brown markings with strips of fur fabric and stitches in brown wool as you feel inclined, using your imagination as to their shape and position.

8 ASSEMBLING
9 WHISKERS
} Work as given for Tabitha Twitchit, page 105, Nos. 8 and 9 but consult the picture of Ribby when attaching arms so that they are in the correct position to hold her umbrella and basket.

10 PETTICOAT. We do not see Ribby's petticoat, but she probably wore one if the other Potter characters are anything to go by—it adds to her charm and helps to shape her dress. Make one exactly as given for Tabitha Twitchit's skirt, page 105, No. 10, cutting slightly shorter so that it will not show beneath her dress. (You could add a red flannel petticoat under this if you wished—I feel almost sure Cousin Ribby wore one in order not to take cold.)

11 DRESS. Work as given for Tabitha Twitchit's jacket, page 106, No. 11 from * to * facing the neck edge on the inside instead of binding. Run

narrow elastic into the hems at sleeve edges so that these fit Ribby's arms tightly at the elbows. Take the skirt piece and join the short ends half way across. (The open part is for opening at top of skirt.) Turn back hems on the two open sides to match those on bodice. Gather round top of skirt, pull up gathers to fit base of bodice, pin and stitch bodice to skirt. Try dress on to Ribby (the opening and skirt seam is at centre front). Pin up hem all round bottom of dress so that it just touches the ground and mark position of overlapped front with a pin. Remove dress. Invisibly slip stitch hem and sew three or four press-studs invisibly to inside of bodice opening to fasten. Press and put on to Ribby. Pin or sew on her brooch.

12 APRON. Ribby is obviously wearing her best apron—not the one she uses in the kitchen whilst baking mouse pie! The material therefore needs to be rather rich-looking and for the original a taffeta dress lining was used. Make it exactly as given for Tabitha Twitchit, page 106, No. 13 but make the frill and strings from strips of the matching material.

13 SHAWL. So that it may rest smoothly on Ribby's shoulders, this needs making to shape rather than using the plain triangle that the picture indicates. This may be knitted or crocheted and instructions are given below for both. Crochet really looks more authentic and fits better.

To knit the shawl: Work throughout in garter stitch, using size 9 needles and pale blue double knitting wool. Cast on 3 stitches (centre back point).
1st row: Knit.
2nd row: Inc. in first st. K. to end. Inc. in last stitch. Repeat these two rows until there are 39 stitches on needle.
Work 12 rows straight.
K.14. Cast off 11. K.14 (back of neck).
Now work on the last 14 stitches only.
* K. 14 rows straight.
Decrease on outside edge of every third row until all the stitches are used up. Fasten off wool. *
Join in the wool to other side of neck and repeat from * to *.
Work two rows of double crochet all round the outside edge, using white wool.

To crochet the shawl: No. 9 hook (new range, 3·5) and double-knit wool.
Make 4 chain. Turn, miss the first chain and work 1 double crochet in each of the 3 chain.
Row 1: Make 3 turning chain and work across in trebles, increasing at both ends of the row.
Row 2: Make 1 turning chain, work across in double crochet, increasing at both ends of the row.
Repeat these 2 rows until there are 29 stitches. Work straight for 2 rows.

Next row: Treble 10. Turn.

Work straight on these 10 stitches for 5 rows. Decrease 1 stitch at the outer edge only on every other row until there are no stitches left. Fasten off.

Join on again where the work turned after the 10 treble, by missing the first 9 chain (for neck) and making 3 chain for the first treble. Work across with 9 treble into the next 9 chain (10 stitches).

Work to match the first side, by decreases at the outer edge only, until all stitches are worked away.

Make a contrast edging for the shawl by working 2 rows of double crochet all round with the same hook. Turn the corners by working 3 double crochet in each corner.

14 WOOLLY CAP. Ribby wears a quaint little woolly cap under her bonnet—if you look through *The Tale of Samuel Whiskers* you will see its shape.

To knit the cap: Work in garter stitch. Using pink double-knitting wool and size 9 needles. Cast on 3 stitches (centre front point).

1st row: Knit.

2nd row: Inc. in first stitch. Knit to end. Inc. in last stitch.

Repeat these two rows until there are 21 stitches on needle.

Then increase at each end of every third row until there are 35 stitches on needle.

Next row: K.7, K.2 tog., K.7, K.3 tog., K.7, K.2 tog., K.7.

Next row: Inc. in first stitch. K. to end. Inc. in last stitch.

Knit two rows.

Next row: K.7, K.2 tog., K.6, K.3 tog., K.6, K.2 tog., K.7.

Next row: Inc. in first stitch. K. to end. Inc. in last stitch.

Next row: K.6, K.2 tog., K.6, K.3 tog., K.6, K.2 tog., K.6.

Knit 1 row.

Cast off.

Work 2 rows of double crochet all round outside edge, using white wool.

Work a short length of chain crochet from each bottom corner for strings.

To crochet the cap: No. 9 hook (new range, 3·5) and double-knit wool.

Make 25 chain. Make 1 turning chain, and then work 1 row double crochet in each of the 25 chain. Work all the following rows in treble, with 3 turning chain at the end of each row.

Row 1: 6 treble, increase in the next stitch, 5 treble, increase in the next stitch, 5 treble, increase in the next stitch, 6 treble (28 stitches).

Row 2: Decrease 1 stitch, 4 treble, increase in the next stitch, 6 treble, increase in the next stitch, 6 treble, increase in the next stitch, 5 treble, decrease 1 stitch (29 stitches).

Row 3: Decrease 2 stitches at the beginning of the row and 1 stitch at the end (26 stitches).

Repeat row 3 until there are 3 stitches left. Fasten off.

Make a white edging for the cap as follows:

With the same hook and right side facing work a row of double crochet all
round the cap, with 3 double crochet in each corner.

Work a second row in the same manner. Attach a length of chain to the two
bottom corners.

Put the cap on Ribby's head, point to top of head between the ears and
tie strings under chin, tucking the ends out of sight inside her dress. Put the
shawl round her shoulders.

15 BONNET. Cut a piece of lavender-coloured material approximately 24 × 8
inches (61 × 20 cm) for the brim and another piece approximately 12 × 5
inches (30 × 13 cm) for the back. Using a large stitch on the sewing machine
and matching thread, run gathering threads across these two pieces lengthwise about ¾ inch (2 cm) apart. Lay the buckram back piece on the smaller
gathered cotton piece (Fig. 71A) and pull up gathers so that this piece is a
little more than double as wide as the buckram. Fold the cotton piece over
and tuck in the edges. Pin, then oversew all round except for one side, which
was folded (B). The buckram stiffener is now covered on both sides by ruched
material. Cover the brim in the same way, having the fold round the long,
outer curved edge (C) and pulling the rows of gathers up more tightly
towards the inner curve (D). Tuck in the raw edges at short ends. Pin then
oversew these (E). Cut away surplus material at inner curve then tuck in
these edges. Pin then oversew.

Cut the ribbon in half and tie together, again with a neat bow. Sew bow
to centre front of brim. Sew ribbon to brim as shown, catching here and
there. Turn back each ribbon at short end of bonnet and oversew firmly (F).
Then turn ribbons down again, leaving the long ends to tie under chin (G).
On the wrong side oversew inner curve of brim to outer curve of back. Turn
right way out and tie on to cat over woolly cap. If it slips give Ribby a small
hat pin, providing she is not intended for a very small child.

16 UMBRELLA. Cut a circle of the same material as Ribby's apron approximately 8½ inches (21·5 cm) in diameter (draw round a dessert plate) (Fig.
72A). Divide the circle as evenly as possible into ten sections, marking at
the edge with tailor's chalk or pins. Draw a line curving slightly inwards
from one point to the other as shown by Fig. 72B. Cut round these lines so
that the edge of the circle has inverted scallops all round it. Turn back, tack
and machine the tiniest possible hem all round the edge (C). If using a
Tricel or similar material, burn a tiny hole in the centre of circle with the
point of an iron or a piece of hot wire (D). Pleat the circle along the broken
lines on Fig. 72, so that these lines will fold inwards towards the handle.
Tack and press these pleats. When sharply pleated remove tacks. Run a

Fig. 71 Making Ribby's bonnet

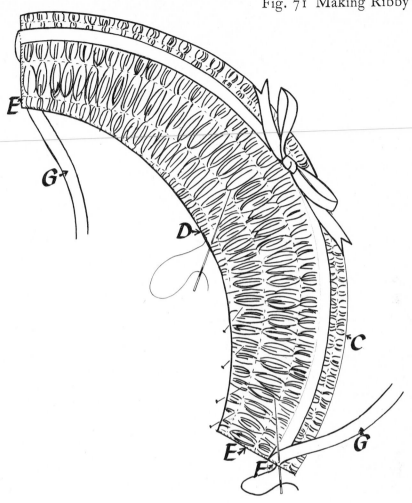

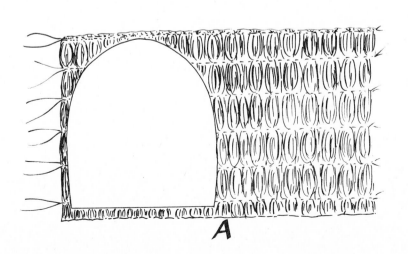

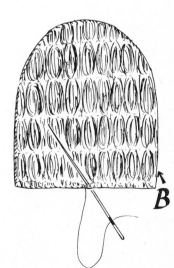

needle and matching thread through all the points (E). Smear a little
adhesive round burnt out circle and slip the prepared handle (see page 292)
down centre of pleats and out through hole. Look at picture and when
enough of the point protrudes, squeeze and pinch the taffeta round the hole

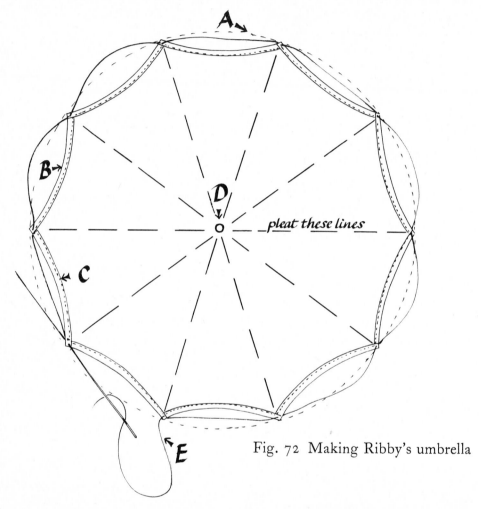

Fig. 72 Making Ribby's umbrella

to the handle until it sticks. Put a tiny spot of adhesive just inside each top
point, pull up the gathering thread tightly and fasten off. Press the points
to handle until they stick. Sew the umbrella to Ribby's hand.

MOPPET

'*Mrs. Tabitha dressed Moppet . . . in a clean pinafore . . .*'

Refer to the pictures in *The Tale of Tom Kitten* and in particular to that on page
23, as well as to the colour plate opposite page 124 of this book.

A cuddly toy with removable pinafore, approximately 8 inches (20 cm) high.

Materials

$\frac{1}{8}$ yard (12 cm) white fur fabric for main parts.

Tiny scrap of black fur fabric for ears and markings.

Tiny scrap of grey fur fabric for tail and markings.

*Scraps of pink felt (Petal 52) for ear linings, paws, foot pads and nose.

*Scraps of green and white felt for eyes.

*Black stranded cotton for claws and mouth.

*Black brush bristles for whiskers.

*Kapok for stuffing. Finished toy weighs approximately 3 ounces (85 grammes).

*$\frac{1}{4}$ yard (23 cm) white poplin or lawn for pinafore.

*White bias binding for neck and armholes.

*Odd pieces of broderie anglaise for trimming (or 1$\frac{1}{4}$ yards (1 metre 5 cm) 1$\frac{1}{2}$-inch (4-cm) wide if buying specially).

*Two small press-studs.

Method

For making markings by patching, and for marking by felt pen, see page 17.

1 CUT OUT the pieces as given on pages 207–9 using white fur fabric for all furry parts except the ears and tail. Cut the ears in black and the tail in grey fur fabric (31 pieces).

2 EARS. Work as given for Ribby, page 109, No. 2, but use black fur fabric for main part and grey for the tiny piece stuck inside. Shade with a black felt pen.

3 HEAD. Work as given for Tabitha Twitchit, page 102, No. 3 with these alterations:

(A) Follow the pictures of Moppet in Tom Kitten's book.

(B) Take the tiniest possible turnings on all head seams in order to get the fullest possible effect of the delicate, kittenish features. On a knitted material several lots of oversewing, using double thread, may be sufficient. The original was sewn in this way.

(C) Use three strands of cotton only for mouth and grey fur fabric for patches.

4 EYES. Work as given for Tabitha Twitchit, page 103, No. 4 from * to * then carefully stick the green iris in place and using a black felt pen, indicate the pupil as shown on pattern.

5 ARMS. Work as given for Tabitha Twitchit, page 103, No. 5.

6 TAIL. Work as given for Tabitha Twitchit, page 105, No. 6 using finely-cut fur fabric snippings for stuffing so as to weight the kitten at the back

and help her to stand well. Instead of one large patch, sew three or four black crescent-shaped markings to top side of finished tail.

7 BODY. Work as given for Tabitha Twitchit, page 105, No. 7 using finely-cut snippings of fur fabric to stuff back of base of body to weight the kitten, and looking at the pictures of Moppet, and Plate 7 opposite, for body markings. These are a series of slightly crescent-shaped stripes and for the original both grey and black fur fabric was used.

8 ASSEMBLING. Work as given for Tabitha Twitchit on page 105, No. 8. Add a few grey fur fabric markings to top of arms.

9 WHISKERS AND FINISHING OFF. Add a few small whiskers each side of mouth and in front of ears (see Fig. 11, page 18). Add a few felt-pen markings to face and body if you wish—these help to merge in the rather solid patches.

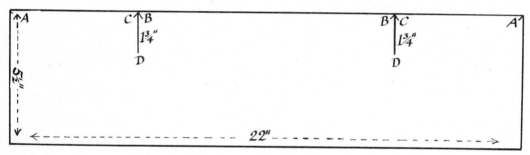

Fig. 73 Plan for skirt of kitten's pinafore

10 PINAFORE. Cut a strip of white poplin $5\frac{1}{2} \times 22$ inches (14×56 cm) for the skirt. Fold this in half and then in half again and cut two slits for armholes $1\frac{3}{4}$ inches (4·5 cm) long at these two points—see plan in Fig. 73. Gather along top of centre section B–B, pull up to fit front of yoke B–B, tack skirt to yoke on the wrong side. Similarly, gather two back sections C–A and A–C, pull up to fit corresponding yoke sections and tack. Machine yoke to skirt A–C, B–B and C–A. Neaten raw edges inside.

Using white bias binding, bind all round both armholes D–C–B–D, also neck. Turn back a narrow hem all down both sides of centre back of pinafore. Stitch. Sew two press-studs in place to fasten, one at neck and one at base of yoke. Sew a narrow frill of broderie anglaise round neck. Turn in and gather the curved edge of epaulettes marked by broken line on pattern, pull up gathers to fit top of armholes (yoke part only between B and C) tack, then stitch in place. Try pinafore on to kitten and pin up bottom hem so that it just clears the ground, then remove it. Stitch a piece of broderie anglaise about 1 inch wide all round bottom edge, machining along both

Plate 7 The fur markings on Moppet and Mittens. *Left:* by patching.
Right: by felt pen.

Plate 8
Finishing
off Mrs.
Tiggy-winkle's
prickles with
glue

edges of trimming. Press and put on to kitten. Press and adjust Moppet to stand firmly.

N.B. To make the kitten's markings by the felt pen method, use grey fur fabric for the ears instead of black, then work as described on page 17, referring to Plate 7.

MITTENS

'Now keep your frocks clean children—you must walk on your hind legs.'
Refer to the pictures in *The Tale of Tom Kitten*, as well as to Plate 7 on page 117 and the colour plate opposite page 124 of this book.
    A cuddly toy with removable pinafore, approximately 8 inches (20 cm) high.

Materials
    ⅛ yard (12 cm) beige fur fabric for main parts.
    ⅛ yard (12 cm) white fur fabric for body gusset, hands and feet (the 'mittens'!).
    Scraps of brown fur fabric for ears and markings.
    Also, all those items marked * as given for Moppet on page 115.

Method
    1 CUT OUT all the pieces as given on pages 207–9 using brown fur fabric for the ears, beige for tail, base, head, head gusset and inner arms and white for body gusset and underchin gusset.
        Cut the body and outer arms in beige except for the small portions indicated by lines of OOOOO on pattern—cut these in white, remembering to cut both the beige and white portions larger so as to allow for joining (35 pieces in all).
        Before starting work, piece together the beige and white parts on arms and body, making a complete piece the shape of the pattern (31 pieces).
        Work through Nos. 2–10 as given for Moppet on pages 115–16 using brown fur fabric for the ears and markings and beige for the small pieces inside the ears. Finish off with felt pen markings on face and body, in a reddish-brown to give the 'marmalade' appearance which shows up in some of the pictures in *The Tale of Tom Kitten*.

TOM KITTEN

'She took all sorts of elegant, uncomfortable clothes out of a chest of drawers, in order to dress up her son Thomas.'

Refer to the many pictures in *The Tale of Tom Kitten*, as well as to the colour plate opposite page 124 of this book.

A cuddly toy approximately 8 inches (20 cm) high with removable hat, buster suit and butterfly.

Materials

⅛ yard (12 cm) beige fur fabric for main parts of body.

Scraps of white fur fabric for front of face and underchin gusset.

Scraps of pink felt (Petal 52) for foot pads, paws and nose.

Scraps of white, green, black, brown and orange felt for ear linings, eyes and butterfly.

Black stranded cotton for claws and mouth.

Black brush bristles for whiskers.

Kapok for stuffing. Finished toy weighs approximately 3 ounces (85 grammes).

12 × 18 inches (31 × 46 cm) blue felt (Muscari 99) for buster suit.

Scrap of white cotton 'edging' for collar.

8 small pearl buttons.

12 × 9 inches (31 × 23 cm) yellow felt for hat.

Oddment of blue bias binding for trimming

Round elastic for hat.

A small, shallow jar-lid approximately 2 inches (5 cm) diameter for crown of hat.

A small gold safety-pin to fix butterfly to paw.

Light and dark brown (or black) felt pens for marking.

Method

1 CUT OUT the pieces as given on pages 210–12 (20 pieces); also the head gusset, outer arms, inner arms, ears, tail, nose, paws, eyes and iris, as for Moppet and Mittens on pages 207–9 using beige fur fabric for all the furry parts, white felt for the ear linings and eyes, and pink felt for the paws and nose (18 pieces); also the underchin gusset and the front part of head (nose side of broken line) in white fur fabric and the back part of head in beige fur fabric, using the pattern for Moppet and Mittens on page 209 (5 pieces), (43 pieces in all).

N.B. Remember to cut the two parts of head to allow for seaming the white and beige parts together.

2 EARS. Work as given for Ribby, page 109, No. 2, but use beige fur fabric for the main part and the tiny piece stuck inside and white felt for the linings.

3 HEAD. Join the two white and two beige parts of head together so that you

have two complete sides of head, then work as given for Tabitha Twitchit, page 102, No. 3, with these alterations:

(A) Follow the pictures of Tom Kitten in his book.

(B) Take the tiniest possible turnings on all head seams in order to get the fullest possible effect of the delicate, kittenish features. On a knitted material several lots of oversewing, using double thread, may be sufficient. The original was sewn in this way.

(C) Use three strands of cotton only for mouth and do not add any patches.

4 EYES. Work as given for Tabitha Twitchit, page 103, No. 4 from * to * then carefully stick the green iris in place and using a black felt pen, indicate the pupil as shown on pattern. (N.B. Tom's eyes are larger and more 'amazed' looking than his dainty sisters'!)

5 ARMS. Work as given for Tabitha Twitchit, page 103, No. 5.

6 TAIL. Work as given for Tabitha Twitchit, page 105, No. 6, using finely-cut fur fabric snippings for stuffing to weight Tom at the back and help him to stand firmly. Do not add any patches.

7 BODY. Join body gusset to one side of body J–K. Join on other side of body J–K–S. Turn right side out; stuff firmly. Gather all round top edge S–J–S and pull up, tucking in raw edges as you pull. Fasten off securely.

8 LEGS. On the outer legs join the top darts 7–8. Place each outer leg on an inner leg, right sides facing, and join them M–N and O–P. Insert the foot pads, matching N and P (note they go in *sideways*, probably the opposite way to what you expect) and stitch all round N–P–N. Turn right side out and stuff firmly. Work four black stitches for claw divisions on each foot just as you did on the arms.

9 ASSEMBLING. Ladder stitch head to top of body and the legs and arms in the positions shown on pattern. Place the arms at any angle you wish but if you want the butterfly to sit on one paw, make sure that arm is extended at a suitable angle. Place the legs evenly so that Tom will stand. Finally sew on the tail, pinning carefully first to get the right angle—this touches the ground at the back and together with the legs forms a kind of tripod, so that the kitten stands very firmly.

10 WHISKERS AND MARKINGS. Add a few small whiskers each side of mouth (see Fig. 11, page 18). Looking carefully at the pictures of Tom, make his markings with light and dark brown (or black) felt pen, taking particular care over his face (see opposite page 124).

11 BUSTER SUIT TOP. On the wrong side join the two fronts to the back A–B and C–D. Fold the sleeves in half (remembering to reverse one to make a pair) and join seams C–E. Insert sleeves into armholes, matching Cs and having the bulges to the back and cut-away part to the front. Turn right side out. Make two small buttonholes as shown on pattern and sew buttons to correspond on the other side. Sew a narrow piece of trimming (the solid,

scalloped edge of a piece of broderie anglaise?) round the neck for a collar. Put the top part of suit on to Tom.

12 TROUSERS. On both pieces join the two darts X–Y on the wrong side except for the small portions towards the top of each one indicated by short lines. Work buttonhole stitch round these four gaps and make two more buttonholes on *one piece only* (the front) as indicated towards the top at each side edge of pattern. Place the two pieces together, right sides facing,

Fig. 75 Butterfly's body

Fig. 74 Tom Kitten's hat

and join side seams V–Z and small V-shaped crutch seam P–O–P. Turn right side out and on the back only cut a slit for tail as indicated by broken line in centre of pattern. Put trousers on to Tom and mark positions for buttons with pins. Two at the front and two at the back of the top of suit to hold the trousers up and one at each side on back half of trousers to fasten these (the front overlaps the back a little). Remove suit. Sew on the six buttons and replace suit.

13 THE HAT. Cut two circles of yellow felt about 4 inches (10 cm) diameter. Place them together and bind all round the edge with blue bias binding to match buster suit, pulling the binding as tight as you can (the brim is double). Now go all round the felt near to binding, stretching it as much as you can by pulling between fingers and thumb. This is to make the brim curl upwards in the typical sailor shape of the period and is not as difficult as it sounds. The tight binding helps! Cut a circle of yellow felt to fit top of jar lid and stick it in place. Cut a strip to fit all round the edge and stick this in place. Oversew all round top edge. This is the crown of hat. Stand covered lid in centre of brim and ladder stitch it in place, working all round one stitch alternately on bottom of covered edge of lid and one on brim. Stretch a piece of blue ribbon or binding tightly round crown and stick in place, leaving two ends to hang down back about $3\frac{1}{2}$ inches (9 cm) long. Cut 'fish-tails' in the ends of these (Fig. 74). Sew a piece of fine round elastic to each side of hat so that when put on the back of Tom's head it will stay firmly in place, the elastic under his chin.

N.B. There is no need to cut away a hole for the head.

14 THE BUTTERFLY. In many of the pictures in Tom's book he is seen gaily chasing a butterfly. Our kitten has one perched on his hand.

Take the brown wing piece and looking at the pattern on page 211 for shape, on both sides stick a black tip to each wing and four small orange markings. Embroider white spots and black veins. Take the body piece and starting at the wide end, roll it up. Secure point by sticking or stitching (Fig. 75). Sew wings to body, catching them upwards at an attractive angle. Sew a small gold safety pin to underside of butterfly's body so that you can pin it to Tom's paw. (If you prefer, fasten it to the paw with a press-stud—one half on the butterfly and one on the paw.)

MISS MOPPET

'*Miss Moppet holds her poor head in her paws and looks at him through a hole in the duster.*'

Refer to the picture on page 24 of *The Story of Miss Moppet*, as well as to the colour plate opposite page 141 of this book.

Miss Moppet is obviously the same kitten as Moppet in *The Tale of Tom Kitten*, so make up a kitten, working exactly as given for Moppet, page 114, sewing her arms on at the angle shown in the picture. Tie her head up in a piece of old blue check duster or gingham. Make a slit for her to peep through then twist and model her paws to hold the duster, either stitching them in place or fastening with press-studs. Tie a piece of bright pink ribbon round her neck.

MISS MOPPET'S HASSOCK

Materials

A piece of foam rubber 3 × 3 × 1 inch (8 × 8 × 2·5 cm).
Scraps of pink felt (Cyclamen 67). If buying—12 × 9 inches (31 × 23 cm).
A small piece of hessian for base.

Cover the foam with felt by oversewing a piece top and bottom and a strip all round the edge. Cover the base with a piece of hessian, turning in the raw edges and oversewing all round. Cut two tiny felt circular tabs (pattern, page 183) fold, stitch round broken line and sew one to each side of hassock. Sit Miss Moppet securely on the hassock by sewing press-studs to her footpads and the other halves to the hassock and another stud, one half to her tail and the other to edge of hassock. She can then be taken off and put on.

MISS MOPPET'S MOUSE

'The Mouse comes very close.'

Refer to the picture on page 24 of *The Story of Miss Moppet*, as well as to the colour plate opposite page 141 of this book, and to Plate 33, page 286.

A miniature felt mouse $2\frac{1}{2}$ inches (6 cm) high.

Materials

Scraps of beige felt (String 32) over from other animals—for the body.
Scraps of pink felt (Petal 52) for hands, feet, ear linings, nose and tail.
Scraps of green felt (Lime 1) for jacket.
Scraps of very narrow red ribbon for tie.
Six pipe cleaners for stiffening tail and arms.
Black and white stranded cotton for eyes.
Brown and beige stranded cotton for hairs.
Black brush bristles for whiskers.
A blazer button for weighting about $\frac{3}{4}$ inch (2 cm) diameter.
A little kapok for stuffing.

Method

1 CUT OUT the pieces as given on page 183 (19 pieces).
2 BODY. Take the body gusset and on the wrong side join a body piece to each side A–C–D. Join one side of head gusset to one side of body A–B. Join the other side of head gusset to the other side of body A–B then continue down centre back, joining the two body pieces together A–B–E. Turn right way out, pushing out point of nose well and stuff very firmly.

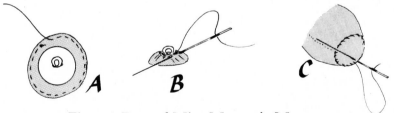

Fig. 76 Base of Miss Moppet's Mouse

Take the blazer button and cut a rough circle of fawn felt a little larger. Run a gathering thread all round the edge (Fig. 76A). Pull up gathers and fasten off (B). This forms a slightly heavy yet flat base so that the mouse stands firmly. Push the shanked side into the base of body and oversew in place, working all round (C).

3 EARS. Stick each pink lining to a fawn felt ear. Fold in half at base and

stitch. Make a hole each side of head as shown on pattern by pushing the points of your scissors into the head. Push base of ears into holes, linings facing outwards (look at picture). Ladder stitch in place.

4 NOSE AND EYES. Cut the smallest possible circle of pink felt. Gather round the edge, pull up and sew to tip of nose (Fig. 77). Looking at picture, embroider eyes, a tiny white and black spot on each side of head. Take a few stitches right through the head from one eye to the other, pulling tightly to sink them a little.

Fig. 77 Mouse's nose

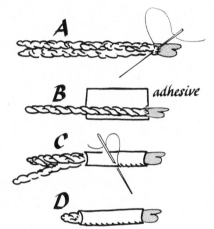

Fig. 78 Making mouse's arms

5 HAIRS. Using beige and one or two different shades of brown Sylko, embroider hairs on head and lower part of body which will not be covered by jacket, working as described on page 76 under 'Finishing off head', No. 10, for Samuel Whiskers.

6 FEET. Stick the feet together in pairs. Fringe fat end as shown on pattern to indicate toes. Looking at picture stick feet to base.

7 BOW TIE. Make a tiny bow from a scrap of very narrow, red ribbon and looking at the picture on page 34 of *The Story of Miss Moppet*, stitch this to front of mouse's neck.

8 JACKET. On the wrong side, join dart 1–2. Put jacket round mouse and stitch at front each side of tie.

9 ARMS. Take the hands and stick them together in pairs. Fold two pipe cleaners in half and stitch one to each hand—the folded loop of the cleaner to the straight end of hand (Fig. 78A). Twist the ends of cleaners together. Take the sleeve pieces and lay a hand complete with pipe cleaner on each one (pointing finger to the top). Stick the straight edge of hand to sleeve with a very small amount of adhesive (B). Fold the sleeve over neatly, over-sew along lower edge (sleeve seam) (C). Take an odd length of pipe cleaner and push it down into arm to fill it out well (C). Cut off surplus ends of pipe

The visitor was a neighbour, Mrs. Ribby; she had called to borrow some yeast. "Come in, Cousin Ribby, come in . . ."

The Tale of Samuel Whiskers

Mrs. Tabitha Twitchit and her kittens, Moppet, Mittens and Tom Kitten: "Now keep your frocks clean, children!"

The Tale of Tom Kitten

Mr. Jeremy stuck his pole into the mud
and fastened his boat to it. Then he
settled himself cross-legged and arranged his
fishing tackle.

The Tale of Mr. Jeremy Fisher

cleaners leaving only about ½ inch (2·5 cm) protruding. Press these short ends well together (D).

10 ASSEMBLING. Look at picture and push the points of your scissors or a large packing needle into each side of mouse in the position you want the arms (make the hole right through jacket into body). Push the short stubs of pipe cleaners on arms well into these holes then ladder stitch sleeve to jacket very neatly, working all round the top of sleeve. Bend the arms to the position required.

11 TAIL. Cut 4 inches (10 cm) off a pipe cleaner and cover it with pink felt as shown for Samuel Whiskers (Fig. 48C, page 78) but omit the foam rubber as this mouse is so tiny he needs a very slim tail. Make a hole in centre lower part of back with the point of your scissors. Push the end of tail well in. Ladder stitch in place and with brown Sylko, embroider a few hairs from body on to tail to soften the join and fatten the end. Bend tail to shape.

12 WHISKERS. Add a few whiskers to each side of face. If you look at the picture on page 34 of *The Story of Miss Moppet* you will see that they are rather long. To make whiskers see Fig. 11, page 18.

Stand your mouse beside Miss Moppet's hassock, poking her with his finger!

Other Characters

The toys in this section do not have any obvious friends and relations with which to group them, so they have been put all together in this section to keep each other company.

Many of the greatest favourites of all are here, some being very easy indeed to make (Mr. Jeremy Fisher) and some not quite so easy (Mrs. Tiggy-winkle).

MRS. TIGGY-WINKLE

'. . . a very stout short person . . . Her print gown was tucked up and she was wearing a large apron over her striped petticoat. Her little black nose went sniffle, sniffle, snuffle, and her eyes went twinkle, twinkle; and underneath her cap—where Lucie had yellow curls—that little person had PRICKLES!'

Refer to the many pictures in *The Tale of Mrs. Tiggy-winkle*, as well as to the colour plate on the back cover and jacket of this book.

An 8-inch (20·5-cm) high, flat-based model for nursery decoration. (Unsuitable for play because of her prickles.)

Instructions for making her clothes-basket are on page 272; clothes-horse, page 293; iron, page 294; table, page 293.

Materials

Scraps of long pile brown fur fabric for head (see note 1 below).

Two black boot buttons for eyes (see note 2 on next page).

Scraps of light brown felt for ears and hands. Black for nose; very light beige for claws.

Scraps of crisp, white cotton material for cap and apron.

27 inches (69 cm) ½-inch (1·5-cm) wide white tape for apron strings.

22 × 5 inches (56 × 13 cm) pink/white flowered cotton material for print skirt.

12 × 7 inches (31 × 18 cm) 'open' check cotton material for blouse (Potter's (Cepea 4419) 2970–4).

15 × 5 inches (38 × 13 cm) striped denim (stripes running the short way), for petticoat (see note 3 below).

Odd piece of cream or white curtain lining or similar for skirt base.

Circle of thick card the size of a tea cup for base.

A small pebble for weighting.

Fourteen pipe cleaners for stiffening arms.

10 inches (25·5 cm) wire for body frame.

½-inch (1·5-cm) wide medical adhesive tape for binding.

About 25 wooden cocktail sticks with points both ends and brown paint for prickles.

Kapok for stuffing. Finished toy weighs approximately 7 ounces (200 grammes).

Notes on materials

1 FUR FABRIC. This needs to be a very long pile fabric and if shaded lightly looks realistic. A small piece of simulated fur trimming from a large store was used for the original. It is important that the pile runs in the correct direction as it eventually becomes prickles. It is therefore suggested that the cardboard pattern templates are taken to the store so that they may be tried on the material and an economical-sized piece selected.

2 BOOT BUTTONS. Old-fashioned boot buttons make perfect eyes for this model and many family button bags seem to contain them. However, if not available, substitute jet beads or some other type of button about the same size.

3 STRIPED DENIM. If difficulty is experienced in finding material of a suitable proportion and colour, buy a piece of plain saffron-coloured material and sew on stripes, using narrow ribbon or binding. The colours in the original were taken from page 24 of Mrs. Tiggy-winkle's book.

Method

1 CUT OUT the pieces as given on page 213 (22 pieces).

2 PREPARING THE PRICKLES. Paint the cocktail sticks brown (using household paint or car enamel spray). The simplest method is to stick them into a piece of 'Oasis' or polystyrene and spray or paint them. When dry, reverse the sticks and paint opposite ends. Allow to dry thoroughly and put away until needed.

3 HEAD. On the wrong side of both head pieces join the small darts 1–2. Slit from O²–P. Run a gathering thread from O¹–P on both pieces, pull up thread so that O¹ rests on O² and join small seams O–P. These two steps give fullness to the sides of the face. On the head gusset join the small dart

as indicated by broken lines. (This is at bridge of snout and helps to make it stand up well.) Join one side of head to one side of head gusset A–O. Join under chin gusset to same side of head C–D. Take the other side of head and join it to these pieces E–C–2–D and A–O–B. Turn right side out, easing the top of head down through opening with a blunt stick. Insert small 'end of snout' piece, matching As and oversewing on the right side. (This piece will not show on the finished toy—it is merely used to keep stuffing in place.) Stuff head firmly, pushing out snout well and filling out cheeks sideways. Gather round neck pull, up and tuck in, losing it completely among the long pile.

4 FEATURES AND EXPRESSION. This is the most important part of making Mrs. Tiggy-winkle—the part which gives her own individual character and personality. Work slowly and carefully, referring constantly to the pictures in her book. Using small, sharp scissors, trim away the fur fabric, starting at the nose and working all round 'snout' and up as far as eye position. (The head will look rather like a lion at this stage—don't worry, this is quite right.)

5 NOSE. On the nose piece, join the two tiny darts, oversewing on the wrong side. Turn right side out and put on to face, straight side on top, so that it covers end of snout. As you stitch it in place (using a tiny, neat hemming stitch) try to keep it small, tip-tilted and cheeky—not spread out or flat. Finish off by taking a few stitches right through snout from one side of edge of nose to the same point on the other side and pulling tightly to slim it.

6 EYES AND EARS. Insert boot button eyes, taking position from the pictures and noting that they are fairly wide apart but pulled well in so that they are tiny and twinkling. Sew on felt ears, curving them as you work and embedding them deep in the fur so that they hardly show. (The head still looks nothing like a hedgehog.)

7 HANDS. Place the pieces together in pairs and on the right side oversew them neatly together all round except for short, straight ends (Fig. 79A). Bend back about 1½ inches (4 cm) on the end of ten pipe cleaners (B). Push one of these up into each finger (C). Plait or twist together the five pipe cleaners protruding from each hand (D). Stuff the main part of each hand, pushing small pieces of kapok in with a cocktail stick (E). Embroider a few prickles on the back of each hand, using one strand of dark brown cotton (F).

8 CLAWS. Smear one side of a claw with Copydex and stick it to the end of a finger—half of it on the finger and half protruding (Fig. 79G). Whilst the adhesive is still wet, press the end of finger and the protruding part of claw together, sideways, between your finger and thumb so that the sides of protruding part meet and stick together, making a slim claw (H). Repeat this on each finger, pressing and shaping each claw carefully. When all are

quite dry, curl the claws forwards a little and press the sides of hands together to slim hand and close fingers.

9 BODY FRAME. Bend the wire in half and press tightly together. Bind with adhesive tape to make a body foundation (Fig. 80A). Take the hands and using three more pipe cleaners twisted between them join together so that the finished piece measures 13 inches (33 cm) from the claw tips of one hand to those on the other (B). Bind this to the body wire 2 inches (5 cm) from top using another pipe cleaner, then a piece of adhesive tape (C).

10 BLOUSE. Look at picture and make sure the checks on your material run the correct way, i.e. diagonally. Fold the piece in half lengthwise and cut sleeve seams as Fig. 81. On the wrong side machine these two seams. Turn right side out and put blouse on to body frame, making a small hole at centre of top for wire to come through. Run a gathering thread round both sleeve edges, taking a narrow turning as you work. Pull up gathers to fit hands and stitch each sleeve firmly to a hand so that just the fat part of each hand shows. Make sure the thumbs are at top of hand and that the sleeve seam matches lower seam on hand.

11 ASSEMBLING HEAD AND BODY FRAME. Bend top (shorter) part of body wire backwards a little. Spread Copydex sparingly on top part of blouse in a circle about 1 inch (2·5 cm) diameter round point where wire protrudes through hole. With pointed scissors make a hole in base of head and channel up into it at centre of neck gathers. Push top of body wire right up into hole so that the blouse rests under head. Press so that they stick together firmly (Mrs. Tiggy-winkle has no neck, so sticking a wide portion of head to blouse will help to achieve this rather podgy appearance). Place on one side to dry thoroughly and carry on with the skirts.

12 SKIRT BASE. Work as given for Aunt Pettitoes, page 60, No. 5 from * to *. Have the card circle for base the size of a tea cup and the strip for side 5 inches (12·5 cm) wide. Fix a small pebble to *one side* of wrong side of card base level with the seam—using Copydex and adhesive tape for absolute security.

Mrs. Tiggy-winkle leans forward when finished and the stone will keep her from tipping over. The reason for placing it near the seam is so that you will know where it is later. Turn right side out. Run a gathering thread all round top edge taking $\frac{1}{2}$ inch (1 cm) turning. Stuff firmly for $3\frac{1}{4}$ inches (8 cm) then pull up gathers to centre, making an almost flat top. Fasten off gathers leaving a small hole in centre for the foundation wire to pass through.

13 STRIPED PETTICOAT. Join the short ends on the wrong side. Turn up the narrowest possible invisible hem, using tape or binding. Press hem. Gather round top edge (no need to take a turning). Put over skirt base, pull up gathers and leaving the hole in the centre for wire to pass through, stitch

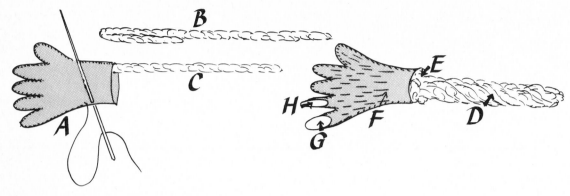

Fig. 79 Mrs. Tiggy-winkle's hands

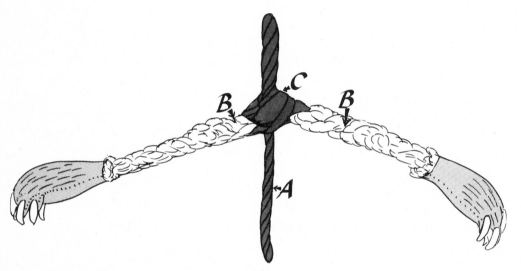

Fig. 80 Mrs. Tiggy-winkle's body frame

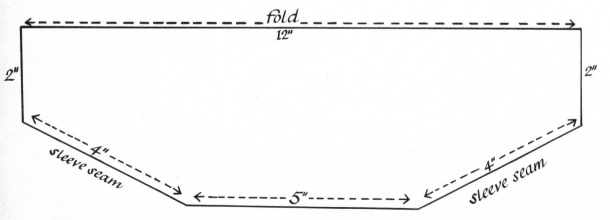

Fig. 81 Plan for Mrs. Tiggy-winkle's blouse

petticoat to base all round the hole. It should just touch the ground all round.

14 JOINING TOP AND BASE. Stitch head to blouse all round edge of circle of adhesive which should now be quite dry. Stuff blouse very firmly pushing small pieces of kapok well down into sleeves and completely embedding pipe cleaners. Bend arms forward as you work. Make the body part very full (look at pictures constantly). Push a pencil down through hole in centre of skirt to make a channel inside the base, then push body wire well down into it. Bend wire so that Mrs. Tiggy-winkle leans forward and arrange her so that the seam on the base and therefore the stone are at centre back. Ladder stitch bottom edge of blouse to skirt base, working right through striped petticoat (note: she has a very fat waist).

15 PRINT SKIRT. On the wrong side machine short ends together. Machine a narrow hem all round bottom edge. Gather round top edge, turning in about $\frac{1}{2}$ inch (1 cm) as you work. Put on to toy, pull up gathers and stitch in place all round bottom edge of blouse. There is no need to adjust length in any way as the skirt will eventually be tucked up.

16 WRISTS. If you look carefully at the pictures of Mrs. Tiggy-winkle you will see that she has what appear to be tiny fur cuffs, but which are presumably hairs and prickles showing below her sleeves. Cut two narrow strips of fur fabric left over from the head. Trim off pile to the length shown in pictures and stick round wrists.

17 FINISHING OFF FACE. Now is the time to turn your lion-like animal into a hedgehog. Looking at pictures and using the family glue pot and a piece of wood, tease and coax the fur pile all round face into small pointed bundles to represent the soft quills (Plate 8 p. 117), working as far back as will show when cap is in position and pulling the few under the snout to each side, horizontally. Leave to dry overnight. N.B. If a glue pot is not available clear Bostik may be used but it is more difficult to cope with.

18 CAP. Using a saucer for a pattern, cut a circle of crisp, white cotton material. Machine the narrowest possible hem all round edge. Run a gathering thread all round outside $\frac{1}{2}$ inch (1 cm) from edge. Pull up so that cap will fit right over head—look at pictures. Pin in position, tucking the frill in at the back so that it doesn't show and pushing kapok inside to give a firm, rounded finish. Using a long, slim needle and strong thread, stitch firmly to head all round the line of gathers.

19 APRON. * Cut a piece of matching white material 4 × 6 inches (10 × 15 cm). Machine a narrow hem round the two short and one of the long sides. Gather along the other (the top) edge, taking a narrow turning to the back as you work. Pull up gathers to $3\frac{1}{2}$ inches (9 cm). Pin centre of tape to back of centre top of apron. Machine tape to apron along both edges and two short ends, covering the raw edges and gathers on apron and leaving an even

length of tape each side for strings. * If you look at page 28 of her book you will see that Mrs. Tiggy-winkle's print skirt is fastened up at the back with a large pin. You can either do it that way or gather along the hem at back, pull up, tuck into a bustle effect and stitch in place. Tie on apron.

20 PRICKLES. Break the prepared sticks in half making about 50 prickles and looking at pictures, insert them into cap, back of blouse and striped petticoat by pushing a needlework stiletto or large packing needle through outer covering and well into stuffing to make a channel then pushing in a piece of stick with a small dab of Copydex on the end.

Mrs. Tiggy-winkle can now be arranged as you want her. Hands folded in front by means of stitching or small press-studs, or holding her iron or some of her laundry.

MRS. TIGGY-WINKLE'S IRON HOLDER

The handle of Mrs. Tiggy-winkle's iron was hot and on page 31 of her book we see her picking it up with a quilted holder. This can easily be made by machine quilting a small piece of bright pink material and backing it with yellowy green felt. The edges have a slim piece of green cord or thick wool stuck or stitched round them with loops at the corners. The original was 1½ inches (4 cm) square which seems about the right size in proportion to Mrs. Tiggy-winkle.

OTHER ACCESSORIES FOR MRS. TIGGY-WINKLE

If you have made her table, clothes-horse and clothes-basket you will need some further odds and ends for Mrs. Tiggy-winkle to use. Cut a piece of flannel or old under-blanket to make her ironing blanket and mark the blue edging with felt pen (page 27 of her book). The currant-wine-stained damask table-cloth hanging on the original clothes-horse was made from a man's handkerchief stained with blackcurrant jam and Sally Henny-Penny's stockings were cut from yellow felt. A red spotted handkerchief that smelt of onions was cut from a suitable piece of material and hemmed. If you read through her book you will have many ideas for filling her clothes basket—Lucie's pinny for instance can be borrowed from Moppet or Mittens.

MRS. TIGGY-WINKLE'S RAG RUG

The very thought of Mrs. Tiggy-winkle's kitchen is enough to convince one that there was a rag rug in front of the fire—no country kitchen with its black-leaded grate, shining fender and stone flags could possibly have been without. On opening the book, there it is to be sure, on the frontispiece, on page 31, and again on page 47, no doubt made by Mrs. Tiggy-winkle during the long winter evenings from all the old vests, pants, trousers and petticoats she could lay her hands on. Those of us whose mothers and grandmothers made such rugs will remember the piles of short pieces of woollen cloth cut from the family's discarded clothes, each one being pulled through the hessian backing with a spiked tool. Mrs. Tiggy-winkle's rug is too small to make with this tool, therefore a special method has been devised.

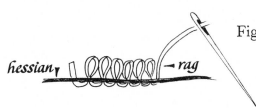

Fig. 82 Making Mrs. Tiggy-winkle's rug

Materials

A piece of hessian or sacking approximately 6 × 10 inches (15 × 25 cm).

A pile of oddments of medium-weight material—Viyella, flannel, jersey cloth, cotton stockinette are all ideal.

A large-eyed tapestry needle or small packing needle.

Method

1 Mark out a design on the hessian using pencil or ball-point pen and leaving about ¾ inch (2 cm) all round the edge for turning back later. A few simple circles or squares are best—nothing elaborate.

2 Cut the materials into strips about ¼ inch (a little less than 1 cm) wide.

3 Thread a strip into the needle and stitch up and down through the hessian backing, leaving a short loop on top and putting the needle down through the same hole you brought it up by. Leave *no* loops on the back, just a short stitch of rag leading to the next hole (Fig. 82). Work in rows in this way, using different colours to make a pattern until the rag is covered closely with loops.

4 Turn the hessian border to the back of rug and stick or stitch in place.

5 With sharp scissors cut through all the loops, then trim off any long, untidy ends.

6 Press well under a damp cloth to give the rug that typical well trodden, much used, flat look.

Mrs. Tiggy-winkle, being a good housewife, would probably not have backed her rug as such a backing held all the grit and dirt and was usually frowned upon!

However, if you want to, there is nothing to stop you backing your own rug with a piece of hessian.

N.B. A rag rug also appears in *Cecily Parsley's Nursery Rhymes*, *The Tale of Samuel Whiskers*, *The Tale of Tom Kitten* and *The Tale of Two Bad Mice*.

MR. JEREMY FISHER

'. . . *he settled himself cross-legged and arranged his fishing tackle.*'

Refer to the picture on page 23 of *The Tale of Mr. Jeremy Fisher*, as well as to the colour plate opposite page 125 of this book.

N.B. Miss Potter spells 'Macintosh' thus—therefore the same version is used here.

Materials

  18 × 12 inches (46 × 30·5 cm) fawn felt for body (String 32).
  Scraps of black and white felt for mouth and eyes.
  Small piece of stockinette (an old sock) for socks.
  Scraps of black Vynide for goloshes.
  Light fawn plastic or paper nylon for macintosh (see note below).
  Eight pipe cleaners for stiffening fingers.
  Two rounded buttons just over $\frac{1}{2}$ inch (1 cm) diameter for eyes.
  Kapok for stuffing. Finished toy weighs approximately 3 ounces (85 grammes).
  Scraps of shiny grey silk for eyes.
  White button thread for his line.
  A bead and matchstick for his float.
  9 inches (23 cm) of something resembling a grass stalk for his rod (see suggestions under No. 11, page 137).
  A piece of red plastic, felt or wool for his worm.
  A polystyrene tile, two shades of green poster paint and green felt for his 'boat'.

Note: Material for macintosh may be difficult to obtain by the yard. A rain hood, make-up cape, shopping bag, child's mac, etc., are all suitable for cutting up and may usually be found in the right colour for a little hunting.

Method

  1 CUT OUT the pieces as given on pages 214–18 (28 pieces).
  2 BODY. Roll the 'back of eye' pieces round into a cone and oversew seams A–B (Fig. 83A). Flatten these pieces and lay on right side of top of body in the position shown by broken lines on pattern, As to centre of head and the

seam A–B in the centre, underneath cone. Neatly and invisibly hem both to head X–A–X on top of body (Fig. 83B). Stuff 'cones' firmly to make a raised back to the eye (Fig. 83C). Take one body side and on the *right* side stab stitch round curved piece X–X, joining it to the curved top of cone on 'top of body' piece X–X. Join on the other body side in the same way. Now on the *wrong* side join the two body sides together C–D and still on the wrong side join body sides to top of body X–C–X then X–E–X. Take the underbody and the extra black piece you have cut to fit the front part to broken line. Stick this black piece on the wrong side of underbody (it will eventually show through to front at edges and indicate mouth). On the *right*

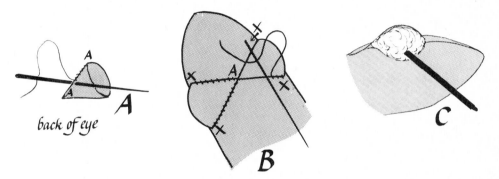

Fig. 83 Making the backs of Mr. Jeremy Fisher's eyes

side stitch underbody to sides of body, stab stitching all round F–D–F and working through the two thicknesses of fawn and one of black felt then on the *wrong* side continue joining sides of body F–E–F leaving opening on one side as shown on pattern. Turn work right side out and check that the stitching is correct. All stitching should be on the *wrong* side except for the mouth and curves over eyes, where the stab stitching on the *right* side should make a neat ridge. Stuff the body very firmly and invisibly close opening.

3 LEGS. Place an inner leg and outer leg together and stitch all round G–H–I on the wrong side. Turn right side out, pushing out point well and stuff firmly. Make the other leg in the same way, remembering to reverse the pieces to make a pair. Sew the legs firmly to base of body at positions shown on Fig. 84. They will cross at front, left over right.

4 ARMS. On each outer arm join the two top darts 1–2 and 3–4 on the wrong side, remembering to reverse one piece to make a pair. Turn the tops of eight pipe cleaners back as shown by Fig. 85A. Then using one of the arm pieces as a guide, twist them together in fours so that there are two pieces, each with four separate fingers and a solid arm (Fig. 85B). Place the cleaners on one side. Place an inner arm on each outer arm and on the *wrong* side join them together J–K and L–M. Turn both arms right way out and slip a

prepared pipe cleaner stiffener into each one. Stab stitch the fingers together on the right side, including a pipe cleaner in each finger (Fig. 85C). Sew arms firmly to body sides in the position shown on pattern and looking at picture for angle at which to place them—the right one *up* to hold his fishing rod and the left one *lower* down to hold the float.

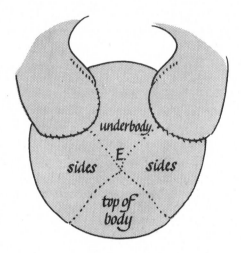

Fig. 84 Position of Mr. Jeremy Fisher's legs

5 EYES (Fig. 86). Take two rounded buttons to make protruding eyes (A). Cut a circle of shiny grey material about half as big again as each button. Gather all round the outside edges (B). Place buttons in centre, pull up gathers and fasten at back of button (C). Stick a large, round, black felt pupil in the centre front of each eye and add a small triangular white felt highlight (D). Sew an eye to each side of head on the semi-circular bulge between X and X as indicated by broken lines on pattern, attaching them first by the shank if there is one and then hemming all round edge of eye.

6 PAINTING MARKINGS. Look at the pictures in *The Tale of Mr. Jeremy Fisher* and using either thick brown and green poster paint or ordinary household paint, or easiest of all, felt-tip pens, add blotches and stripes on head, hands and legs—allow to dry.

7 MACINTOSH. '*Mr. Jeremy put on a macintosh.*' Stitch sleeve seams A–B. Turn right side out. Insert sleeves into holes in macintosh matching As and stitching all round. Slip on to frog, tucking down behind crossed legs. Stick front flap at top corner.

8 SOCKS. Place the pieces together in pairs, right sides facing and oversew all round N–O–P. Turn and stitch a very narrow hem round top N–P–N. Turn right side out and put on frog.

9 GOLOSHES. '*Mr. Jeremy put on . . . a pair of shiny goloshes.*' Place the side pieces together in pairs and on the wrong side join short seams Q–R and S–T. Insert sole, stitching all round Q–S–Q and easing in to fit. Turn right side out and put on to frog.

10 HIS FLOAT. '*He had the dearest little red float*' (Fig. 87). Take a large bead. Paint one half red and one white. Push a piece of cocktail or matchstick through the hole, fixing with adhesive and shaping one end.

11 HIS ROD. '*His rod was a tough stalk of grass.*' Find something fine but strong that looks like grass. The original was a piece of green, split cane from a rolled bamboo and cane dinner mat. You might use a slim twig, green plastic-covered wire or a very small gauge green knitting needle.

12 HIS LINE. '*His line was a fine long white horse-hair and he tied a little wriggling worm at the end.*' Tie about 24 inches (60 cm) of strong white button thread to the end of the rod, keeping firmly in place with a spot of colourless adhesive or nail varnish. Looking at picture, twist the line several times round the rod, put rod into your frog's right hand and pass the line also through this hand. Tie on the float and put it in Mr. Jeremy's left hand, then tie a scrap of red felt or other material to the end for his worm.

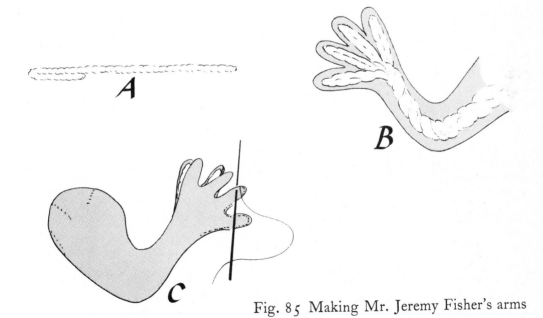

Fig. 85 Making Mr. Jeremy Fisher's arms

13 HIS BOAT. '*The boat was round and green, and very like the other lily-leaves.*' The shape of the leaf is given by a broken line behind the other patterns on page 216. Cut it out from a small polystyrene tile using old scissors and

paint green all over. Add a few streaks and veins in two darker shades of green. N.B. If you have any adhesive suitable for polystyrene, the boat is improved if a piece of green felt is stuck to one side and the markings painted on this.

For his fishing creel see page 279.

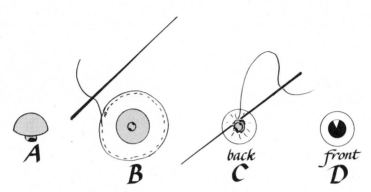

Fig. 86 Making Mr. Jeremy Fisher's eyes

Fig. 87 Making Mr. Jeremy Fisher's float and worm

JEMIMA PUDDLE-DUCK

'*Jemima Puddle-duck was a simpleton, not even the mention of sage and onions made her suspicious.*'

Refer to the picture on the cover of *The Tale of Jemima Puddle-duck*, as well as to the colour plate opposite page 140 of this book.

A felt toy approximately 8 inches (20 cm) high with removable bonnet and shawl.

Materials

12 × 18 inches (30 × 46 cm) white felt for body.
Scraps of yellow and black felt for beak and feet.

Scraps of blue felt and narrow matching ribbon for bonnet.

26 inches (66 cm) wire for stiffening feet and adhesive tape for binding.

Pink/blue paisley material for shawl.

Black and white stranded embroidery cotton for eyes.

Fine white wool for feather markings.

Kapok for stuffing. Finished toy weighs approximately $2\frac{1}{2}$ ounces (70 grammes).

Method

1 CUT OUT the pieces as given on pages 220–1 (24 pieces).

2 BODY. Take one side of body and on the wrong side join on head gusset A–B. Join body gusset to same side of body C–D–F. Join these pieces to the other side G–E–D–C–B–A, leaving an opening A–G on this side. Turn right side out, pushing the top of head down through neck with the help of a blunt stick. Prepare 5 inches (13 cm) of wire (see Fig. 8A and B, page 13). Stuff body very firmly indeed, keeping the top of head as narrow as possible (look at picture), and pushing the wire up into head and down through neck into body as you work (as shown by broken line on pattern), bending it to the correct contour and completely embedding it in the kapok. Close opening, starting at the top and stuffing the neck firmly and carefully as you work.

3 EYES. Following Fig. 88, embroider eyes, then using strong thread and a slim needle, take a few stitches right through head between the two front corners and pull them tightly to sink them.

4 BEAK (Fig. 89). Using Copydex very sparingly, stick the black base piece to the yellow (A). Take the two side pieces and using six strands of black embroidery cotton, take a small stitch on each for nostrils as shown on pattern. On the right side, stab stitch these two pieces together H–I (B). Open this joined piece out and place on top of the black base piece, matching letters (C). On the right side stab stitch together all round J–I–J. Stuff beak very firmly. (The black felt shows through as a dividing line where the beak would open.) Place open end of beak flat against front of head so that the centre of lower edge J–J just covers point A on head. Pin in place, then stitch invisibly all round.

5 FEATHER MARKINGS. Using fine white wool or stranded cotton, take a series of stitches all over the duck to represent feathers, except for a patch round the eye (Fig. 88), under the tummy where the legs will be inserted, and the parts which will be covered by wings.

6 WINGS (Fig. 90). Place the pieces together in pairs and on the wrong side stitch together all round the edge except for openings. Turn right side out. Push just a little stuffing inside, spread evenly through wings. Close openings. Following the two broken lines on pattern, stab stitch right through both wings (A). Embroider a few feather markings on right side except for a

small portion at curved ends (Fig. 90B), remembering to reverse one to make a pair. Sew wings in position round top curve as marked by XXX on pattern —points turning upwards. Work a few more feather markings over join between wing and body to hide it.

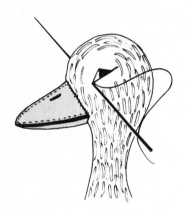

Fig. 88 Jemima's head

Fig. 89 Making Jemima's beak

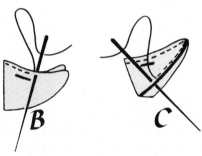

7 FEET (Fig. 91). Cut three pieces of wire, one piece 7 inches (18 cm) long and one piece 3½ inches (9 cm). Bend the 7-inch piece in half like a hair pin and bend the lower ¾ inch (2 cm) on each side sharply forwards at right angles. Bend the lower ¾ inch (2 cm) forwards in the same way on the short piece and place together in the position shown by (A). Using strong pliers press the two halves of bent piece closely together to make a slim leg and bind all three leg wires tightly with adhesive tape (B). Bind the three foot wires by wrapping each one in a small piece of adhesive tape—pressing it on tightly to keep the parts very slim (C). Place a full-size yellow felt leg piece on *top* of the prepared wires (front of leg) and a short foot piece underneath them and stab stitch the two together all round the edge with the wires between them (D). Stab stitch on both sides of the centre wire to keep it in place and along inner side of each outer wire (E). Stick a card stiffener to the underside of each foot (F). Stitch the other full-size felt foot piece to the under side of foot, continuing up leg with the wires inside (G). Make the other leg in the same way.

She laid some more in June: but only four of them hatched. Jemima Puddle-duck said that it was because of her nerves; but she had always been a bad sitter.

The Tale of Jemima Puddle-Duck

Miss Moppet holds her poor head in her paws, and looks at him through a hole in the duster. The Mouse comes *very* close.

The Story of Miss Moppet

Make two slits in the body gusset as shown on pattern and push pointed scissors up into body to make a channel. Push a leg well up into each slit leaving about ¾ inch (2 cm) protruding. Ladder stitch body to legs very firmly, working several times round each one.

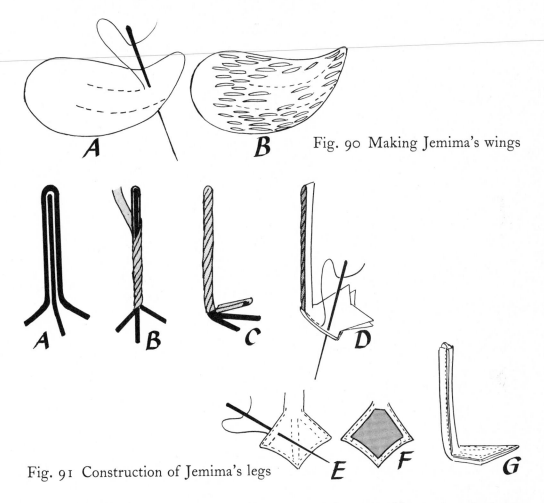

Fig. 90 Making Jemima's wings

Fig. 91 Construction of Jemima's legs

8 BONNET. On the wrong side join the straight part of bonnet to the back piece K–L–K. Join these pieces to the brim M–M. Run a gathering thread along *longest* edge of frill N–N. Pull up gathers to fit straight edge of bonnet, pin in place matching Ns and stitch. Turn right side out. Run a gathering thread along line of gathers where frill joins bonnet. Try on to Jemima and pull up these gathers so that the bonnet fits snugly into neck. Fasten off. Stitch a short piece of narrow matching ribbon to each side and tie on to Jemima's head so that her eyes just show. Finally grasp the top of bonnet brim firmly between thumb and forefinger and work all round the edge pulling and stretching so that it stands well away from Jemima's head and gives the poked effect shown in the pictures in her book.

9 SHAWL. Looking at picture cut a small rectangle of suitable material to fit Jemima. Fringe three sides. Try on to Jemima and with a few stitches adjust to fit, tucking in top end and taking a dart or fold on each side. Fasten in front with a small hook and eye and if you have one, sew on a small yellow bead or button to give the appearance of a clasp as in picture.

JEMIMA PUDDLE-DUCK'S BABIES

'. . . *she was permitted to keep them herself; but only four of them hatched.*'

Refer to the picture on page 58 of *The Tale of Jemima Puddle-duck*, as well as to the colour plate opposite page 140 of this book.

Miniature felt toys approximately 2 inches (5 cm) high.

Materials

Scraps of light yellow felt for bodies (over from Pigling Bland's trousers?).
Scraps of darker yellow felt for beaks and feet.
Black stranded cotton for eyes.
A postcard for stiffening feet.
Kapok for stuffing (the four completed ducklings together weigh less than $\frac{1}{2}$ ounce).

Method

1 CUT OUT the pieces on page 219 (11 pieces for each duckling).
2 BODY. Take one body side and on the wrong side join it to the head gusset A–B and body gusset A–C. Join these pieces to the other body side, stitching all round B–A–C–F. Turn right side out, easing the head down through neck with a small blunt stick and pushing the tail point well out with a cocktail stick. Stuff body firmly and invisibly. Close opening.
3 BEAK. On the right side stab stitch the two pieces together H–G and insert base, stitching all round I–H–I. Stuff firmly and looking at picture sew to front of head in position required, working all round open top G–I–I–G.
4 EYES. Using black stranded cotton make a French knot on one side of head. Pass needle through head and pulling cotton tightly so that the eyes sink into head make a knot on the other side. Fasten off by passing the needle backwards and forwards through head from eye to eye, several times.
5. WINGS. Sew in place round the portion marked by a broken line on pattern only, using a tiny, neat hemming stitch.
6 FEET. These consist of two layers of felt with a card stiffener between them. They are fiddly to make and the simplest method is to stick the card shapes to a piece of felt (Fig. 92A). When dry, cut the surplus felt away all round

card (B). Stick the card side of feet to another piece of felt (C) and when dry cut away the surplus felt again (D). Looking at picture, stick completed feet to base of duckling in position required, making sure he will stand firmly.

Make three more ducklings in the same way, varying the positions of beaks and wings, so that they all have a different appearance. Heads can be pulled backwards or sideways by ladder stitching, i.e. one stitch on neck or body (Fig. 93A) and one on head alternately, whilst pulling the head over in the direction required (B).

Fig. 92 Making the ducklings' feet

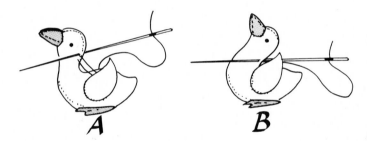

Fig. 93 Pulling the ducklings' heads backwards

'He cut his coats without waste, according to his cloth.' (*The Tailor of Gloucester*)

THE PATTERNS

Note: in the instructions
for cutting out
the various pieces

F = felt
FF = fur fabric

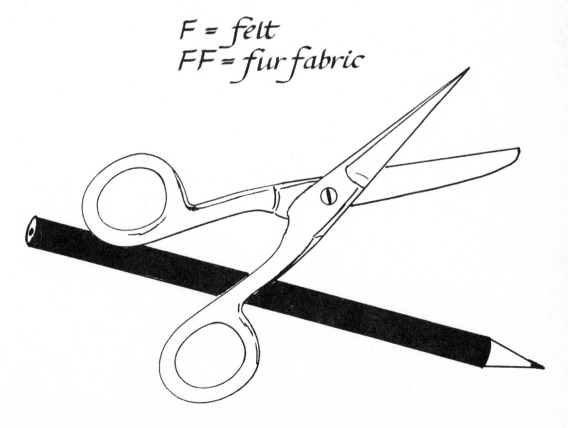

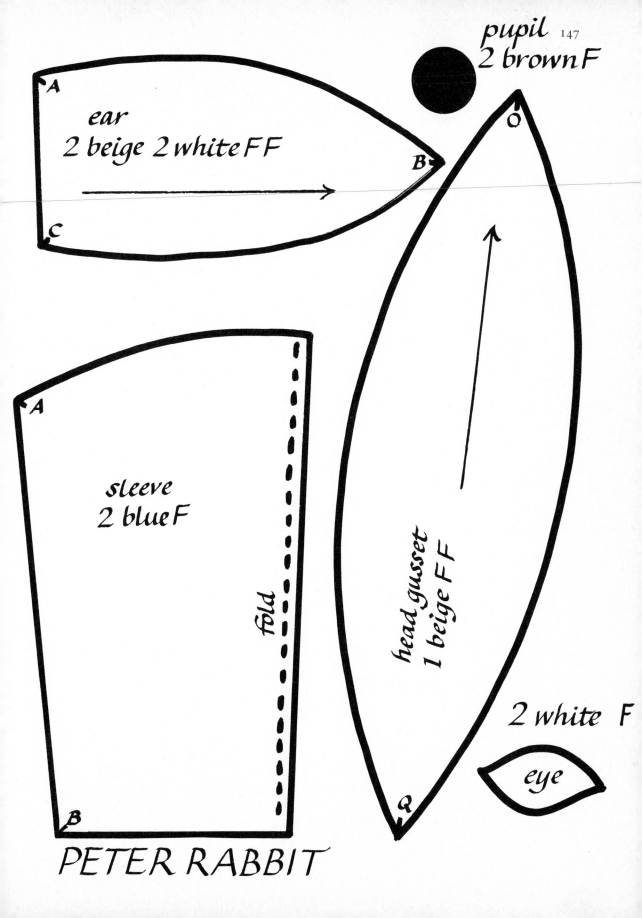

ear
2 beige 2 white FF

A

B

C

pupil 147
2 brown F

O

sleeve
2 blue F

A

fold

head gusset
1 beige FF

B

Q

2 white F

eye

PETER RABBIT

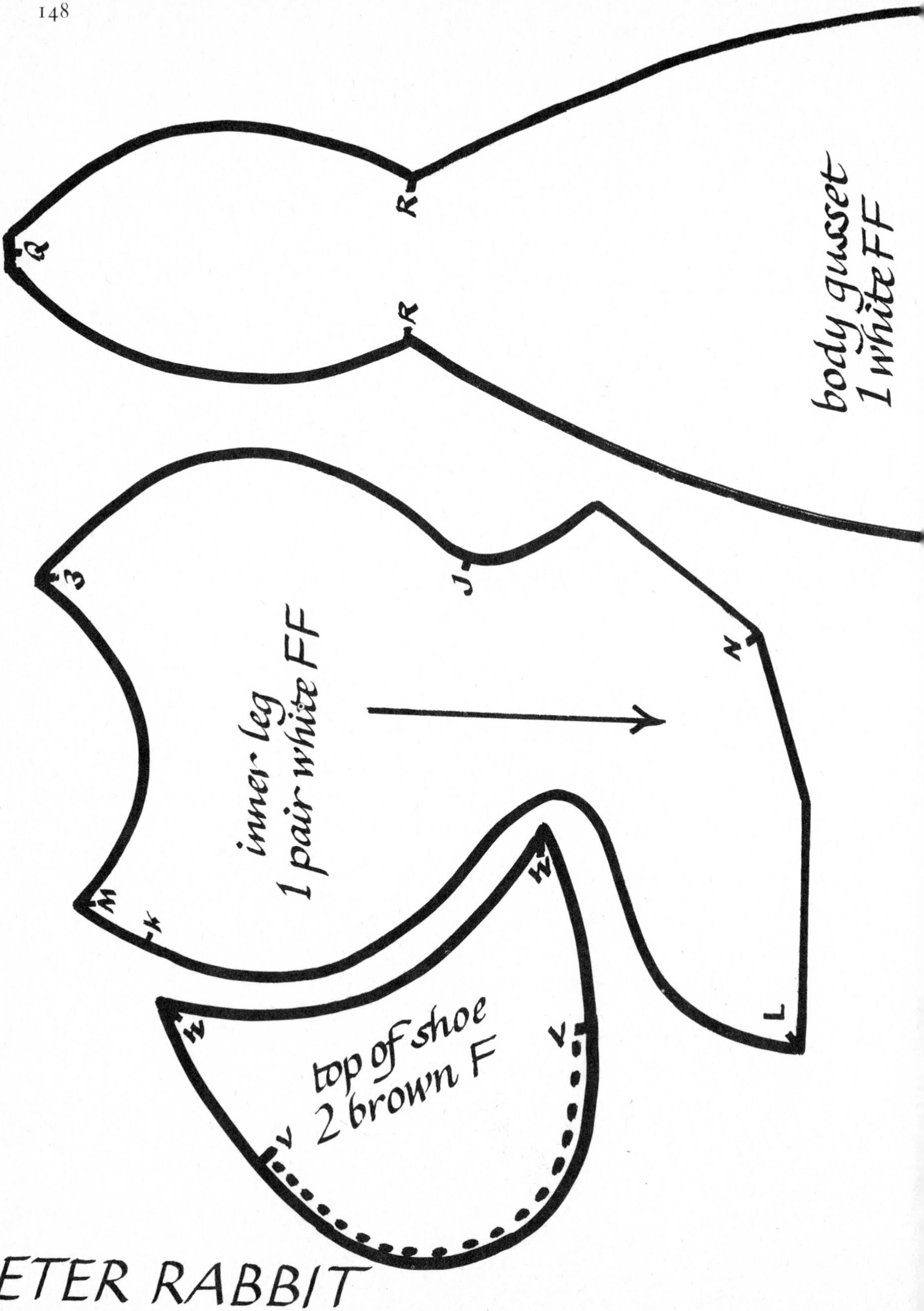

148

Q

R

R

body gusset
1 white FF

3

J

N

inner leg
1 pair white FF

W

M

K

W

L

W

top of shoe
2 brown F

V

V

PETER RABBIT

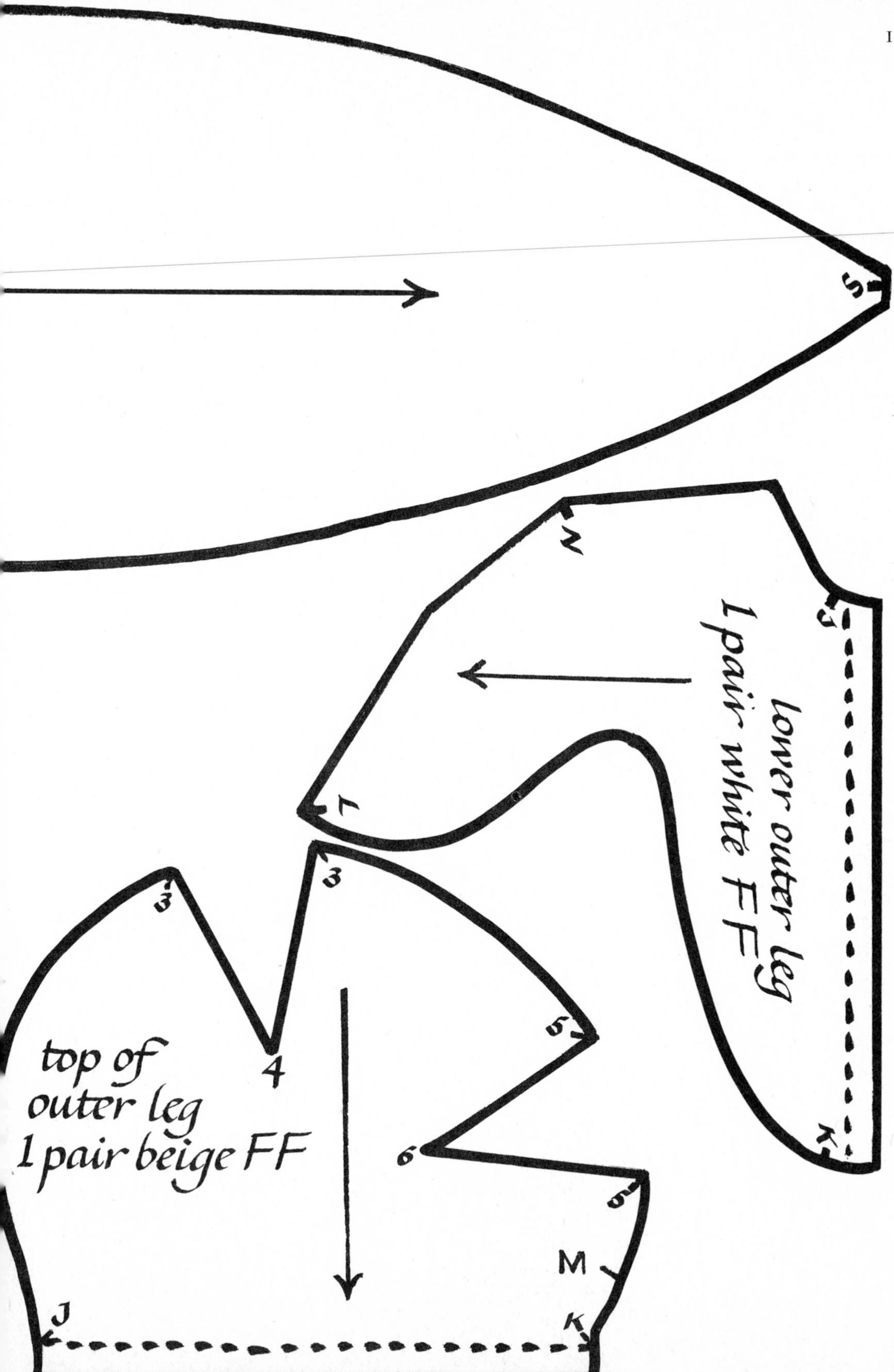

5

2

3

1

3

lower outer leg
1 pair white FF

K

5

top of
outer leg
1 pair beige FF

4

6

6

M

J

K

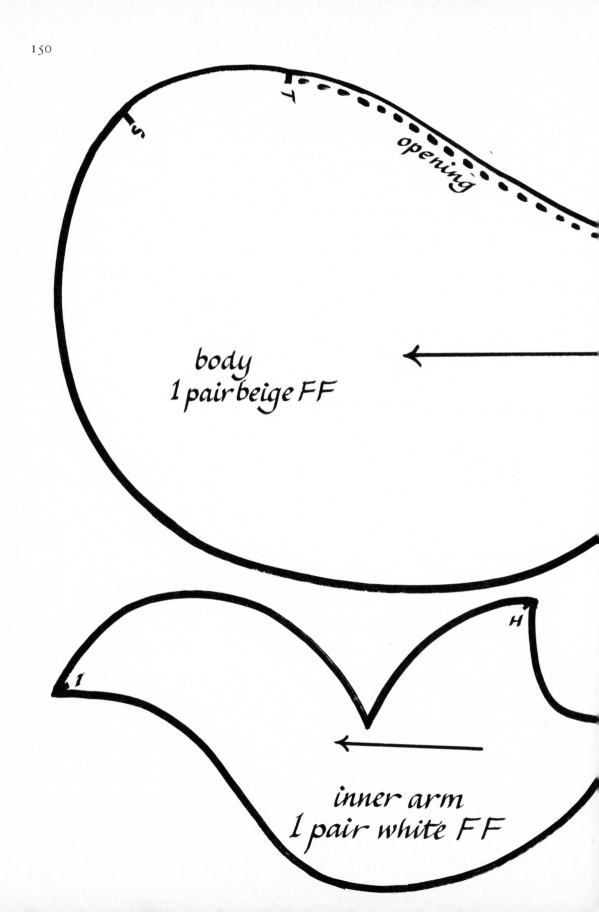

opening

body
1 pair beige FF

inner arm
1 pair white FF

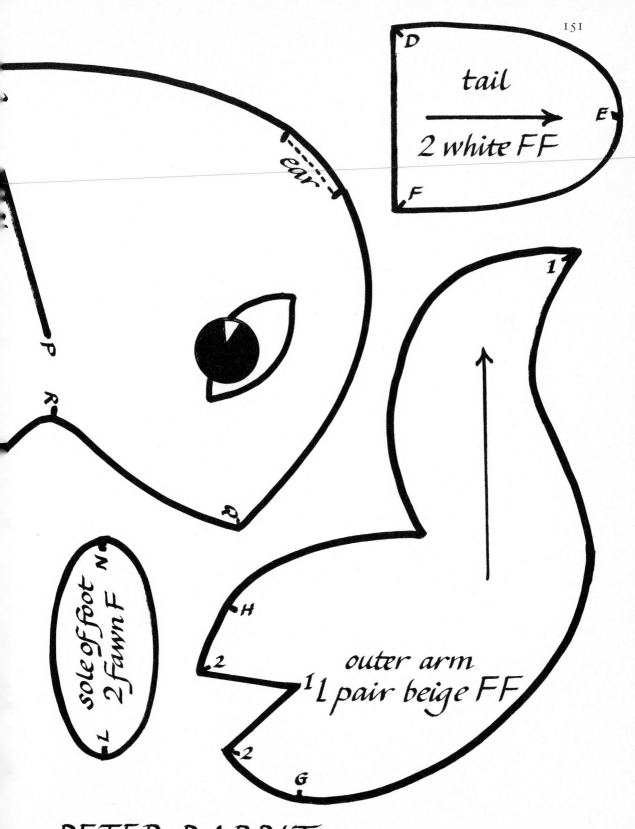

151

tail

2 white FF

outer arm
[1]1 pair beige FF

sole of foot
2 fawn F

PETER RABBIT

152

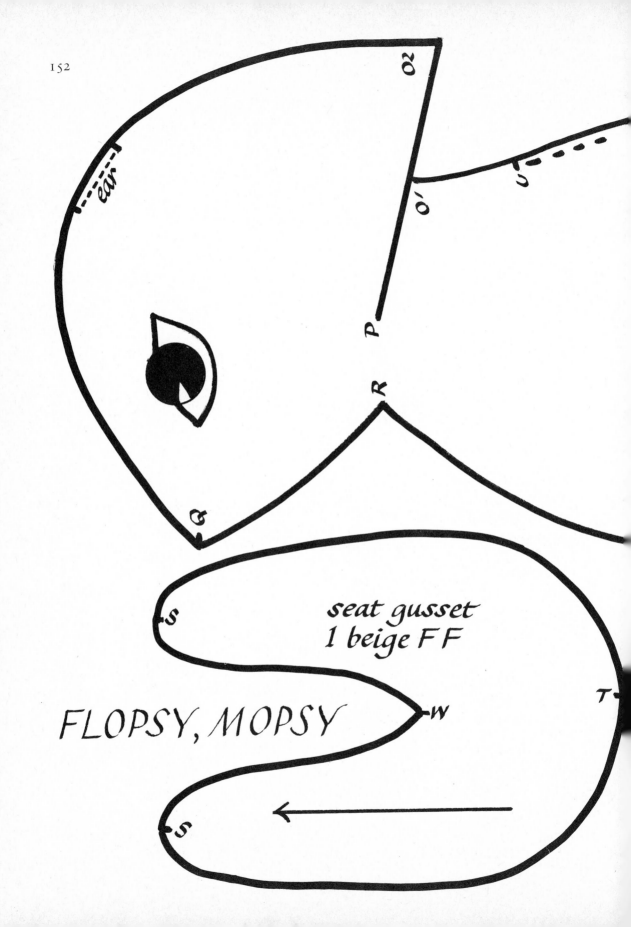

ear

O²

O¹

U

P

R

Q

S

seat gusset
1 beige FF

W

T

FLOPSY, MOPSY

S

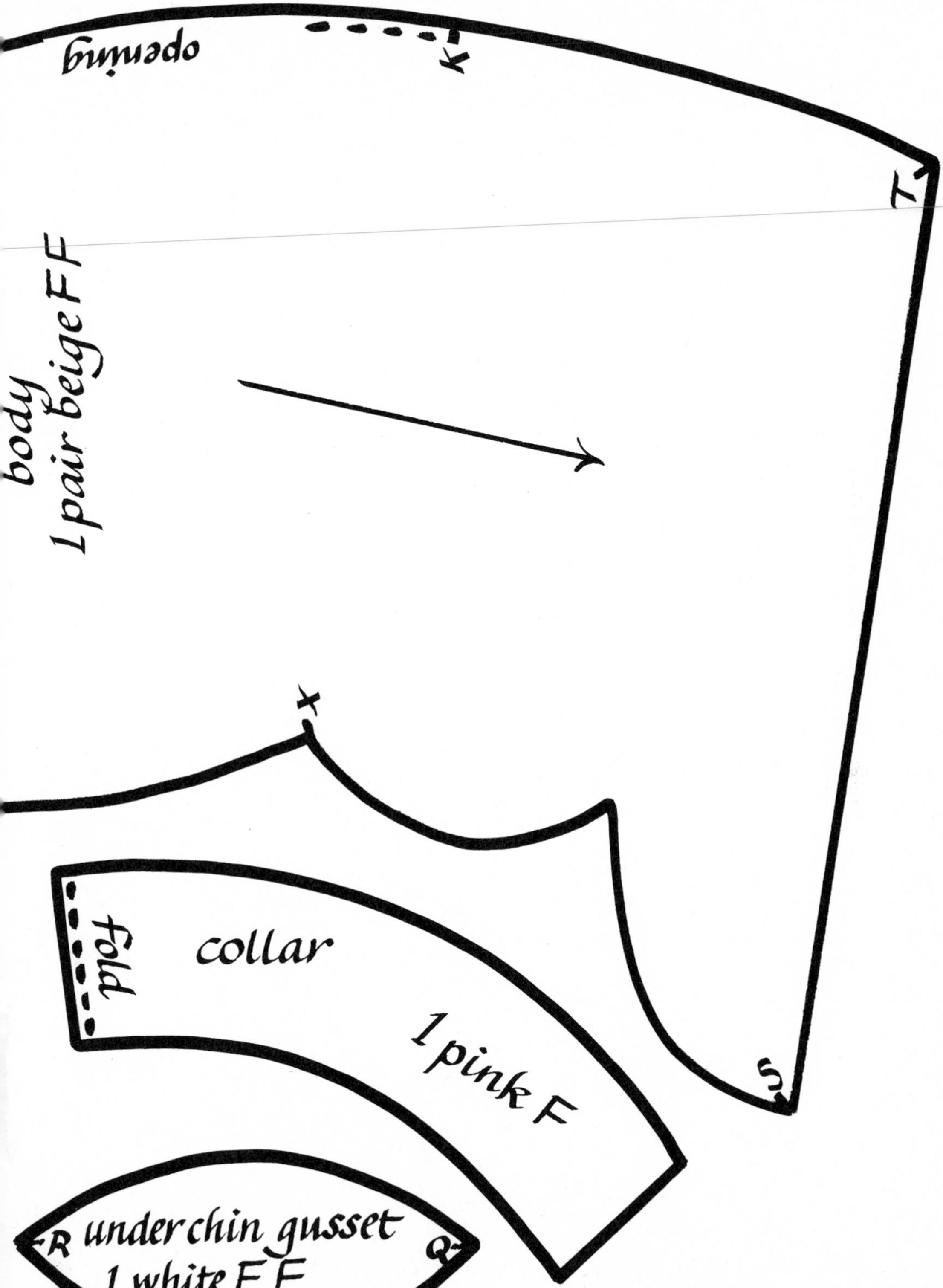

opening

body
1 pair beige FF

T

x

collar

fold

1 pink F

S

R under chin gusset Q
1 white FF

COTTON~TAIL

154

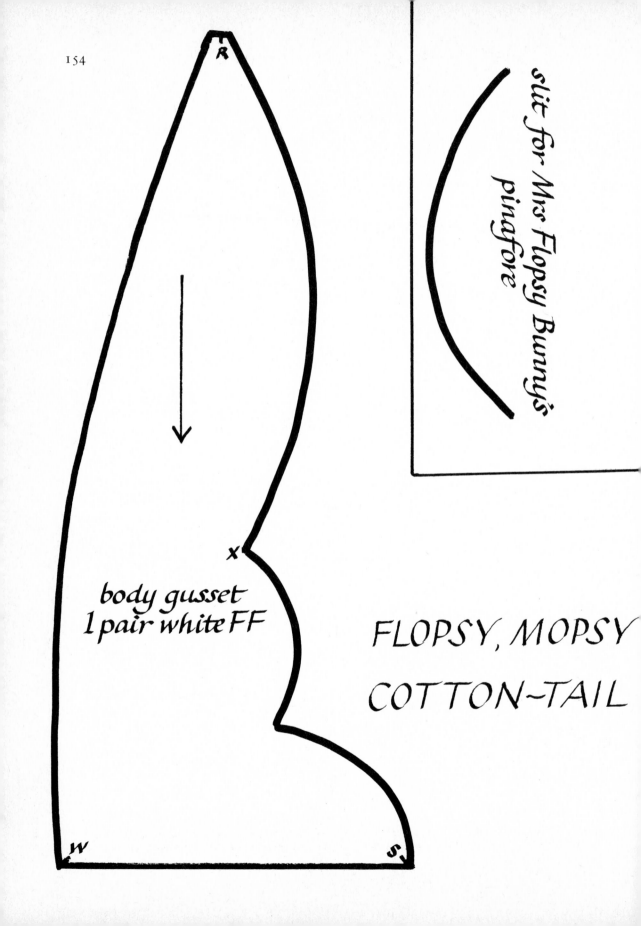

slit for Mrs Flopsy Bunny's
pinafore

R

X

body gusset
1 pair white FF

FLOPSY, MOPSY

COTTON-TAIL

W

S

155

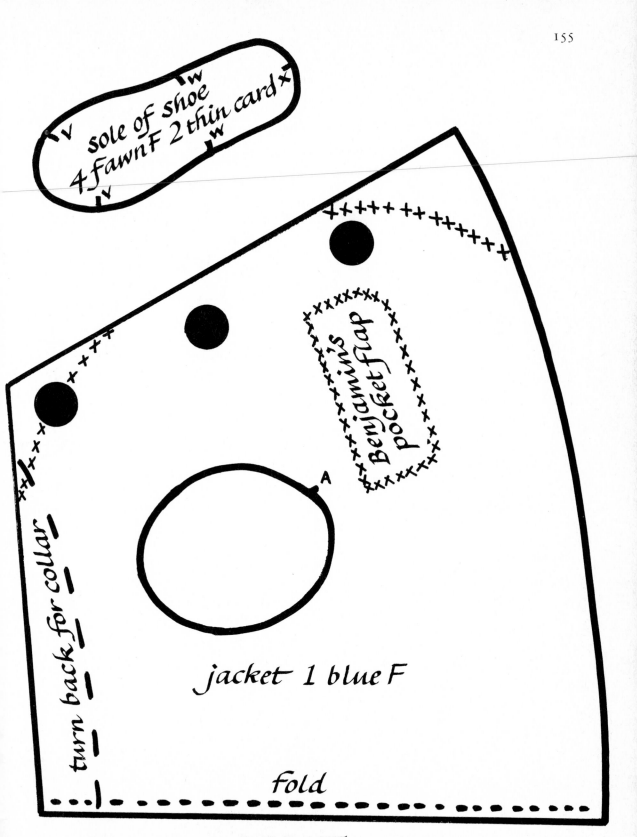

sole of shoe
4 Fawn F 2 thin card

w w x x

v v

Benjamin's
pocket flap

A

turn back for collar

jacket 1 blue F

fold

PETER RABBIT

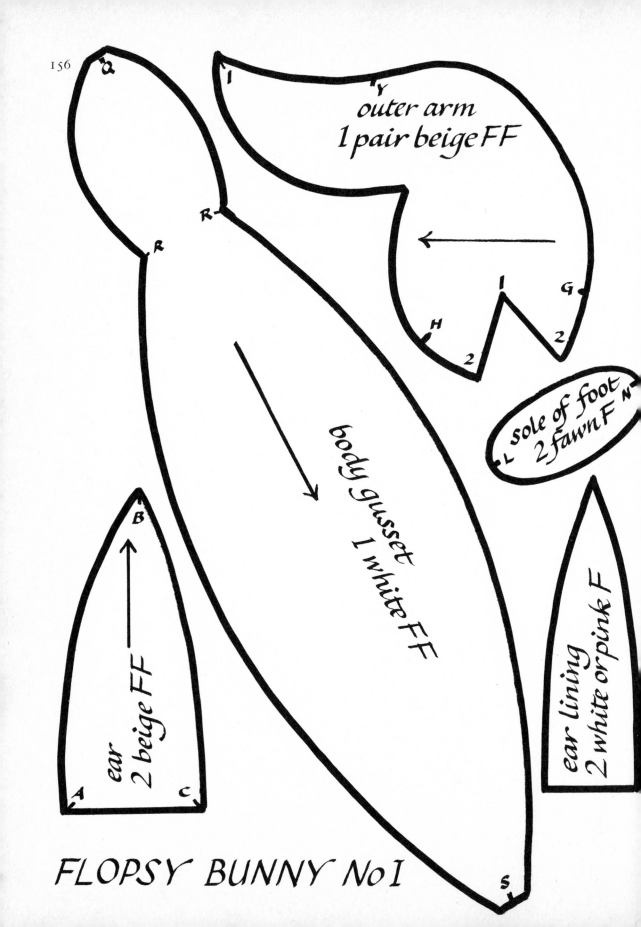

156

outer arm
1 pair beige FF

Y

I

R

R

R

G

H

2

2

sole of foot
2 fawn F

N

L

body gusset
1 white FF

B

ear
2 beige FF

A

C

ear lining
2 white or pink F

S

FLOPSY BUNNY No 1

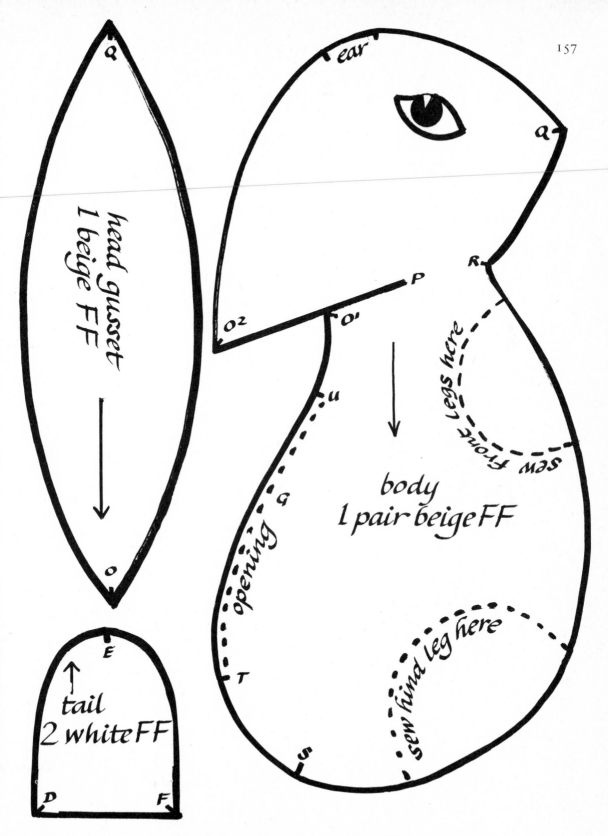

157

head gusset
1 beige FF

Q

O

ear

Q

R

P

O2

O1

u

G

opening

T

S

body
1 pair beige FF

sew front legs here

sew hind leg here

E

tail
2 white FF

D

F

FLOPSY BUNNY No1

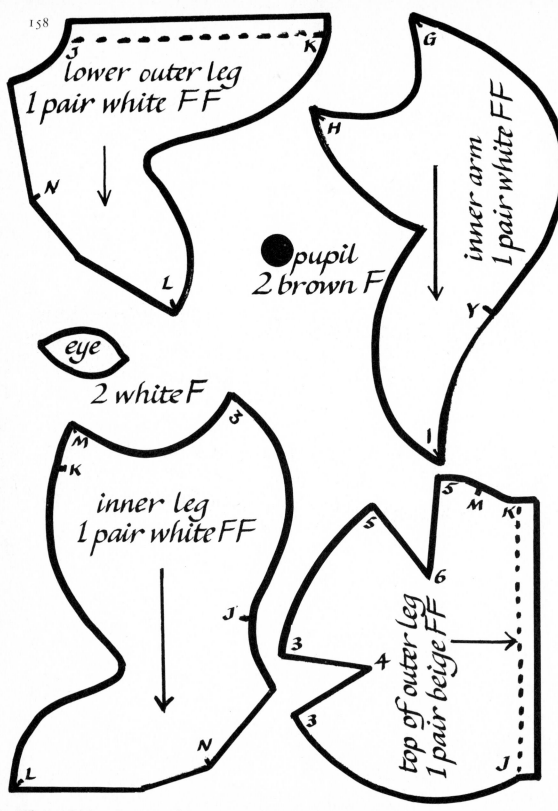

lower outer leg
1 pair white FF

J   K

N

L

inner arm
1 pair white FF

G

H

Y

I

pupil
2 brown F

eye
2 white F

M
K

3

inner leg
1 pair white FF

J

L   N

5   M   K

S

6

3

4

top of outer leg
1 pair beige FF

3

J

FLOPSY BUNNY No1

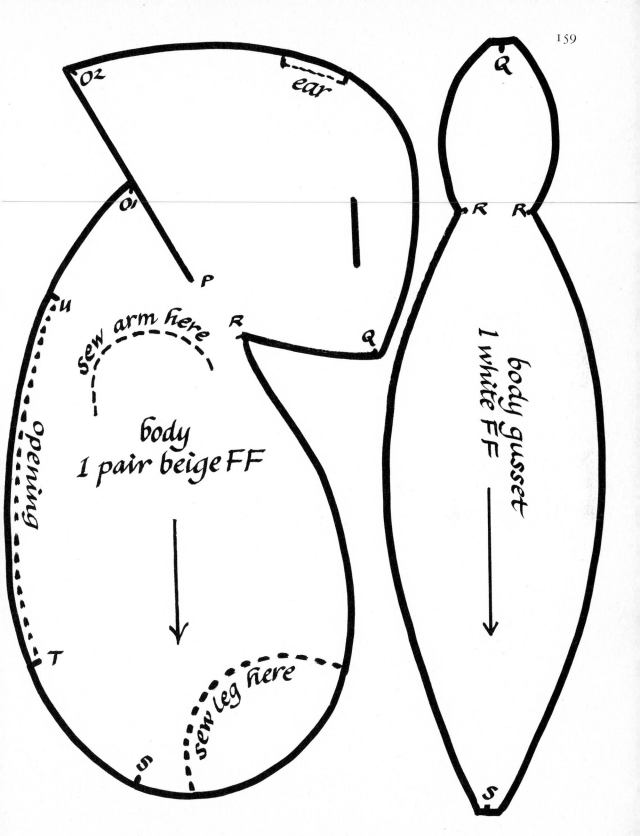

159

ear

O2

O1

P

Q

Q

R

R

R

sew arm here

body
1 pair beige FF

u

opening

T

S

sew leg here

body gusset
1 white FF

S

FLOPSY BUNNY No2

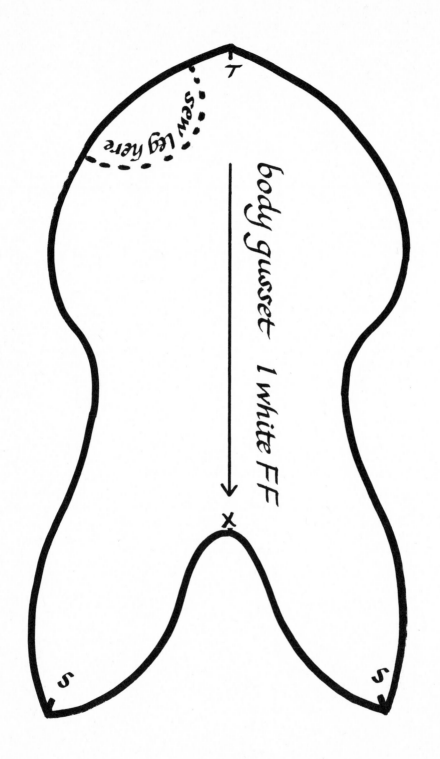

T

sew leg here

body gusset   1 white FF

X

S   S

FLOPSY BUNNIES   Nos 3 & 5

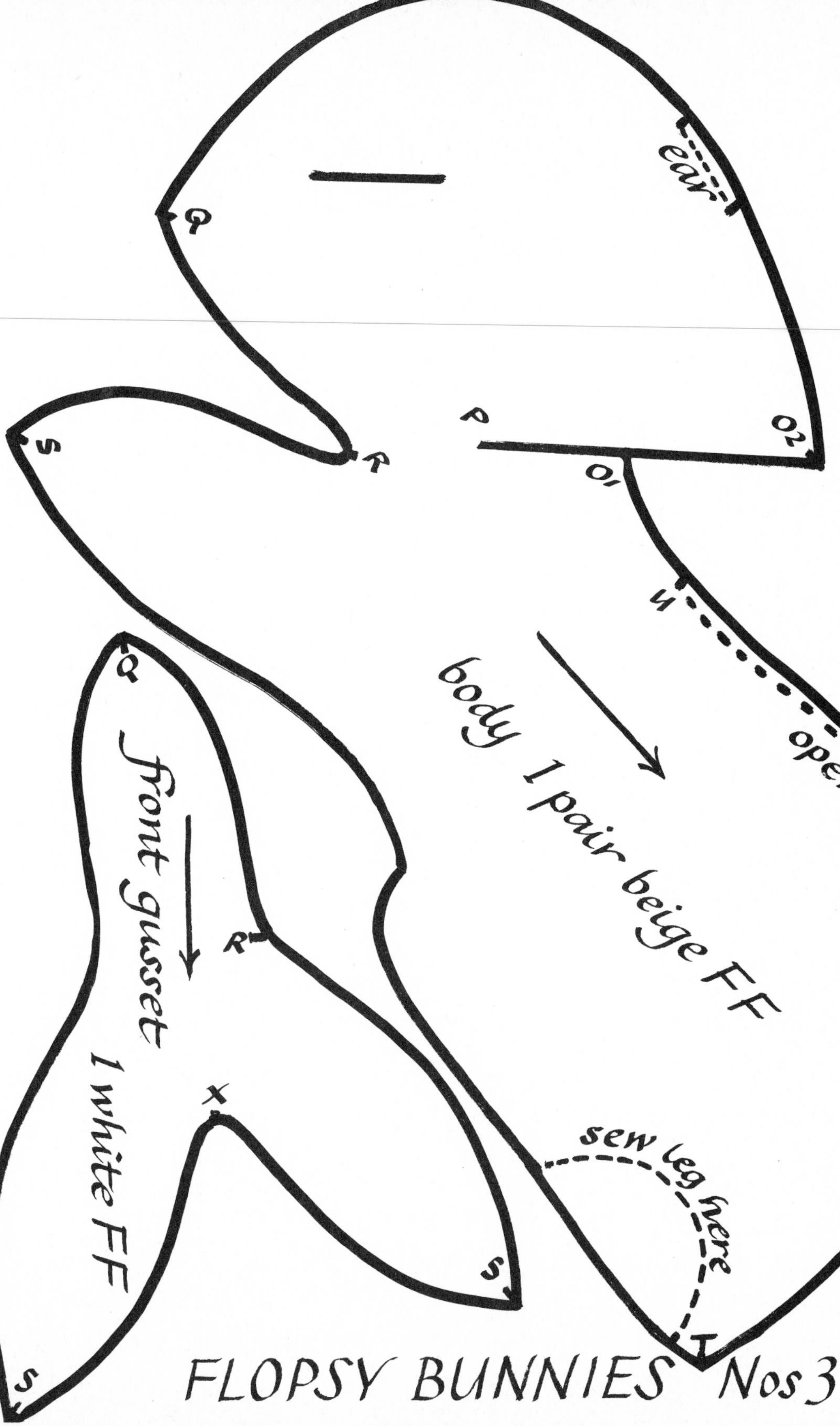

ear

Q

S

R

P

O1

O2

u

opening

body 1 pair beige FF

Q

front gusset

1 white FF

R

X

K

sew leg here

S

T

S

FLOPSY BUNNIES Nos 3 & 5

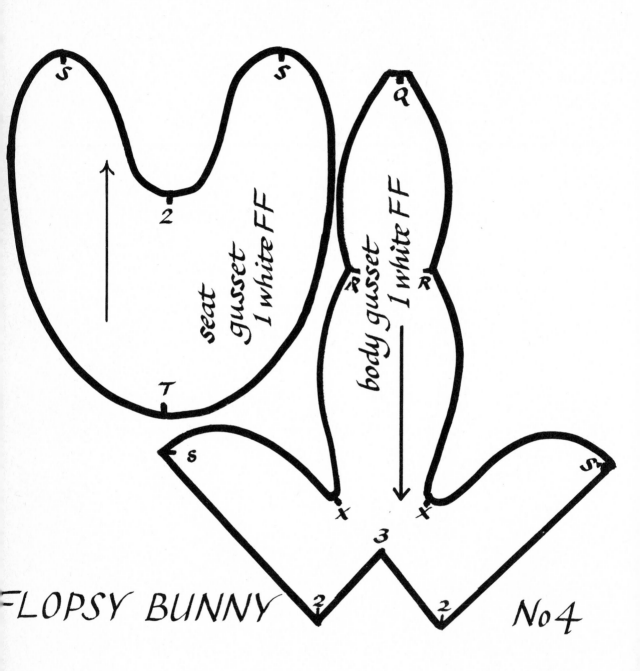

seat gusset
1 white FF

body gusset
1 white FF

FLOPSY BUNNY   No 4

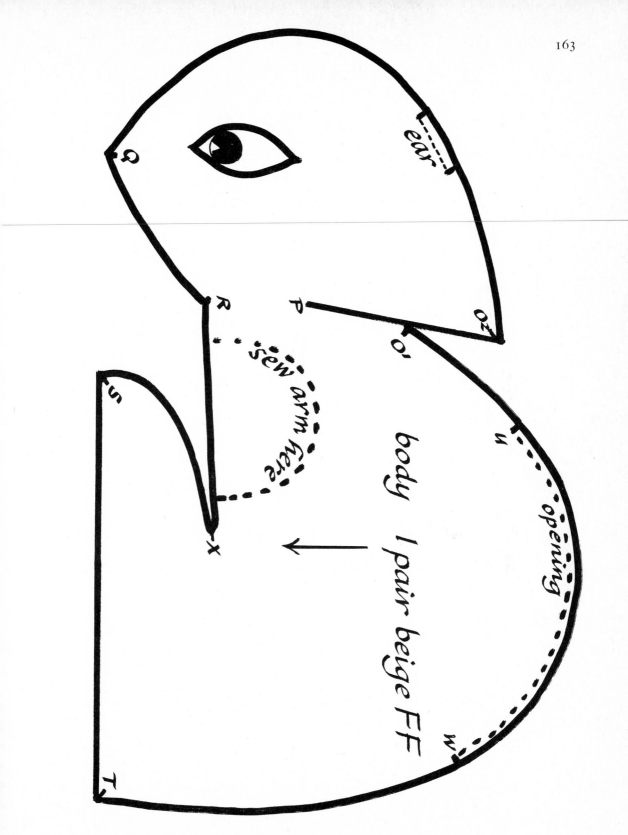

ear

Q

R

P

O'

O

N

S

sew arm here

X

body   1 pair beige FF

opening

W

T

FLOPSY BUNNY No 4

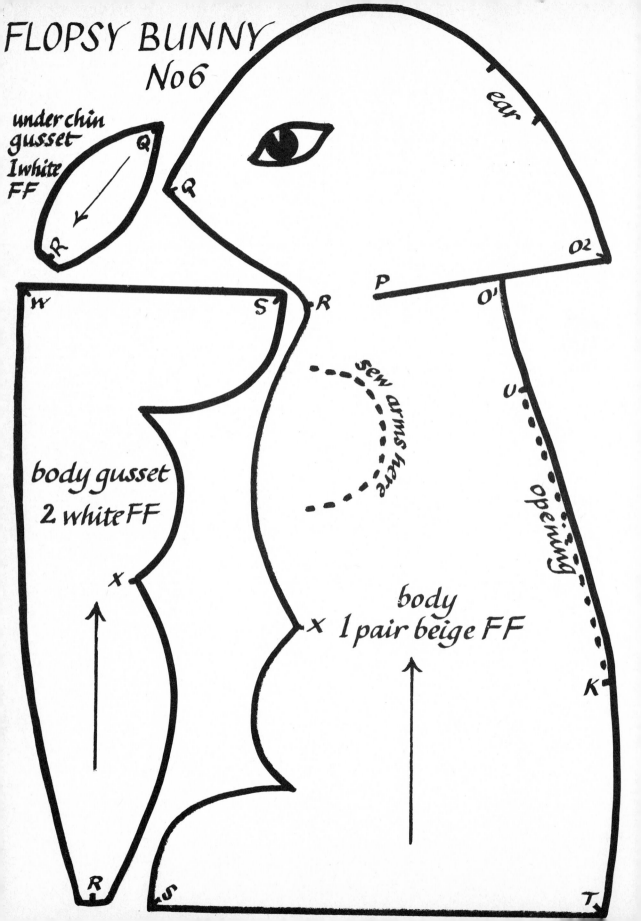

FLOPSY BUNNY
No 6

under chin
gusset
1 white
FF

Q
Q
R

ear
O2
P
O'
R
W
S
U
opening
sew arms here
body gusset
2 white FF
X
X
body
1 pair beige FF
K
R
S
T

back upper   2 grey F

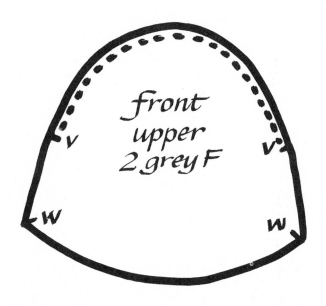

front
upper
2 grey F

heel

12 thick card
2 fawn F

BENJAMIN BUNNY'S
CLOGS

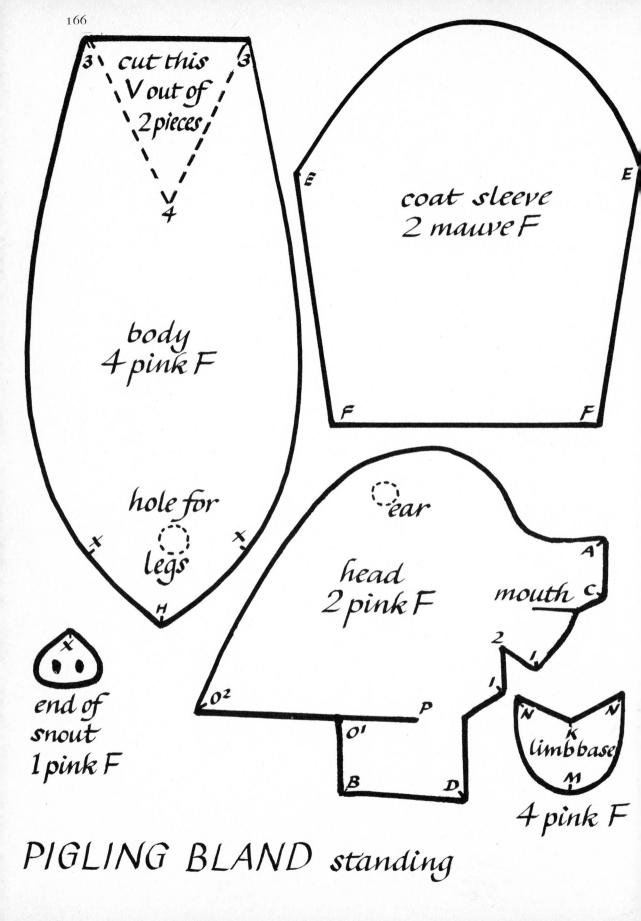

166

cut this
V out of
2 pieces

3   3

4

body
4 pink F

hole for

legs

coat sleeve
2 mauve F

E   E

F   F

end of
snout
1 pink F

head
2 pink F

ear

mouth

A

C

2

1

1

O²

P

O¹

B   D

limb base

N   N

K

M

4 pink F

PIGLING BLAND *standing*

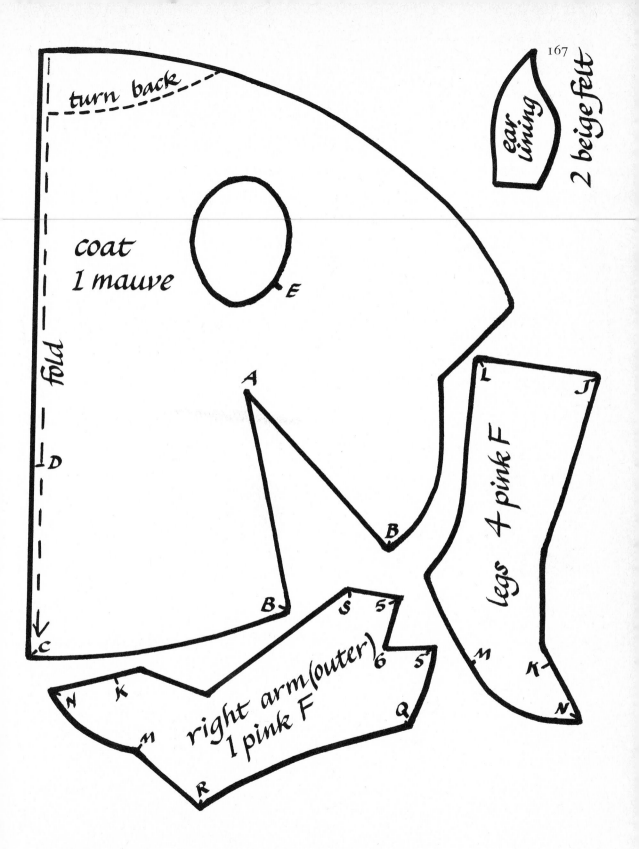

coat
1 mauve

turn back

167
ear lining

2 beige felt

fold

E

A

D

B

B

C

L

J

legs 4 pink F

S S

6 5

N K

M

N

K

M

R

right arm (outer)
1 pink F

Q

K

N

PIGLING BLAND *standing*

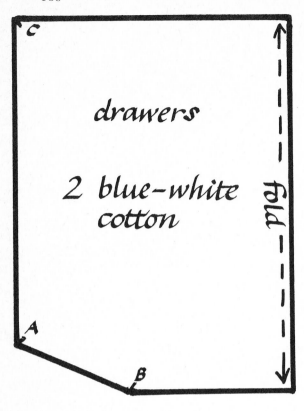

drawers

2 blue-white
cotton

fold

C

A

B

PIG-WIG'S
DRAWERS

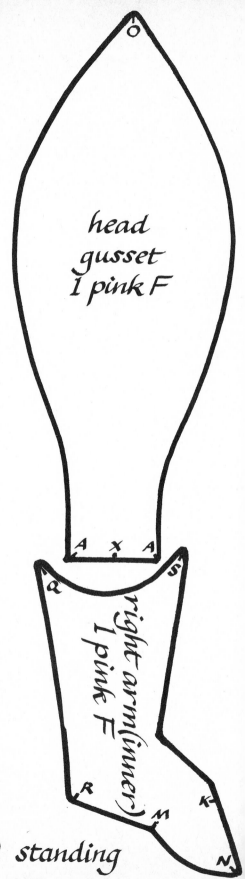

head
gusset
1 pink F

O

A X A

Q S

right arm (inner)
1 pink F

R M K

N

PIGLING BLAND *standing*

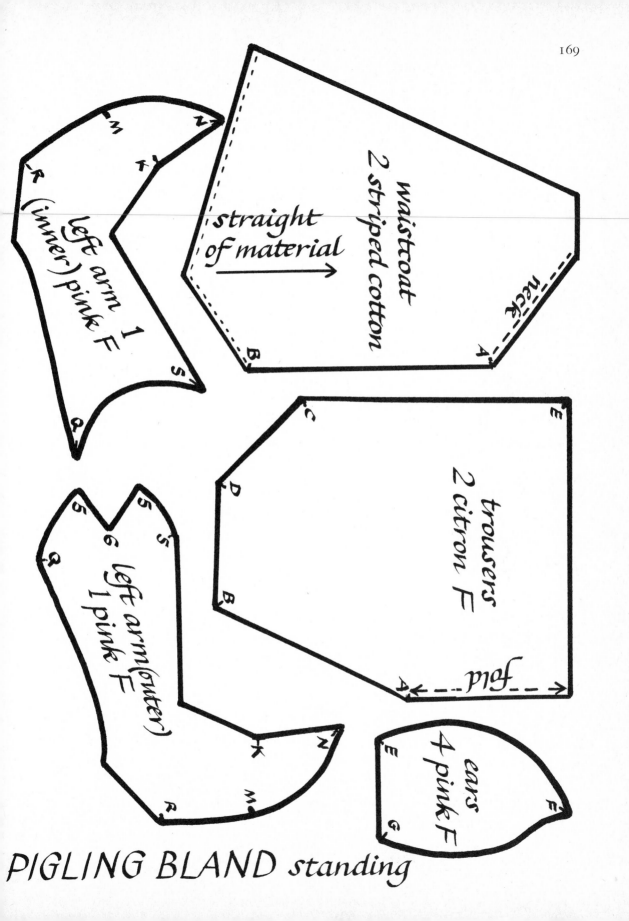

169

left arm
(inner) pink 1 F

straight
of material →

waistcoat
2 striped cotton

neck

trousers
2 citron F

fold

left arm (outer)
1 pink F

ears
4 pink F

PIGLING BLAND standing

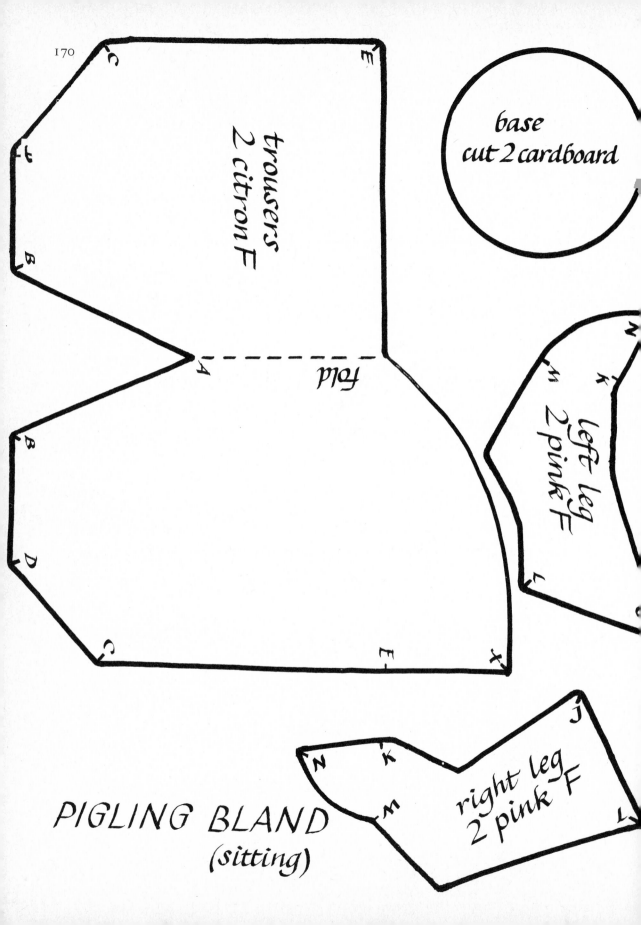

170

base
cut 2 cardboard

trousers
2 citron F

fold

left leg
2 pink F

right leg
2 pink F

PIGLING BLAND
(sitting)

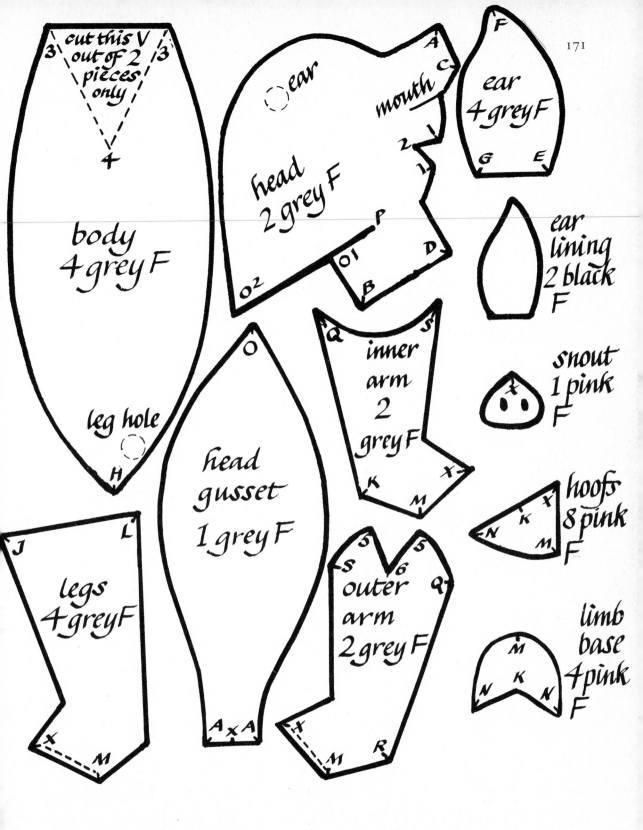

171

cut this V out of 2 pieces only
3   3
+

body
4 grey F

leg hole

legs
4 grey F

J   L

X   M

head gusset
1 grey F

O

H

A   x   A

ear

head
2 grey F

mouth

A
C
2
1
1
P
O1
O2   B   D

inner arm
2 grey F

Q   S

K   X
M

outer arm
2 grey F

S   S
S   6
Q

H   M   R

ear
4 grey F

F

G   E

ear lining
2 black F

snout
1 pink F
X

hoofs
8 pink F
X
K
N   M

limb base
4 pink F
M
N   K   N

PIG-WIG

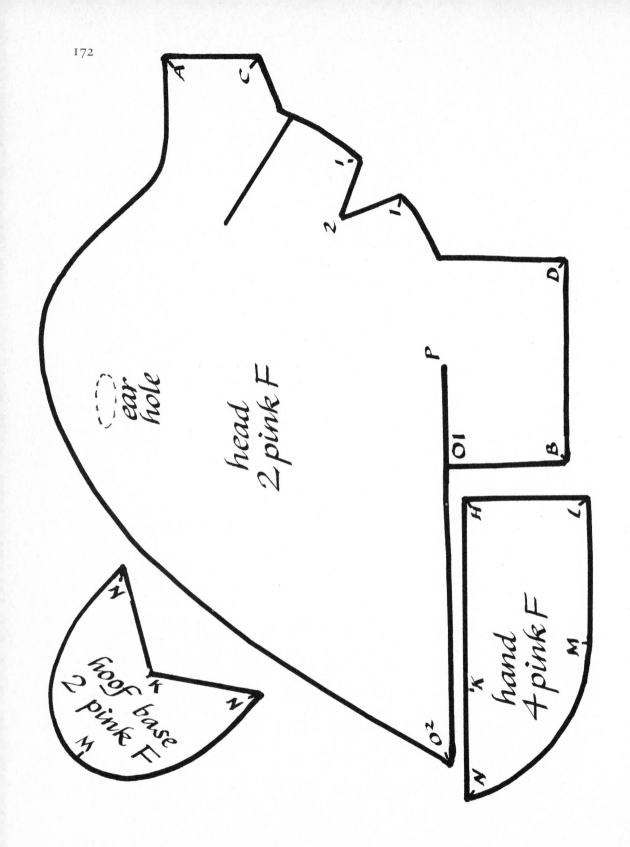

head
2 pink F

ear
hole

hoof base
2 pink F

hand
4 pink F

AUNT PETTITOES

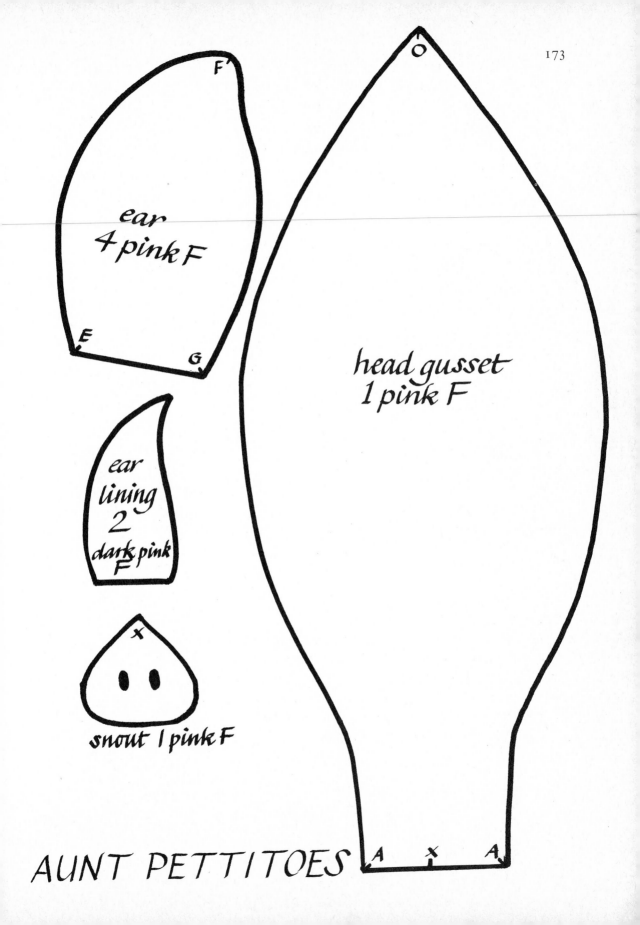

173

ear
4 pink F

F'

E   G

head gusset
1 pink F

O

ear
lining
2
dark pink
F

X

snout 1 pink F

A   X   A

AUNT PETTITOES

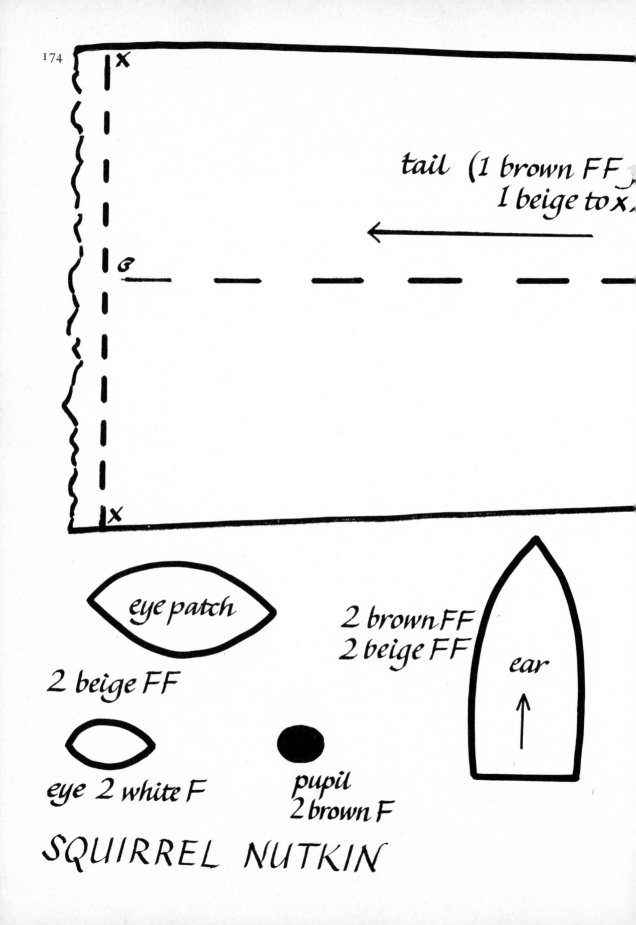

tail (1 brown FF
1 beige to x.

eye patch

2 beige FF

2 brown FF
2 beige FF

ear

eye 2 white F

pupil
2 brown F

SQUIRREL NUTKIN

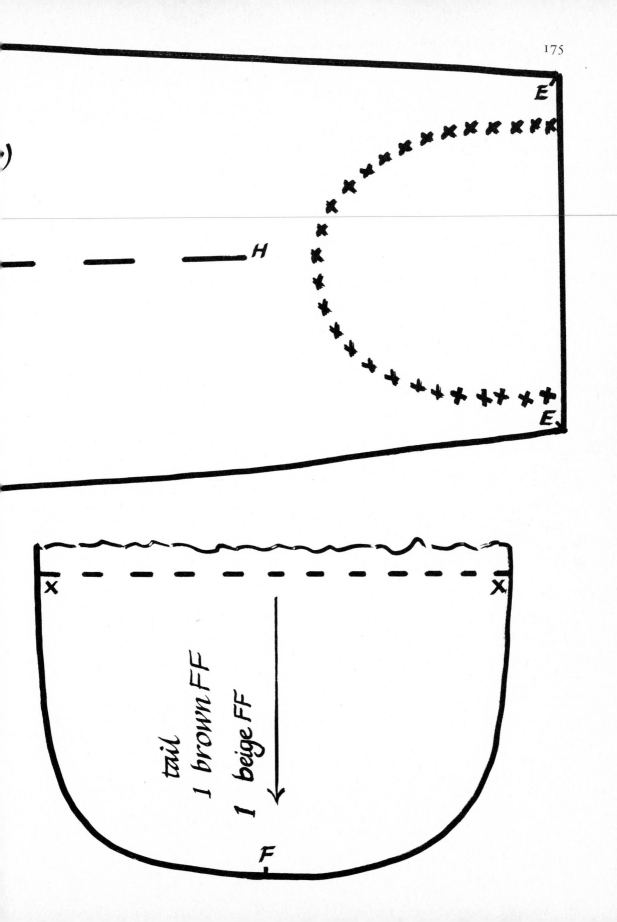

E

)

H

E

X · · · · · · · · X

tail
1 brown FF
1 beige FF

F

SQUIRREL
NUTKIN

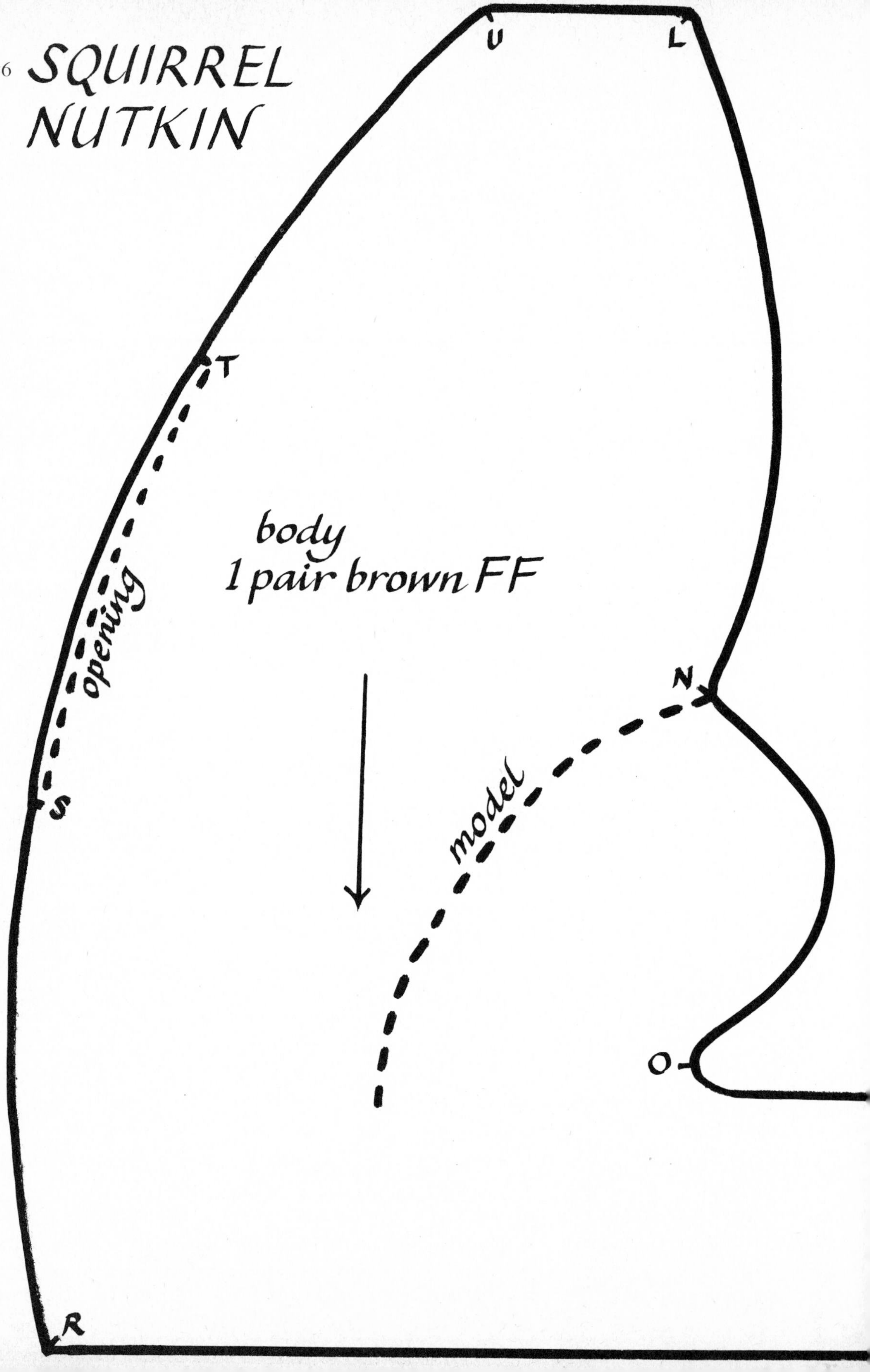

U L

T

body
1 pair brown FF

opening

S

model

N

O

R

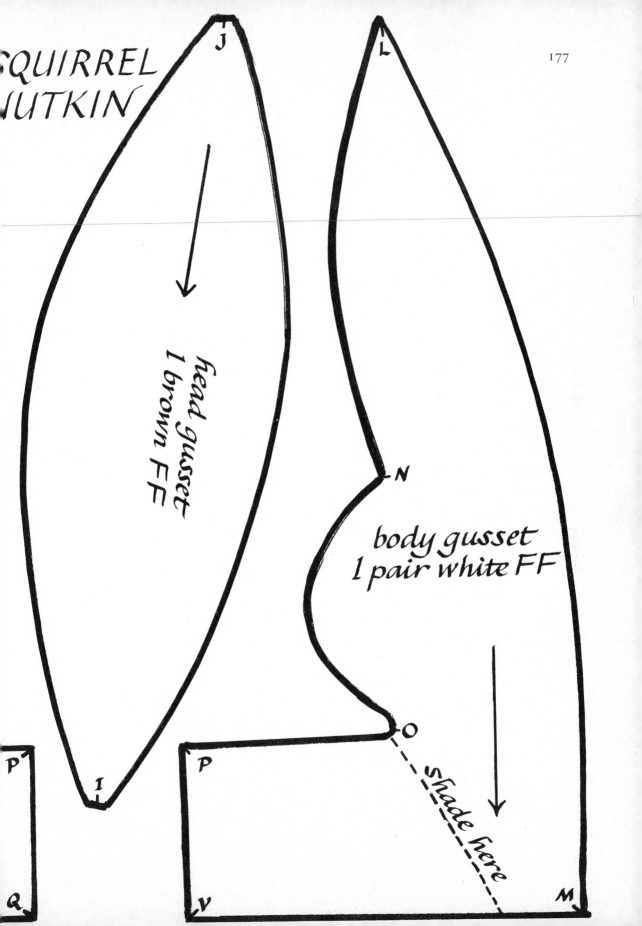

SQUIRREL
NUTKIN

177

J

L

*head gusset
1 brown FF*

N

*body gusset
1 pair white FF*

O

shade here

P

I

P

Q

V

M

178

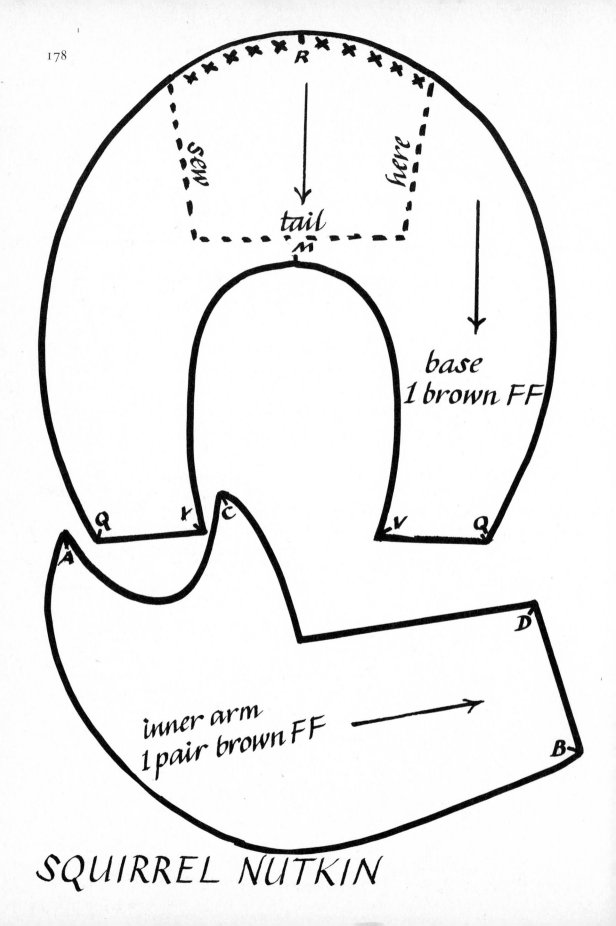

sew here

R

tail

base
1 brown FF

Q r C V Q

A

D

B

inner arm
1 pair brown FF

SQUIRREL NUTKIN

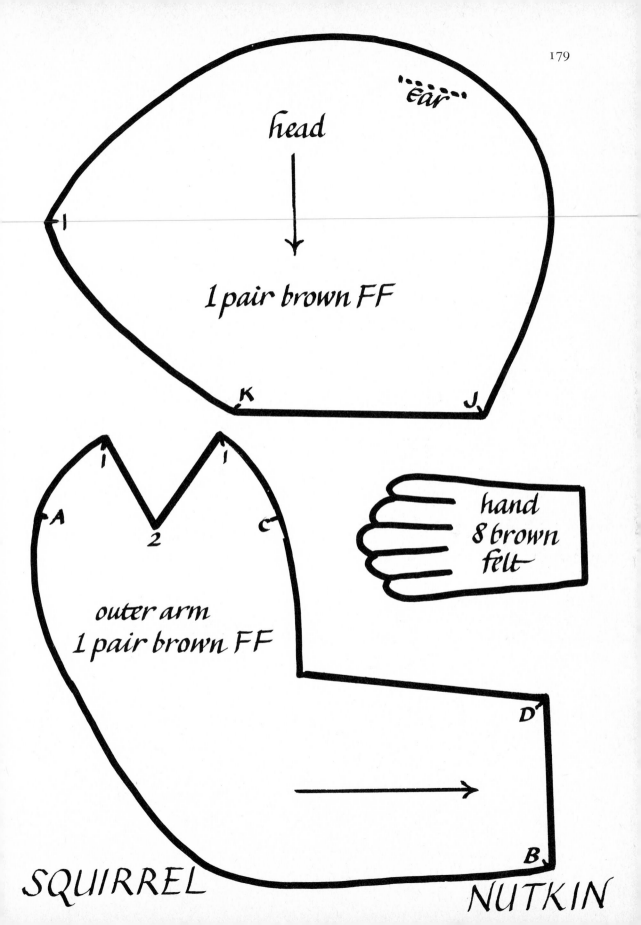

179

head

"ear"

1 pair brown FF

I

K   J

I   I

A   C

2

outer arm
1 pair brown FF

hand
8 brown
felt

D

B

SQUIRREL

NUTKIN

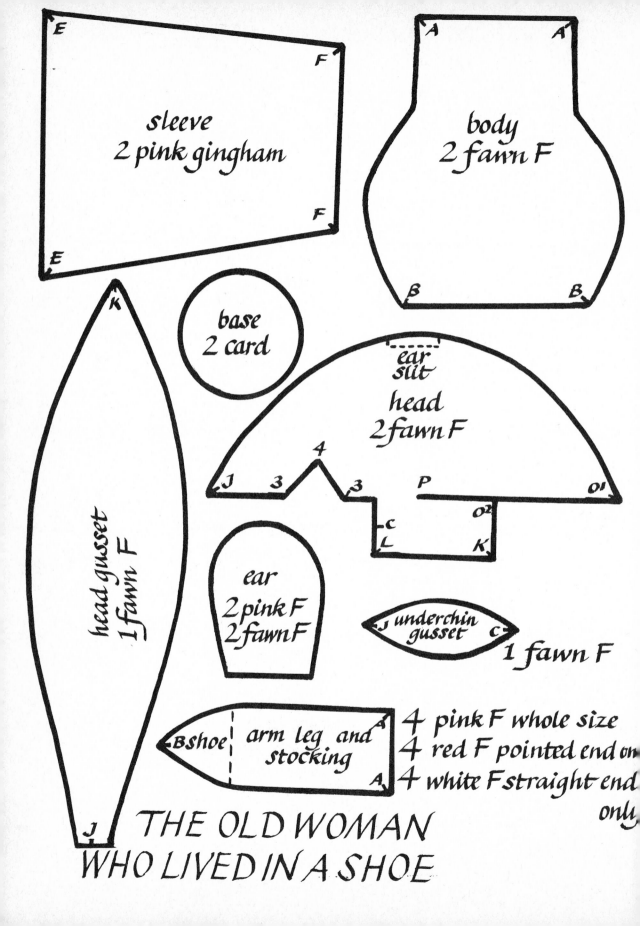

sleeve
2 pink gingham

E   F
F
E

body
2 fawn F

A   A
B   B

base
2 card

ear
slit
head
2 fawn F

4
J   3   3   P   O¹
O²
c
L   K

head gusset
1 fawn F

K

J

ear
2 pink F
2 fawn F

underchin
gusset
J   c
1 fawn F

B shoe   arm leg and stocking   A
A

4 pink F whole size
4 red F pointed end on
4 white F straight end only

THE OLD WOMAN
WHO LIVED IN A SHOE

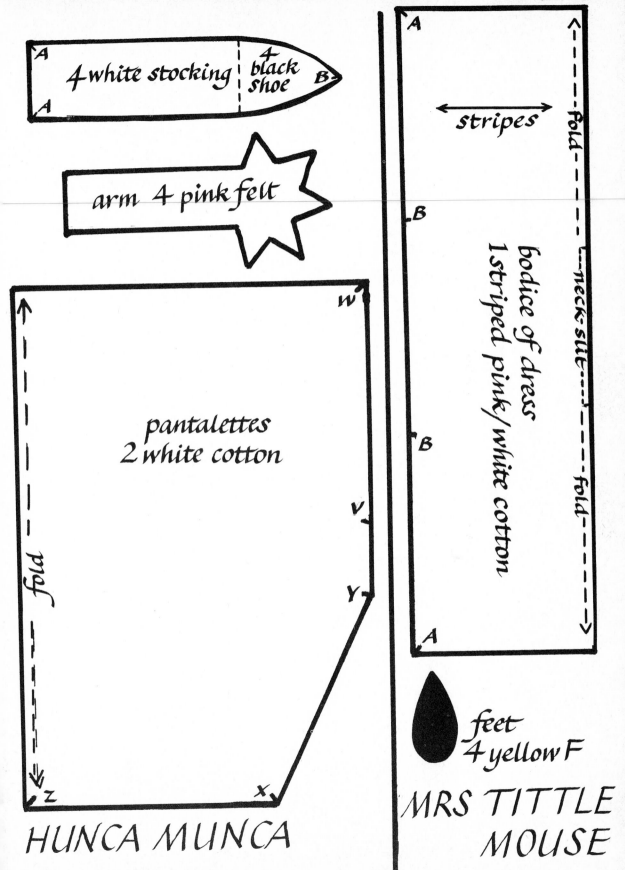

A 4 white stocking 4 black shoe B

A

arm 4 pink felt

A stripes

B bodice of dress
1 striped pink/white cotton

fold neck slit fold

B

W

pantalettes
2 white cotton

fold

V

Y

A

feet
4 yellow F

Z X

HUNCA MUNCA

MRS TITTLE MOUSE

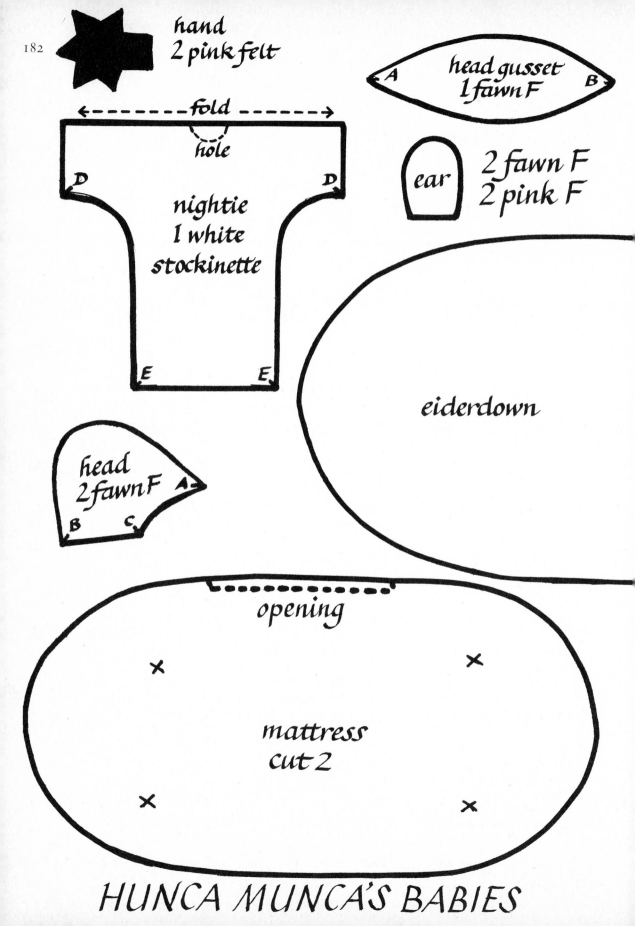

hand
2 pink felt

head gusset
1 fawn F

A   B

fold

hole

D   D

nightie
1 white
stockinette

ear   2 fawn F
      2 pink F

E   E

eiderdown

head
2 fawn F   A

B   C

opening

mattress
cut 2

HUNCA MUNCA'S BABIES

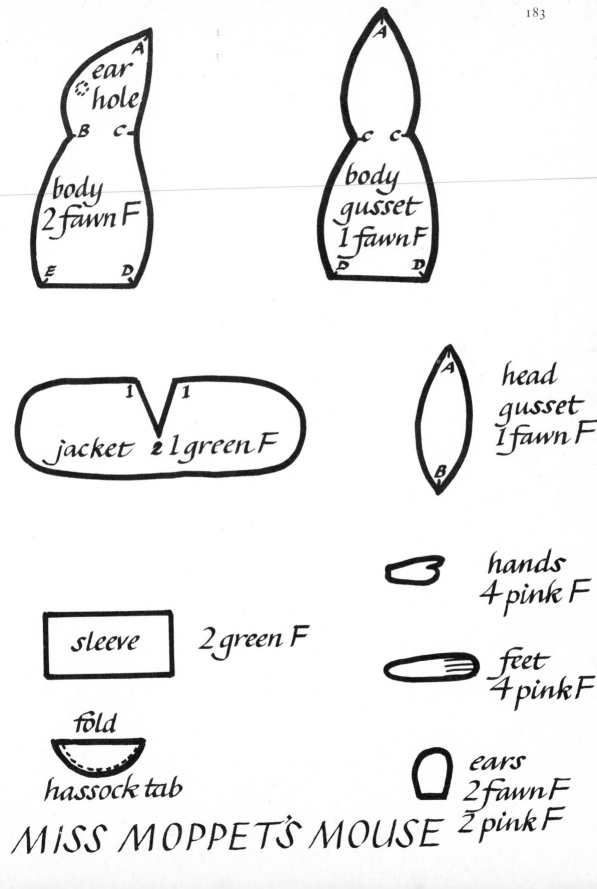

ear
hole

B   C

body
2 fawn F

E   D

body
gusset
1 fawn F

C   C

D   D

1   1

jacket   **2** 1 green F

head
gusset
1 fawn F

A

B

hands
4 pink F

sleeve   2 green F

feet
4 pink F

fold

hassock tab

ears
2 fawn F
2 pink F

MISS MOPPET'S MOUSE

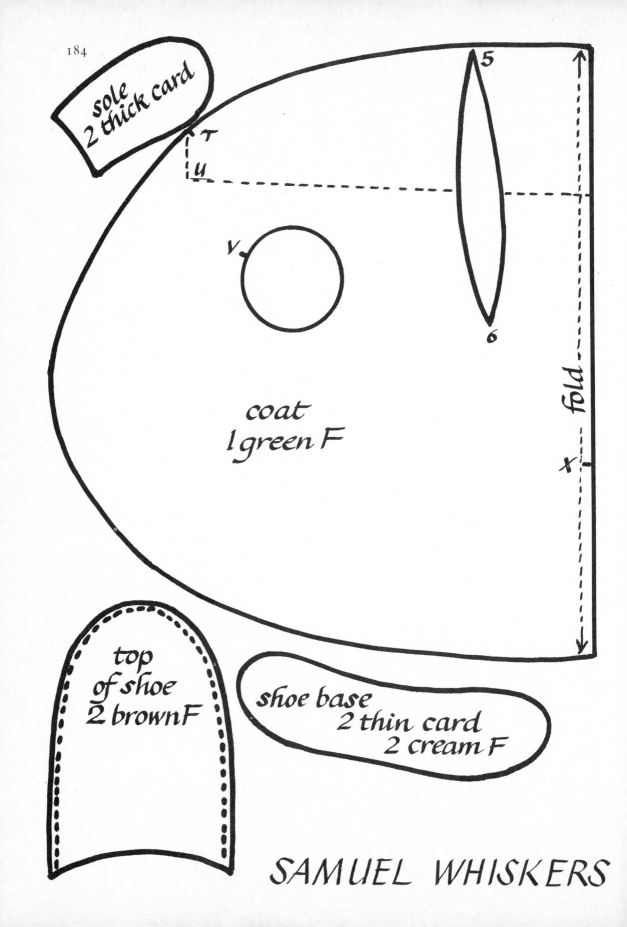

184

sole
2 thick card

T
U

5

6

V

coat
1 green F

x — fold

top
of shoe
2 brown F

shoe base
2 thin card
2 cream F

SAMUEL WHISKERS

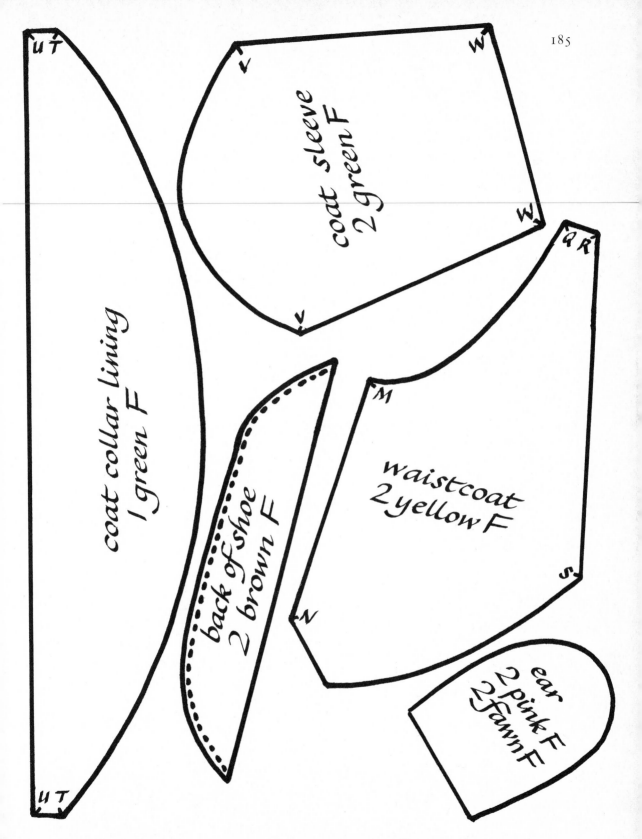

coat sleeve
2 green F

coat collar lining
1 green F

waistcoat
2 yellow F

back of shoe
2 brown F

ear
2 pink F
2 fawn F

SAMUEL WHISKERS

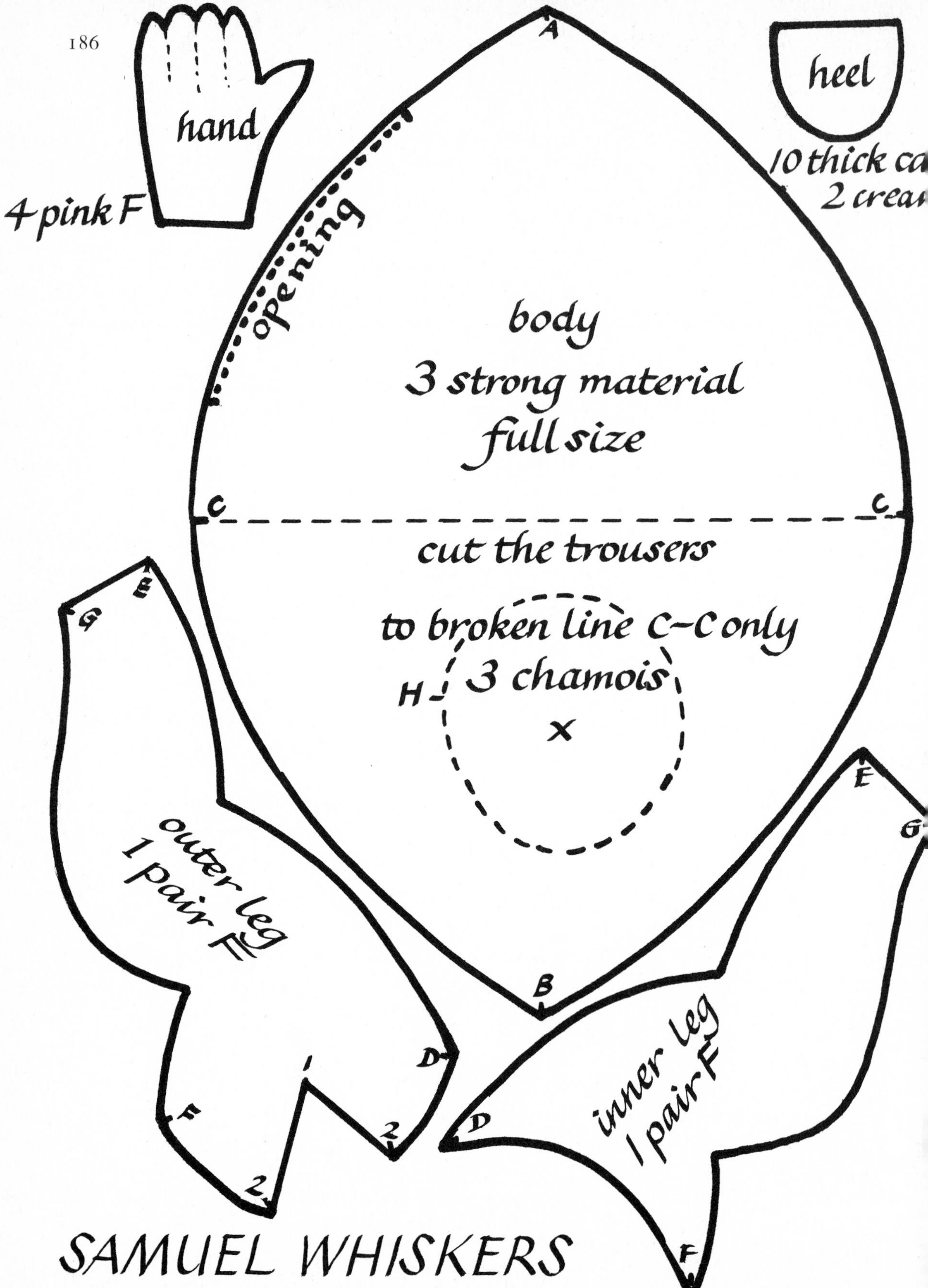

hand

4 pink F

heel

10 thick ca
2 crea

opening

body
3 strong material
full size

A

C   C

cut the trousers

to broken line C–C only
3 chamois

H

×

B

E

G

D

D

outer leg
1 pair F

inner leg
1 pair F

F

2

2

F

SAMUEL WHISKERS

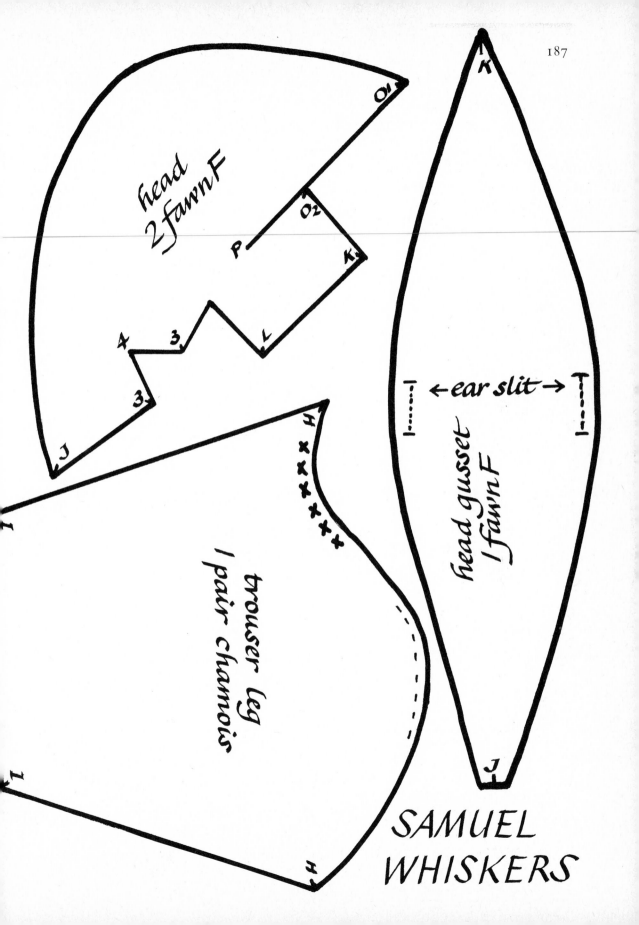

187

head
2 fawn F

O1

O2

P

K

L

4

3

3

J

I

ear slit

head gusset
1 fawn F

K

J

trouser leg
1 pair chamois

H

I

I

H

SAMUEL
WHISKERS

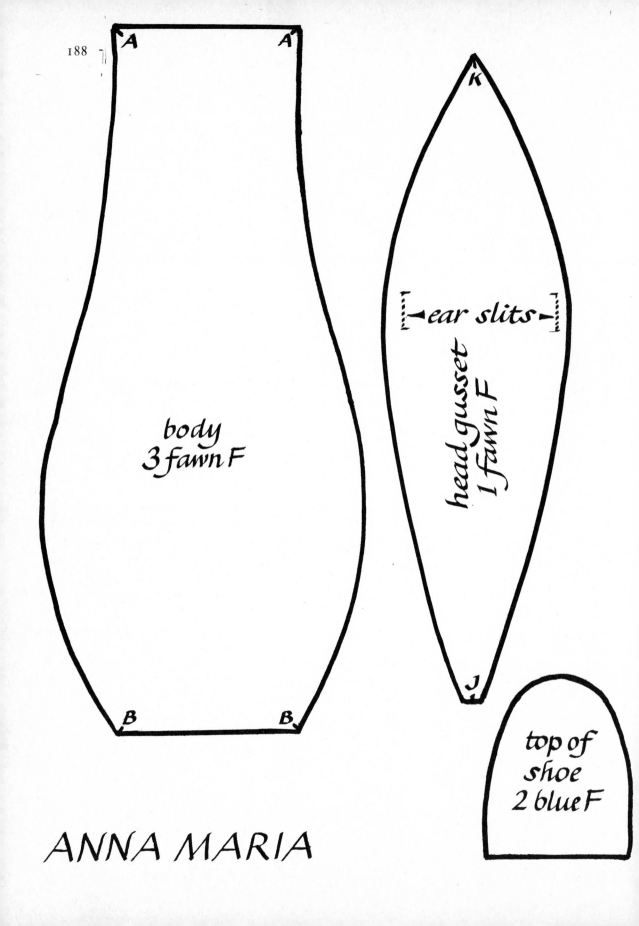

188

A   A

K

ear slits

*body
3 fawn F*

*head gusset
1 fawn F*

B   B

J

*top of
shoe
2 blue F*

ANNA MARIA

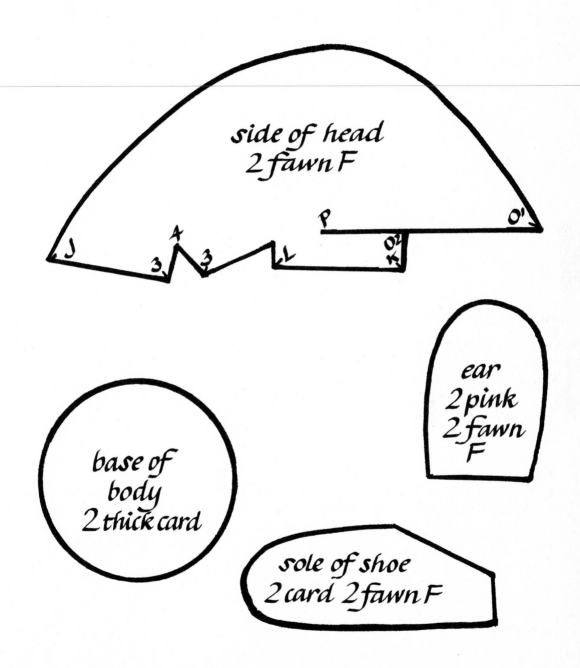

side of head
2 fawn F

P   O'

A
J   3   3   L   O²
                    K

ear
2 pink
2 fawn
F

base of
body
2 thick card

sole of shoe
2 card 2 fawn F

ANNA MARIA

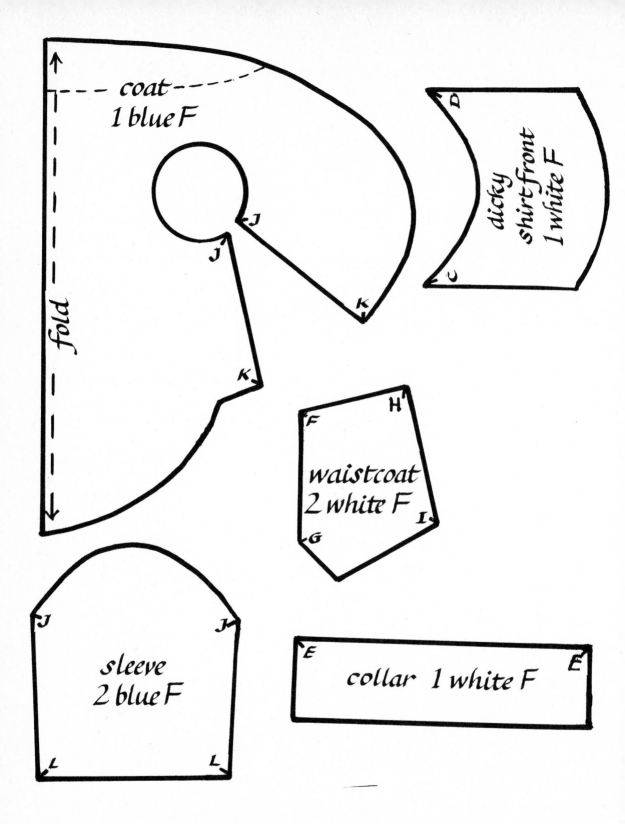

coat
1 blue F

fold

J

J

K

K

dicky
shirt front
1 white F

D

C

waistcoat
2 white F

F

H

G

I

sleeve
2 blue F

J

J

L

L

collar 1 white F

E

E

JOHNNY TOWN-MOUSE

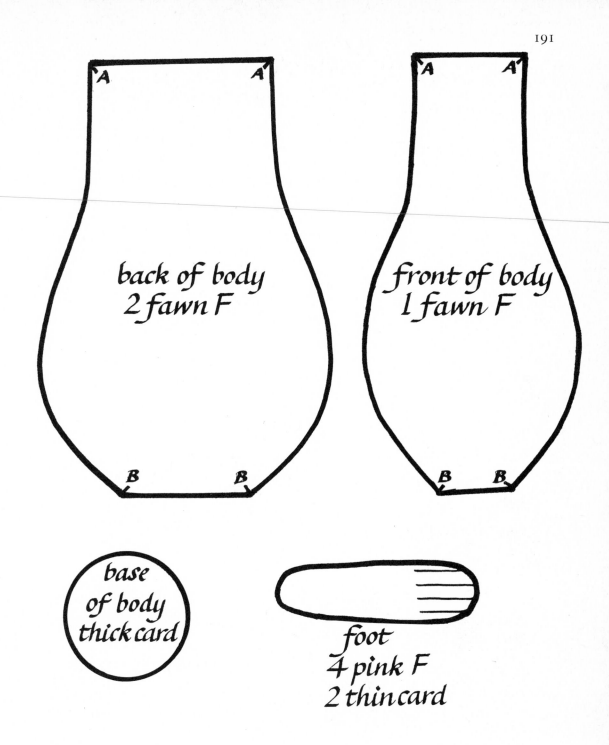

back of body
2 fawn F

front of body
1 fawn F

base
of body
thick card

foot
4 pink F
2 thin card

JOHNNY TOWN-MOUSE

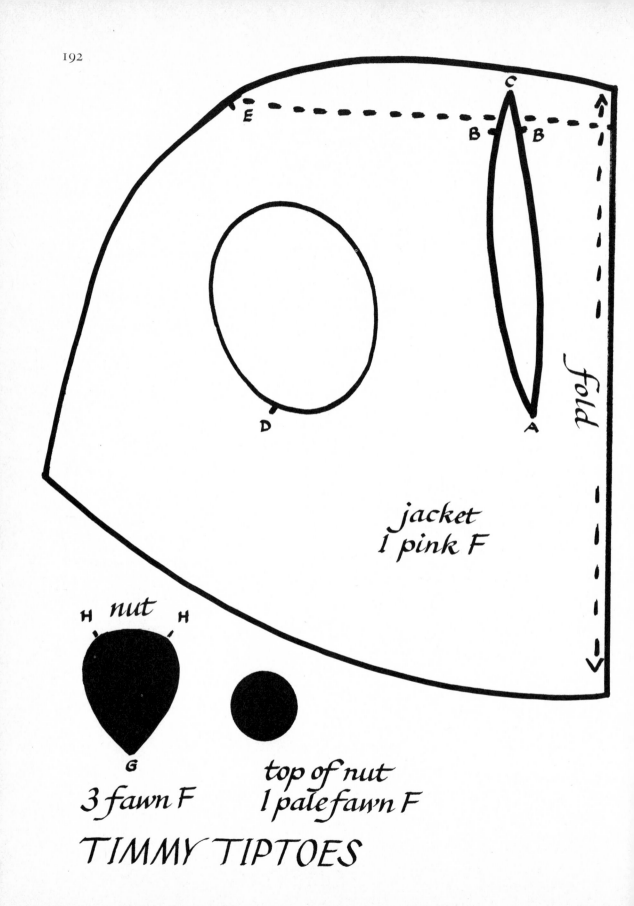

E

C

B B

fold

D

A

jacket
1 pink F

H *nut* H

G

3 fawn F

top of nut
1 pale fawn F

TIMMY TIPTOES

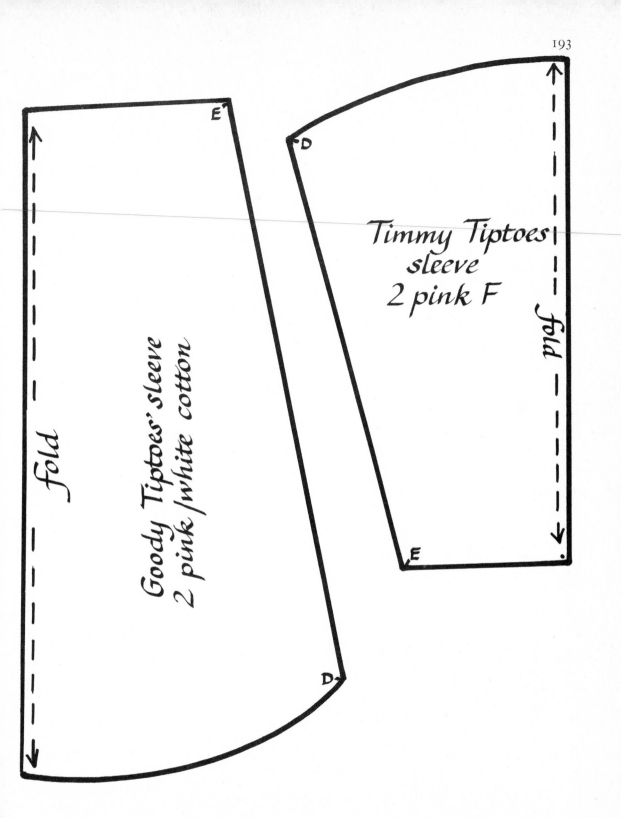

E

D

Timmy Tiptoes
sleeve
2 pink F

fold

Fold

Goody Tiptoes' sleeve
2 pink /white cotton

D

E

TIMMY TIPTOES & GOODY TIPTOES

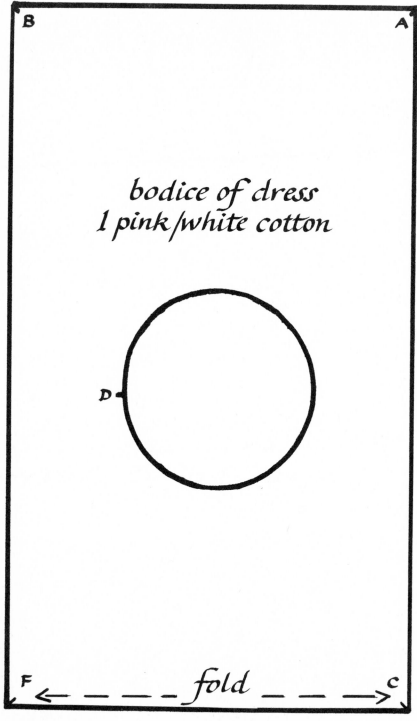

B   A

bodice of dress
1 pink/white cotton

D

F   *fold*   C

GOODY TIPTOES

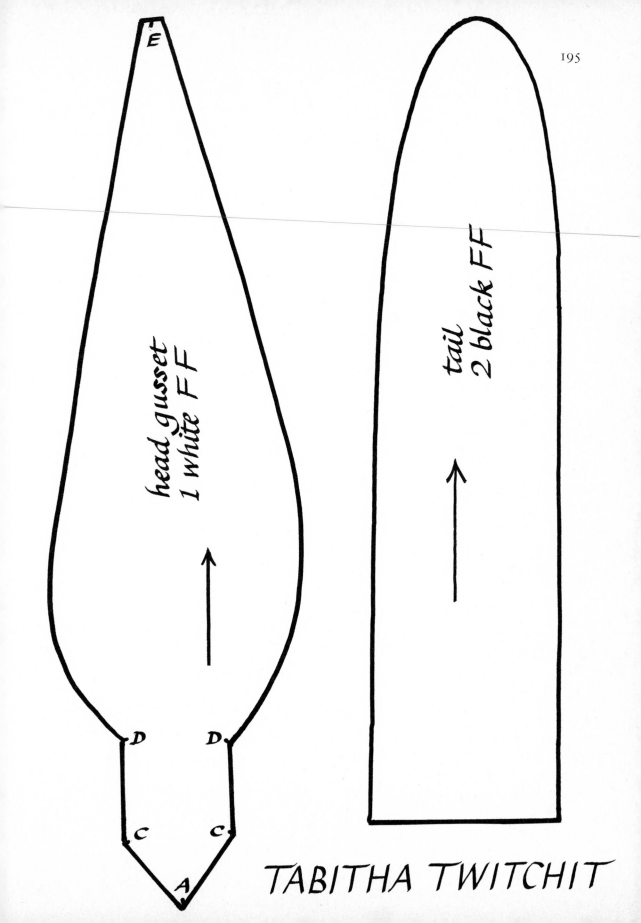

head gusset
1 white FF

E

D   D

C   C

A

tail
2 black FF

TABITHA TWITCHIT

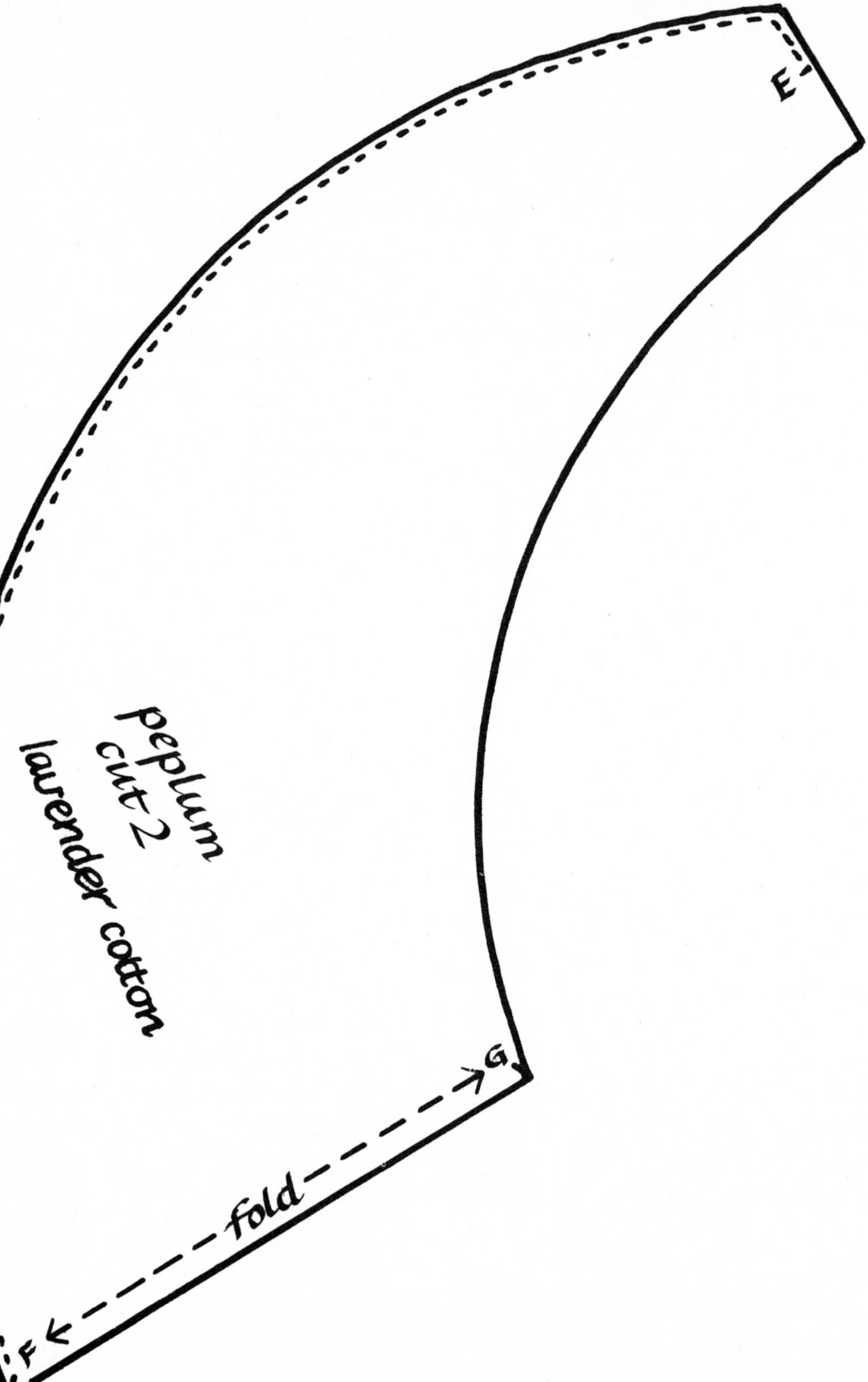

E

peplum
cut 2
lavender cotton

G

fold

F

TABITHA TWITCHIT

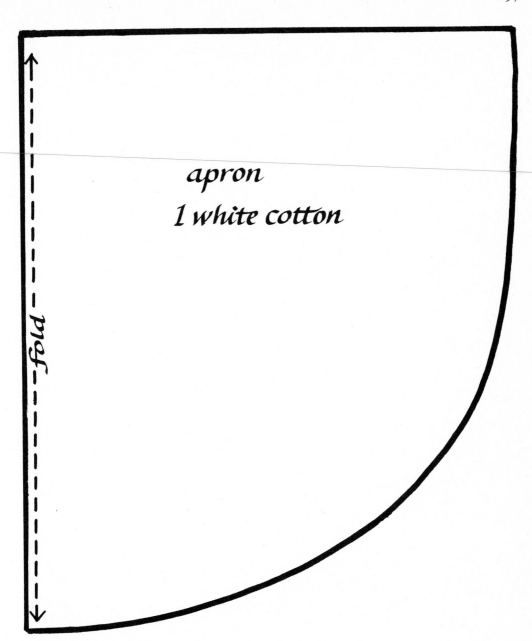

apron
1 white cotton

fold

TABITHA TWITCHIT

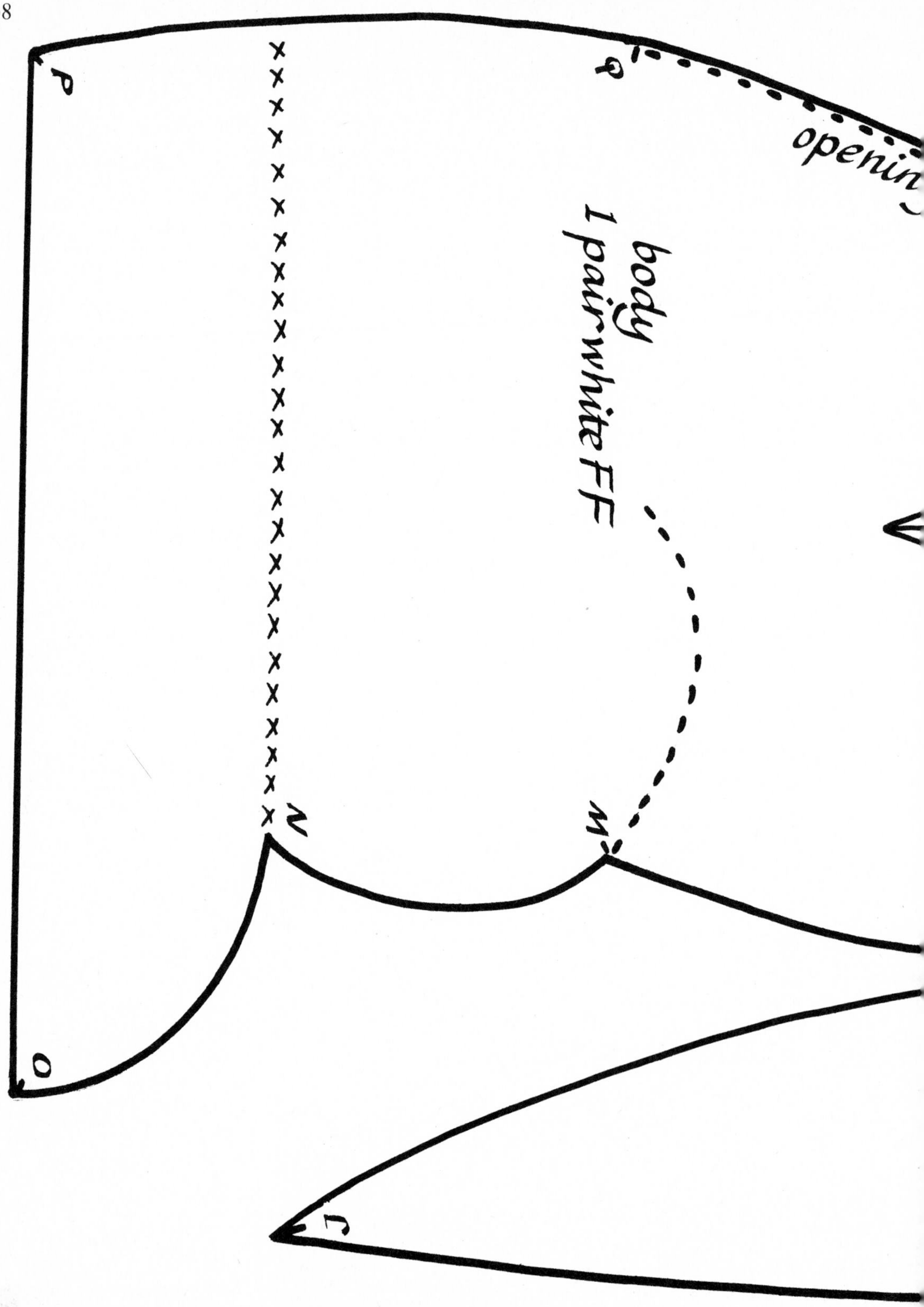

x x x x x x x x x x x x x x x x x x x x x x x x x x x x x x

P

q

opening

body
1 pair white FF

N

m

o

j

TABITHA TWITCHIT

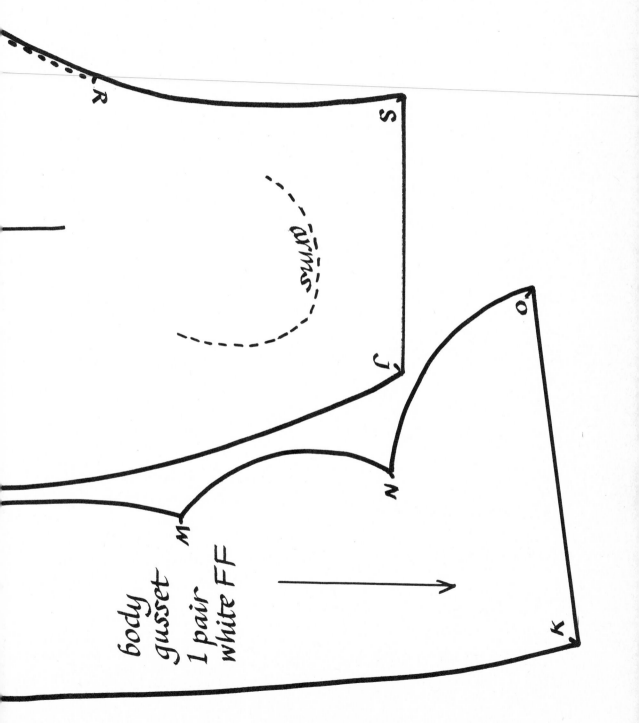

R

S

sew

O

J

N

M

K

body
gusset
1 pair
white FF

TABITHA TWITCHIT

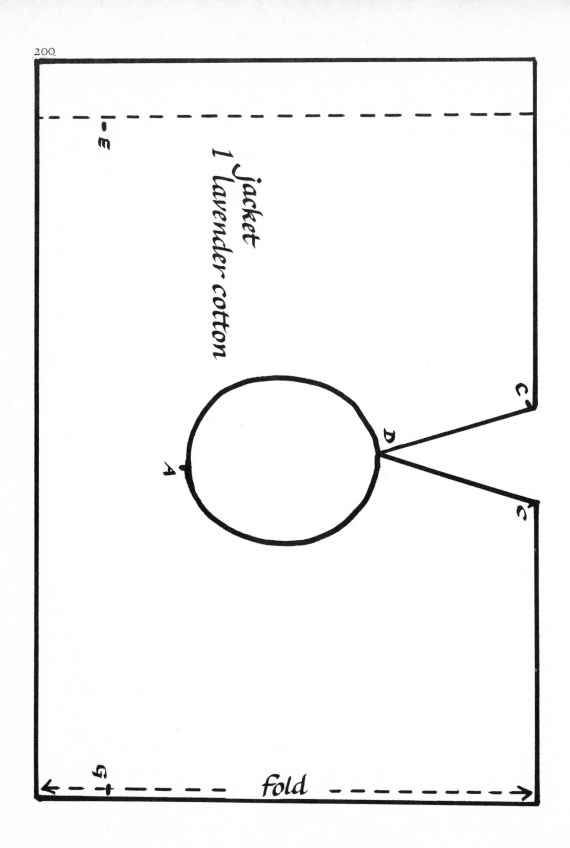

200

Jacket
1 lavender cotton

E

A

D

C

C

G

fold

TABITHA TWITCHIT

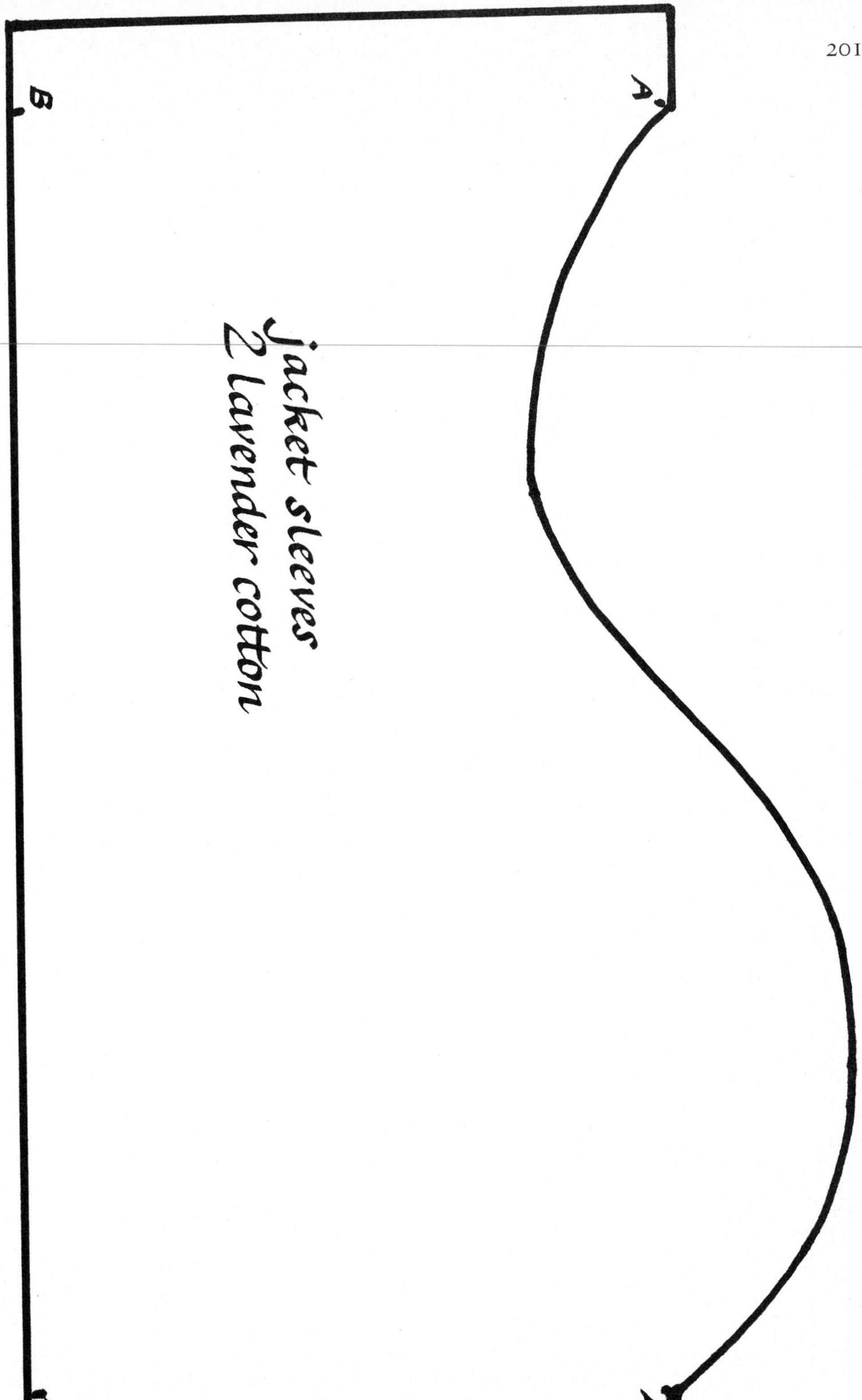

201

jacket sleeves
2 Lavender cotton

B

A

B

A

TABITHA TWITCHIT

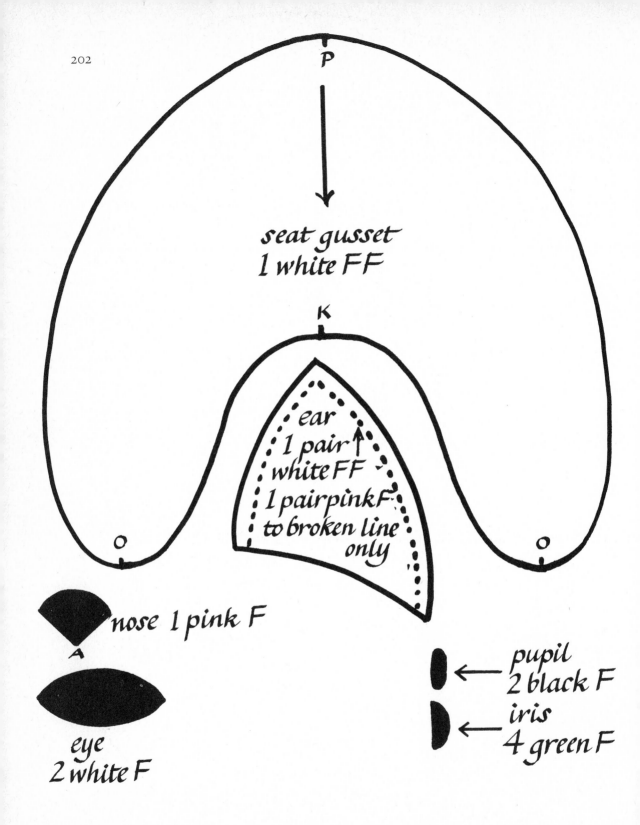

202

seat gusset
1 white FF

ear
1 pair
white FF
1 pair pink F
to broken line
only

nose 1 pink F

pupil
2 black F
iris
4 green F

eye
2 white F

TABITHA TWITCHIT

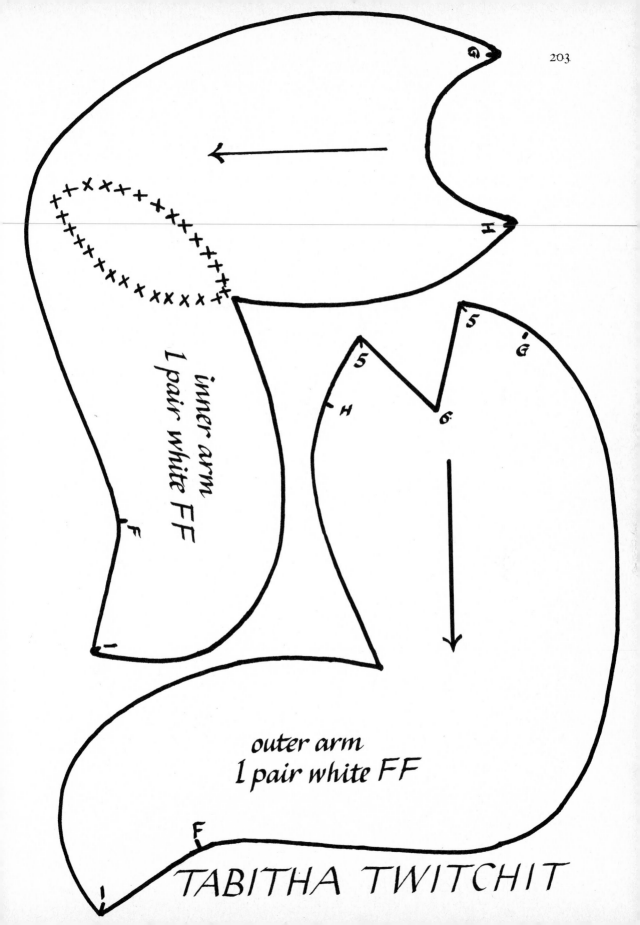

203

inner arm
1 pair white FF

outer arm
1 pair white FF

TABITHA TWITCHIT

204

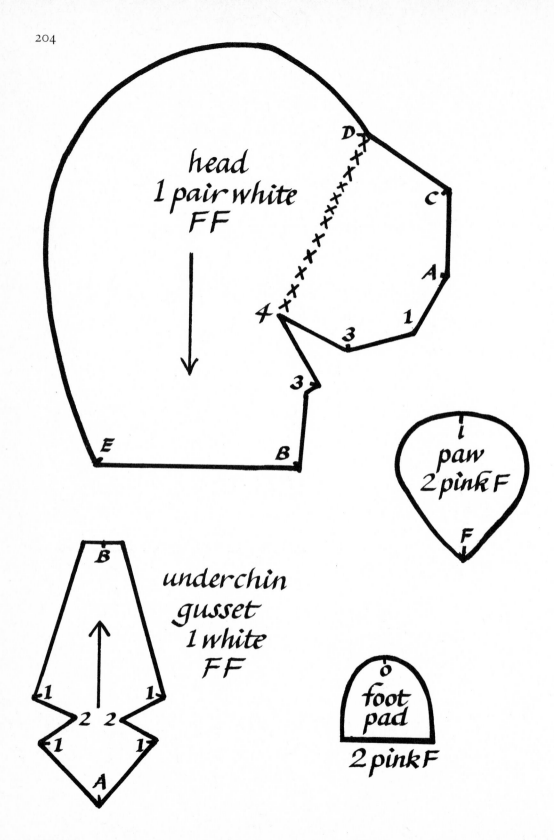

head
1 pair white
FF

D

C

A

1

4

3

3

E

B

paw
2 pink F

1

F

underchin
gusset
1 white
FF

B

1   1

2   2

1   1

A

foot
pad

o

2 pink F

TABITHA TWITCHIT

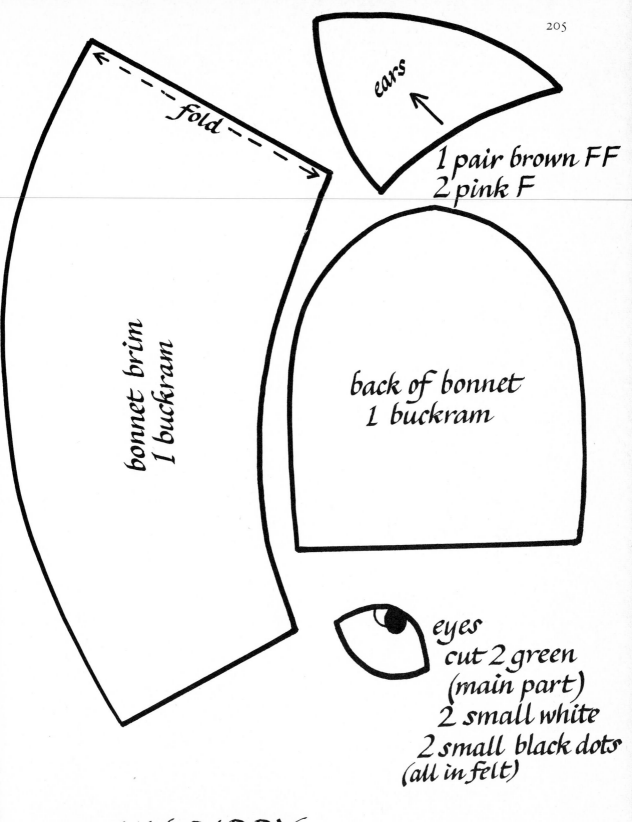

205

ears

1 pair brown FF
2 pink F

fold

bonnet brim
1 buckram

back of bonnet
1 buckram

eyes
cut 2 green
(main part)
2 small white
2 small black dots
(all in felt)

COUSIN RIBBY

206

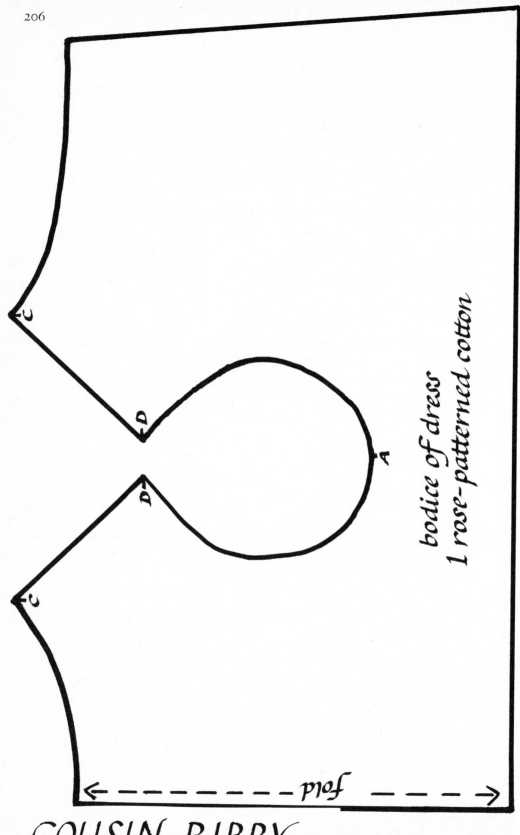

bodice of dress
1 rose-patterned cotton

fold

COUSIN RIBBY

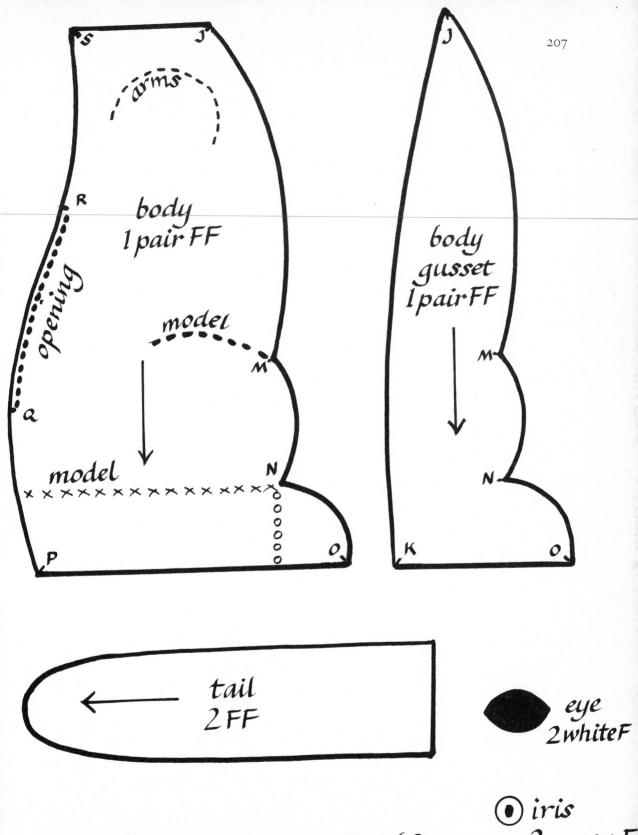

207

body
1 pair FF

opening

arms

model

model
× × × × × × × × × × × × × ×

body
gusset
1 pair FF

tail
2 FF

eye
2 white F

⊙ iris
2 green F

MOPPET & MITTENS

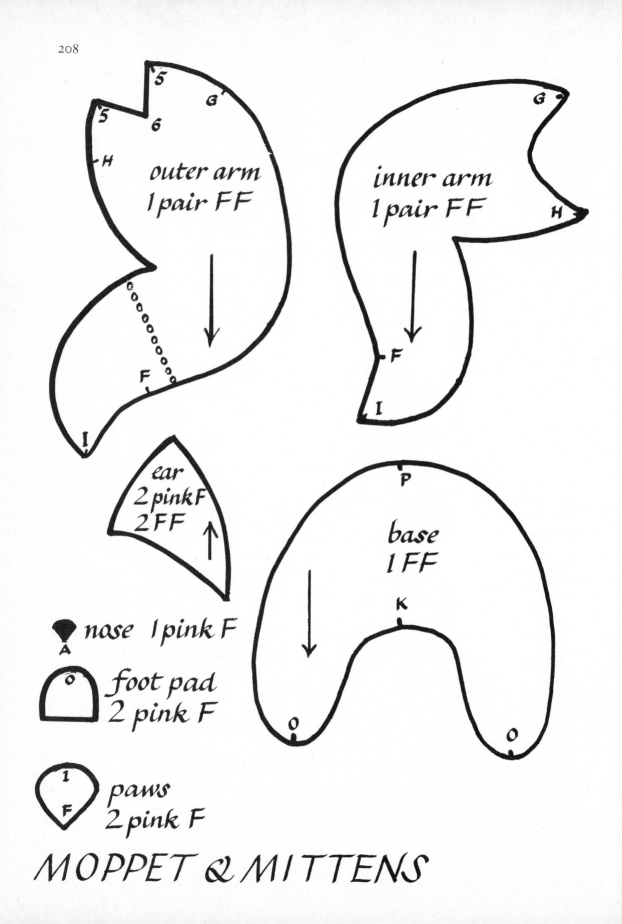

outer arm
1 pair FF

inner arm
1 pair FF

ear
2 pink F
2 FF

base
1 FF

nose 1 pink F

foot pad
2 pink F

paws
2 pink F

MOPPET & MITTENS

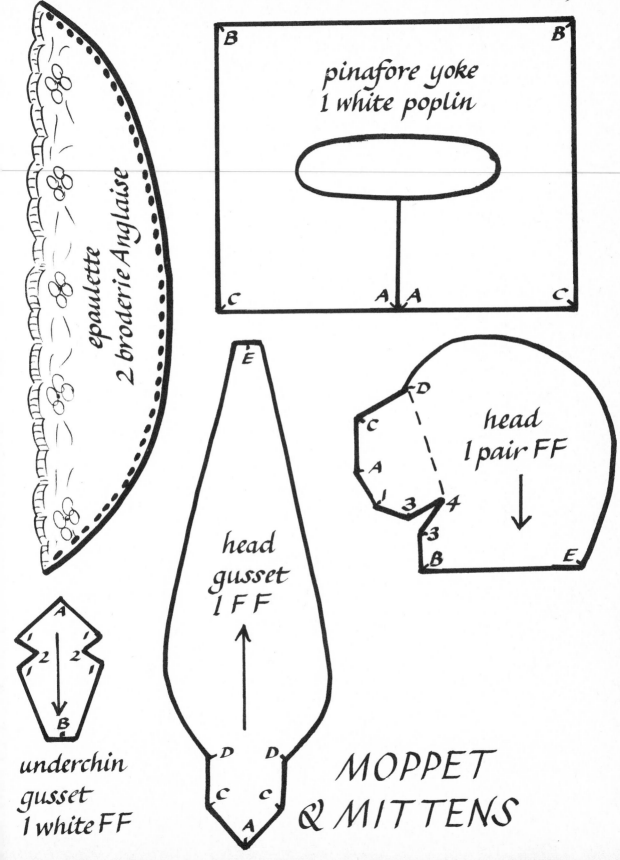

209

epaulette
2 broderie Anglaise

pinafore yoke
1 white poplin

B   B

C   A A   C

E

head
gusset
1 F F

head
1 pair FF

D

C

A

1 3 4

3

B   E

underchin
gusset
1 white FF

A

2 2

B

D D

C C

A

MOPPET
& MITTENS

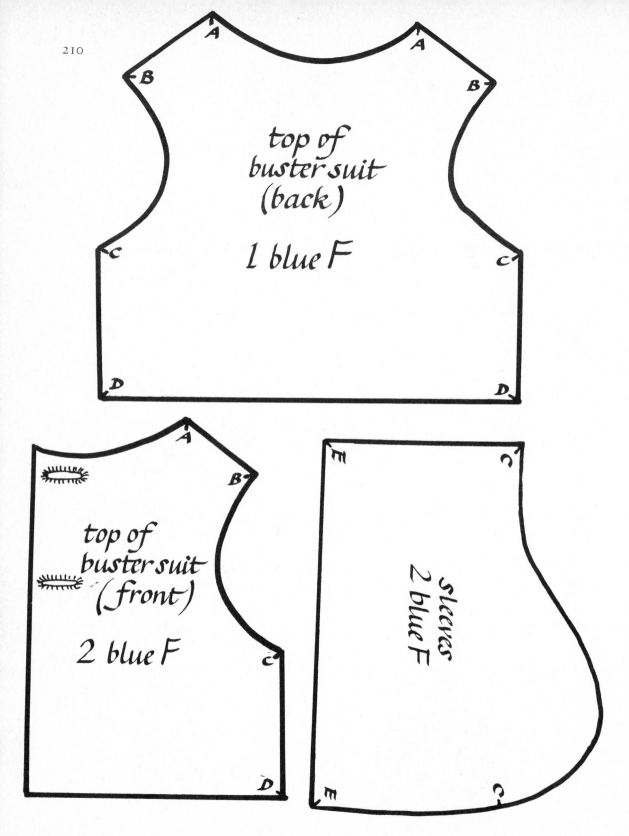

top of
buster suit
(back)

1 blue F

top of
buster suit
(front)

2 blue F

sleeves
2 blue F

TOM KITTEN

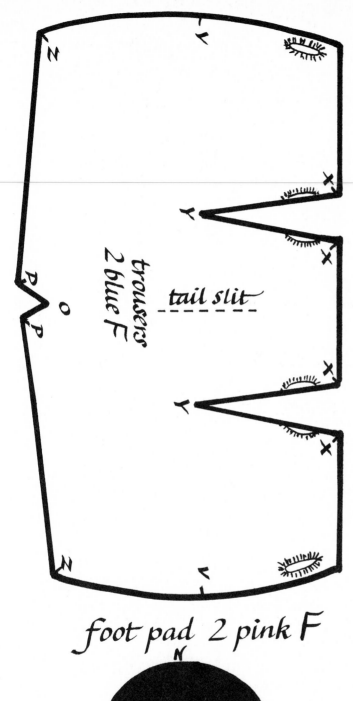

211

butterfly
1 brown F

trousers
2 blue F

tail slit

butterfly's
body
1 brown F

foot pad 2 pink F

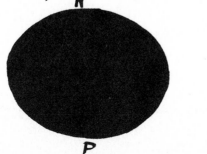

TOM KITTEN

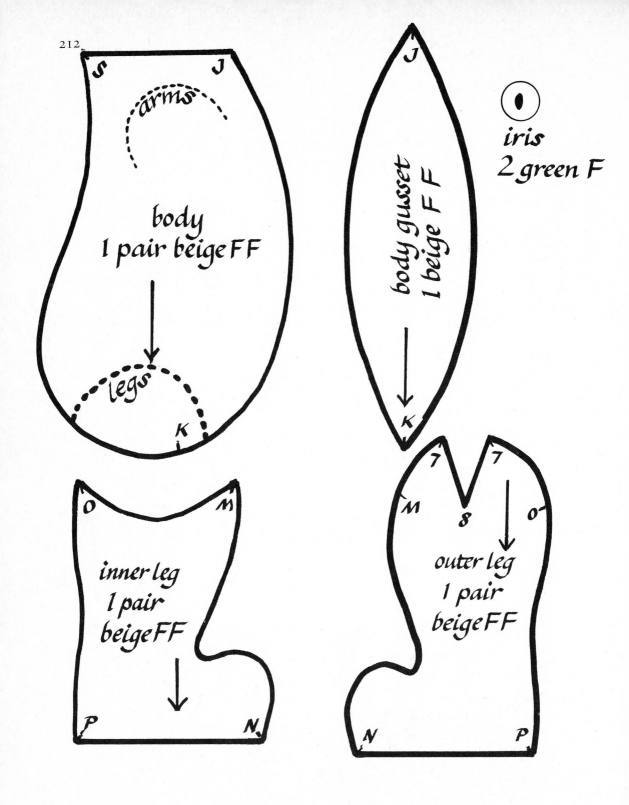

212

S   J

arms

body
1 pair beige FF

legs

K

J

body gusset
1 beige FF

K

iris
2 green F

O   M

inner leg
1 pair
beige FF

P   N

7   7

M   8   O

outer leg
1 pair
beige FF

N   P

TOM KITTEN

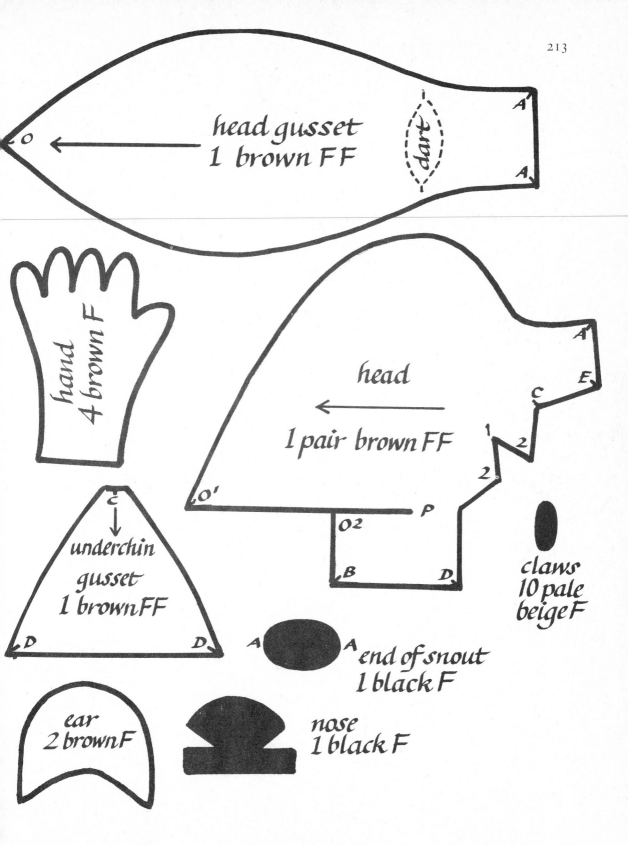

head gusset
1 brown FF

dart

O

A'

A

hand
4 brown F

head

1 pair brown FF

O'

A'

E

C

1

2

2

2

P

O2

B

D

claws
10 pale
beige F

underchin
gusset
1 brown FF

C

D

D

A

A

end of snout
1 black F

ear
2 brown F

nose
1 black F

MRS TIGGY-WINKLE

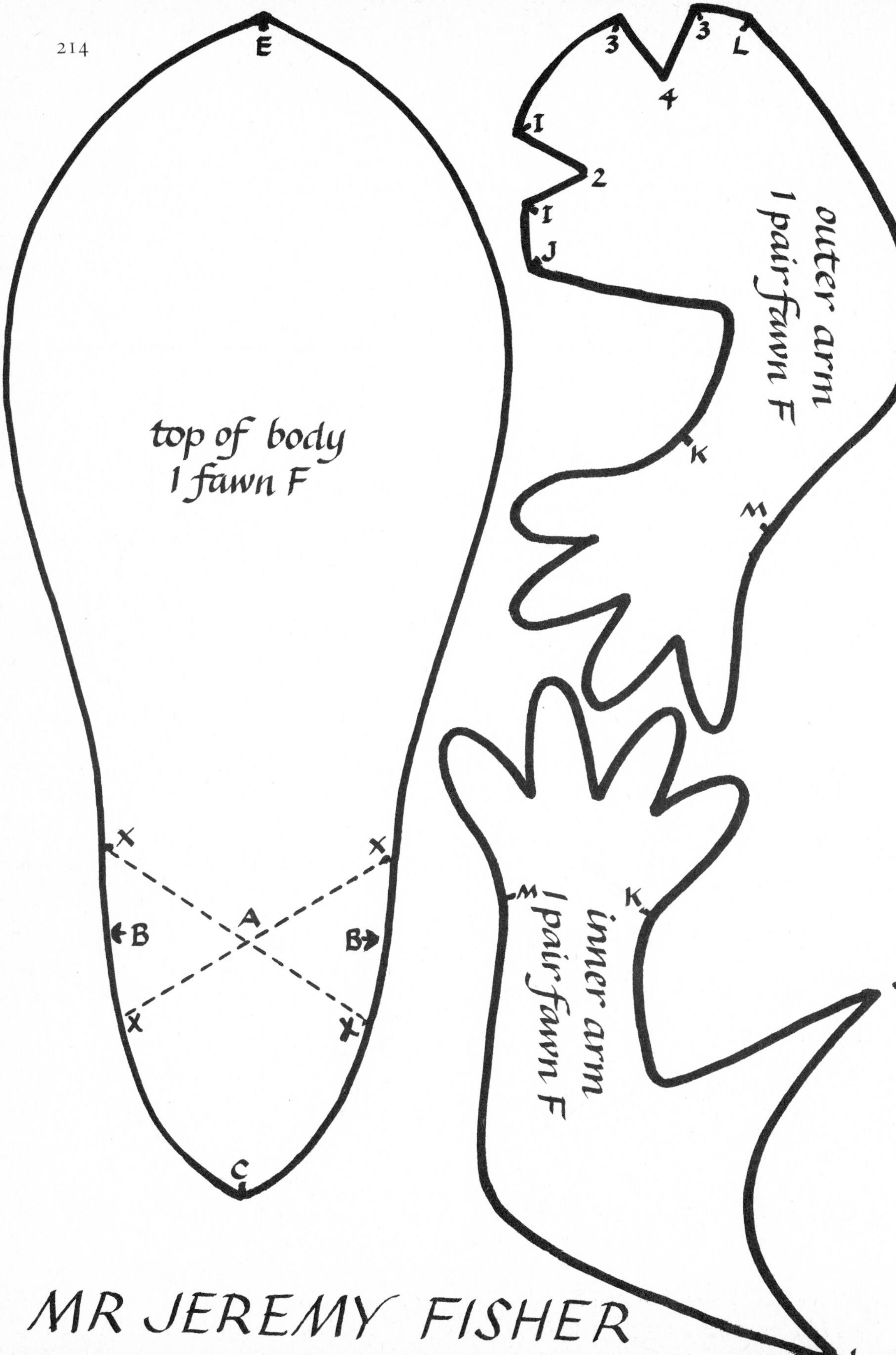

214

top of body
1 fawn F

E

X   X

←B   A   B→

X   X

C

3   3   L
4
I
2
I
J

outer arm
1 pair fawn F

K

M

inner arm
1 pair fawn F

M   K

J

L

MR JEREMY FISHER

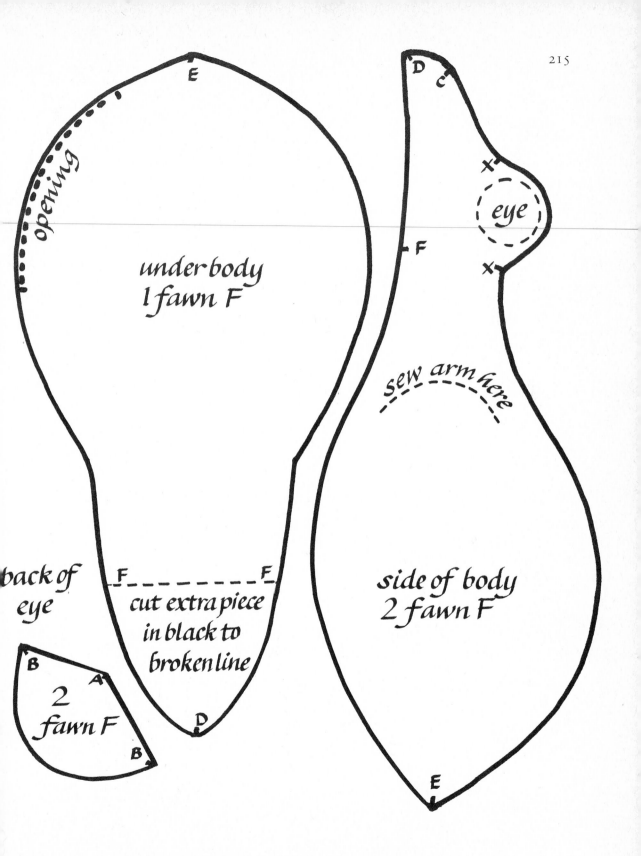

215

opening

under body
1 fawn F

D C

X

eye

F

X

sew arm here

back of
eye

F _ _ _ _ _ _ _ F

cut extra piece
in black to
broken line

B

A

2
fawn F

B

D

side of body
2 fawn F

E

MR JEREMY FISHER

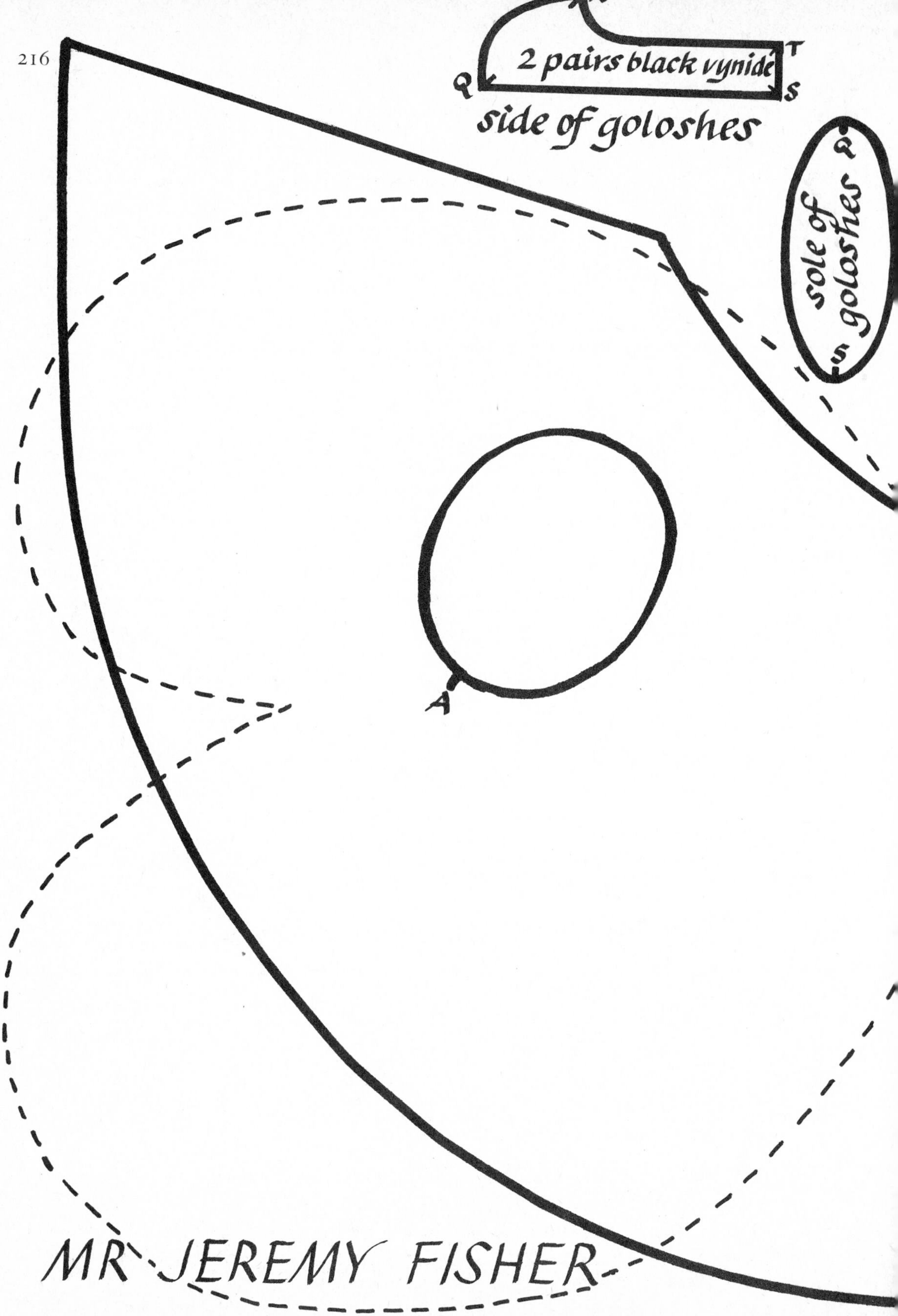

216

2 pairs black vynide

side of goloshes

sole of goloshes

R

Q

T

S

P

P

A

MR· JEREMY FISHER

sock 4 white stockinette

N P

O

macintosh

1 fawn plastic

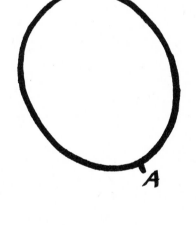

A

MR JEREMY FISHER

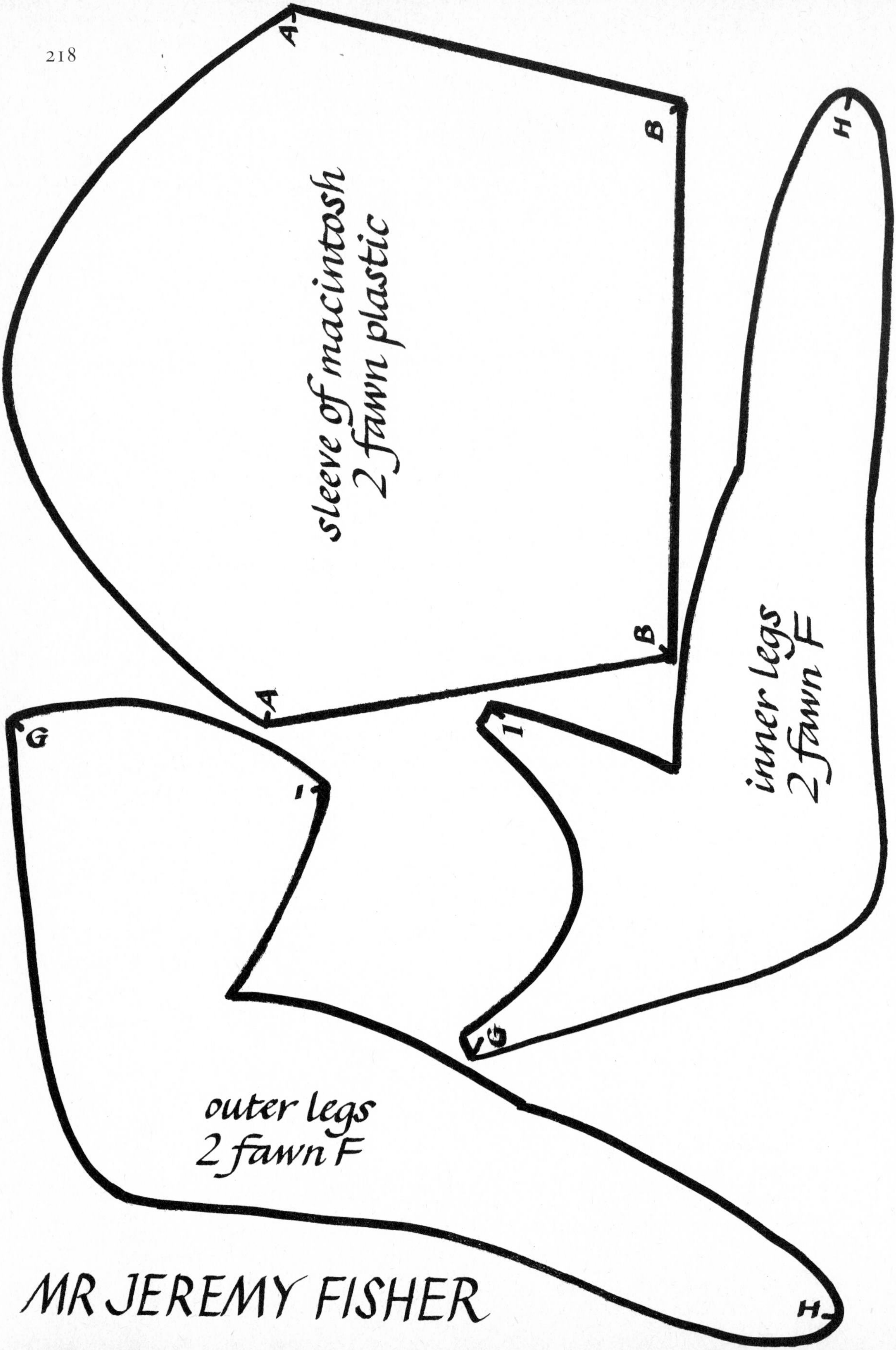

A

B

sleeve of macintosh
2 fawn plastic

H

B

A

inner legs
2 fawn F

G

I

I

G

outer legs
2 fawn F

H

MR JEREMY FISHER

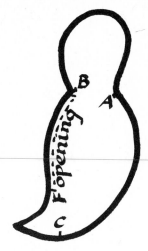

side of
body
2 yellow F

Opening

body gusset
1 yellow F

head
gusset
1 yellow F

wing
2 yellow F

base of
beak
1 dark
yellow F

top of beak
2 dark yellow F

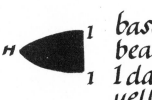

foot
2 card

JEMIMA PUDDLE-DUCK'S BABIES

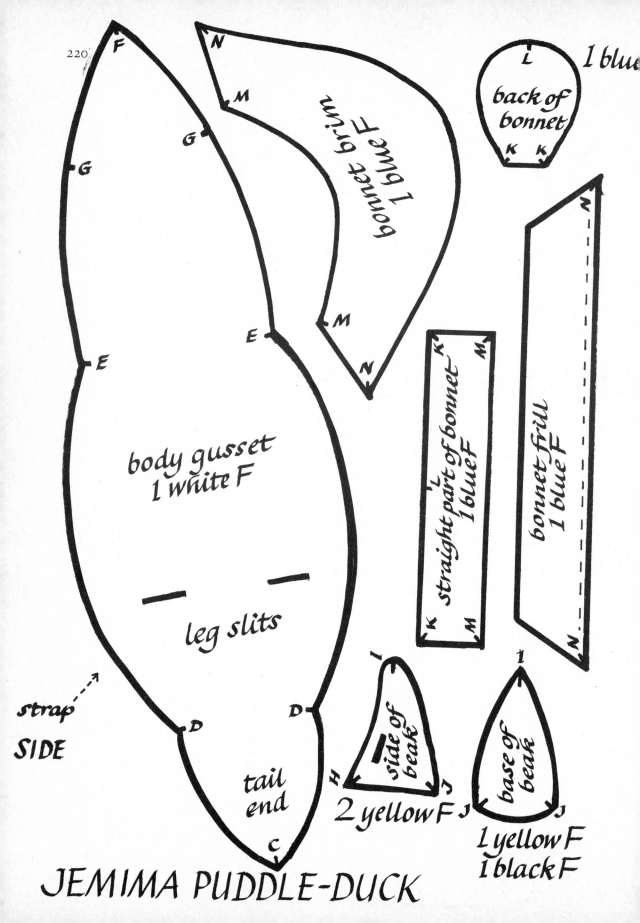

220

F

N

G

M

G

bonnet brim
1 blue F

L

1 blue

back of
bonnet

K K

E

E

M

N

body gusset
1 white F

N

K

M

straight part of bonnet
1 blue F

L

bonnet frill
1 blue F

K

M

leg slits

N

I

1

strap

SIDE

D

D

H

side of beak

J

base of beak

tail
end

C

2 yellow F

J

J

1 yellow F
1 black F

JEMIMA PUDDLE-DUCK

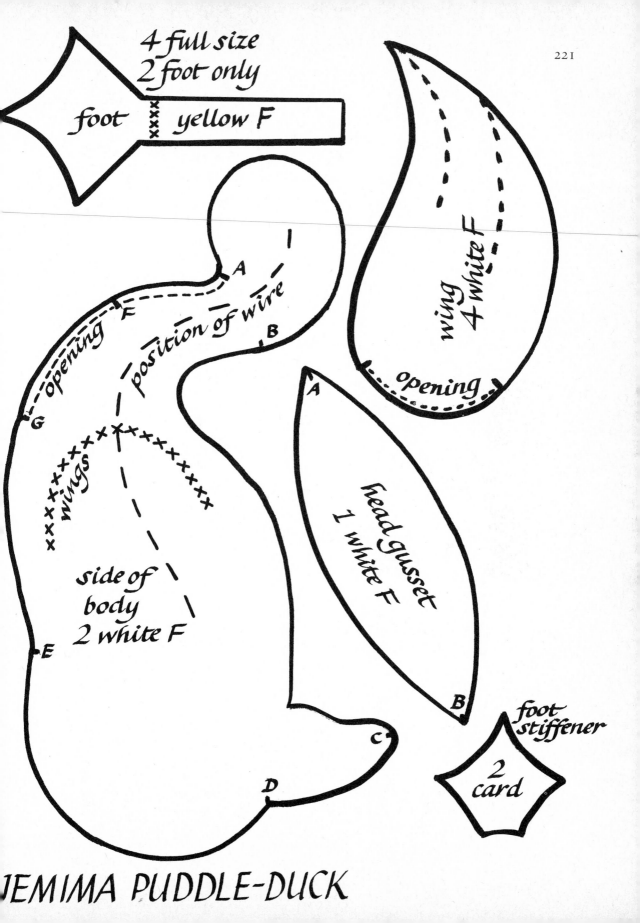

4 full size
2 foot only

foot

xxx yellow F xxx xxx

221

wing
4 white F

opening

A

F
opening

position of wire

B

G

x x x x x x wings x x x x x x x x x x x x x x x x x x

A

head gusset
1 white F

side of
body
2 white F

E

B

foot
stiffener

C

2
card

D

JEMIMA PUDDLE-DUCK

PART TWO
THE BASKETS

Introduction

Making baskets on a small scale is no more difficult—and no easier—than any other form of basketmaking. Due care must be taken, however, to obtain the appropriate sizes of material and certain techniques need to be followed. For it must be remembered that Beatrix Potter did not draw *toy* animals, toy furniture, toy baskets; everything was realistic, and in the case of the baskets they were all the kinds that could be found on any farm or in most households at the time the books were written. The baskets are essentially usable. They are believable too.

What *is* more difficult is to make the baskets look 'worn', look 'used'. For instance, Mrs. Tiggy-winkle's clothes basket, ample and capacious, bent over with many heavy weeks' washing; Hunca Munca's family bulging the stolen cradle out of shape; the basket the squirrels used to carry the huge egg to old Mr. Brown, misshapen by its weighty cargo. You cannot achieve this 'used' effect by simply making the basket rather haphazardly and in fact this point may not worry you so long as you make a fair imitation of the drawing in the book. But my brief was to 'make the baskets as near as possible' to the drawings and so I have suggested here and there doing a little violence—physical violence—to some of the baskets, directions which you can follow or not as you wish.

Another difficult point is that nearly all the original baskets would have been made of willow. White willow, brown willow or buff willow. But to obtain willow fine enough for these small baskets and in small enough quantities is not easy today and so the material used is mostly centre cane. This can be coloured slightly with wood dyes, and in some cases willow *working methods* have been introduced, as the resulting weave gives a more traditional appearance, even though very subtly. Anyone able to obtain willow will, of course, want to use the real thing.

It is interesting to study the baskets Beatrix Potter has drawn. Baskets were made, in those days, into different shapes for different purposes and not for fashion. And each basket has been chosen for the good reason that it was the kind of basket that *would* be used. And each basket adds something to the character of the animal. Which is why it is so important in making these miniatures to really try to copy the original and not just make any old round, oval or square basket as we know them today.

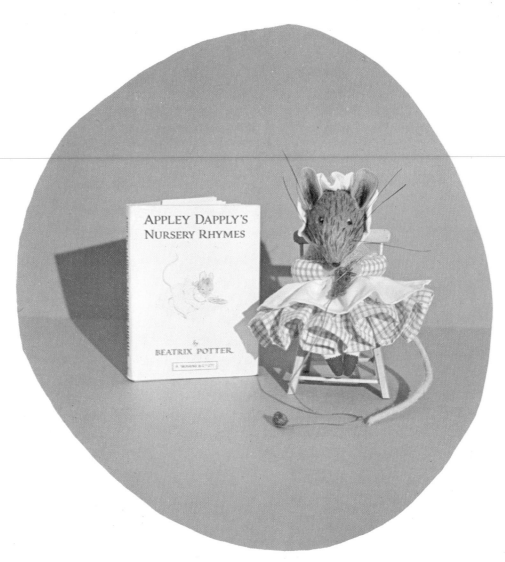

You know the old woman who lived in a
   shoe?
And had so many children she didn't know
what to do?

I think if she lived in a little shoe-house—
That little old woman was surely a mouse!

Appley Dapply's Nursery Rhymes

Hunca Munca has got the
cradle, and some of Lucinda's
clothes.

The Tale of Two Bad Mice

Materials, Tools and Preparation

Materials

As I have already said, most of the baskets used in Beatrix Potter's day would have been made of *willow*, either white willow, which is stripped willow, 'brown' willow, which is willow with its rough skin left on, or willow that has been boiled with its skin on, then peeled, resulting in the familiar tan or 'buff' willow. If you are lucky enough to be able to obtain such willows, from which you will only want to use short lengths from the tops of the finest rods, then you will achieve a more realistic effect than those who can only obtain cane.

But for most of us, *centre cane*,* easily obtainable, will have to suffice, and we must use our ingenuity to obtain as good a likeness of the artist's drawing as we can. Raffia too is introduced for some of the work.

What *is* important is that whatever material you use, willow, cane or raffia, it must be of the appropriate thickness for the size of basket being made. Fig. 94 gives the approximate sizes of cane used, and if other material is substituted care should be taken to use a similar size.

Tools

Since the material used is so fine, most of the tools required will be found in the home. You will need:

A pair of scissors with 4–6-inches (10–15 cm) blades for cutting lengths of cane.

A pair of wire-cutters (similar to a pair of basketmaker's side-cutters) for trimming.

A very sharp knife, such as a Stanley knife No. 199, for pointing the ends of stakes and for cutting cardboard.

A pair of round-nosed pliers for squeezing stakes when bending up.

A stabbing awl, known to a basketmaker as a bodkin (this is a must) (Plate 21, page 258).

* In some counties, centre cane is referred to as reeds, or rattan, but today all craft workers will know what is meant by these names.

A block of wood about 6–7 inches (15–18 cm) long (balsa wood is ideal) to use as a work board (Plate 16, page 238).

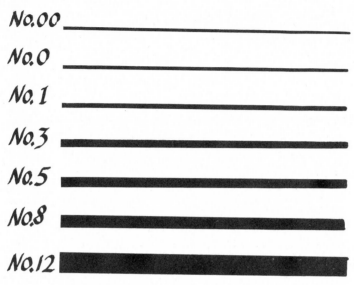

No. 00

No. 0

No. 1

No. 3

No. 5

No. 8

No. 12

Fig. 94 Approximate sizes of cane

Also a small sponge, an old towel, a few small clothes pegs, a tape measure, a ruler, some adhesive tape, glass-paper, pencil, possibly some light wood water dye and some clear varnish or gloss polyurethane and a brush to apply it with.

Preparation

Any dressmaker or embroideress will take care in the preparation of her materials and will study the directions before starting work. It is a curious fact that the beginner in basketry is seized with an immediate urge to get started, and since the cane being used for these small baskets is so fine, it is more than likely that many will try to skip the preliminaries and start work without due care and preparation.

CANE. Always buy the best quality you can obtain. 'Blue tie' or 'red tie' are the better grades. Cane should never be used dry, but on the other hand, over-soaking of cane does spoil the appearance. The cane used for these baskets is mostly Nos. 3 to 000; these are very fine and only need dipping in water, then wrapping in a damp towel, leaving them there for 15 minutes or so. Should any cane not be used up, take care to let it dry out overnight or it may develop spots. Only damp sufficient for immediate use. Thicker cane, such as No. 5 and 8, should be soaked in water for about 5–8 minutes before using.

It is a good idea to keep a damp sponge beside you while working, as the warmth of one's hands tends to dry the cane out all too quickly. A frequent wiping with the sponge will keep the cane supple.

RAFFIA. Raffia comes in various forms. There is the good old-fashioned *garden bass or bast*, which is very difficult to obtain these days. If you can find any, then it is simple to prepare it. Dip it in water, shake well and hang up to dry. This will straighten it. When using it wipe each strand as you need it with a damp cloth. Never work with it really damp, as it will shrink on drying and the work will look loose and untidy.

Then there is the *treated garden raffia*, found in most garden sundriesmen's shops, and usually sold in small hanks quite cheaply. This is delightful to use and needs no preparation or soaking at all. If very creased, it helps if you hold it over a steaming kettle for a few minutes to straighten.

You can also obtain *dyed raffia* from handicraft shops, but the colours are usually rather strong and I could not find one suitable for Squirrel Nutkin's basket. If you do use it, do not soak it, but iron each strand to open it out.

And finally there is artificial raffia, such as 'Raffene' which is very soft, in continuous lengths and again, needs no damping or ironing at all.

RUSHES. Anyone visiting the country in summer cannot fail to see the short tufty meadow rush, growing about 2–3 feet (60–90 cm) high. You can see it in ditches, in clumps on boggy land, in woods and meadows.

These soft rushes—and make sure you have the soft rush and not the hard one which looks almost identical—are ideal for plaiting and are at their best in June, July and August.

Cut well down, getting as long pieces as you can; lay them in the shade for a week or so to dry out. They are then ready for use, though if allowed to dry too much you may need to re-damp them by wrapping them in a damp towel until pliable.

Stockists

Cane, raffia, Raffene
> From most handicraft stores. Garden raffia can also be obtained from garden sundriesmen shops.
> By post:
> Jacobs, Young & Westbury, Bridge Road, Haywards Heath, Sussex.

Working Methods

If you already have a knowledge of simple basketry technique, then you will only have to turn to the individual directions to make whichever basket you choose. If however you are a complete beginner, you will need to learn some basic working methods, and since in basketry you do indeed 'make' the fabric, you have to actually start on a basket—it is difficult to practise the methods otherwise. I suggest therefore that you read through the working methods and then begin on the easiest basket of all—Flopsy's blackberrying basket. That will give you the feel of the material.

The base of any basket should ideally be woven, but to make the directions simple enough for beginners and quite young children to follow, I have introduced wood bases for a few of the baskets. If later, when you have mastered a woven base, you would like to remake rather more realistically, you will be well satisfied with the results.

In each weave there is a rhythm, a repetitive movement, as one has in a knitting pattern. Once memorised the process is simple.

But first a few basketry terms:

Stakes: the uprights, or the cross pieces in the base.
Weavers: the canes used for weaving round the stakes.
Byestakes: additional canes to strengthen the stakes, not always necessary.
Weaves: methods of producing the fabric of the basket.
Stroke: 'stitch', movement.
Border: the finishing stroke at top of basket.
Footing: the commencing stroke below a wood base.

WOOD BASES

The bases required are so small that it is unlikely you would ever find them ready-made. They can be made simply at home. Alternatively you could take a drawing of the sizes required to a handicraft shop who would no doubt cut them for you.

To make the bases

The shapes of the wood bases for the blackberrying baskets and for Hunca-Munca's cradle and birdcage are given in actual size (Figs. 102, 104, 105 and 106). Trace out the shapes and the position of the holes and transfer to plywood ⅛ inch (3 mm) thick. Cut out with fret-saw. Pierce the holes with a drill or a fine gimlet. If this is done slightly on a slant, it helps to position the stakes. The slant should be an outward one. You will need to make the holes big enough to take No. 1 cane (No. 3 for the cradle) when damp (it swells slightly). Smooth the edges of the bases with glass-paper, especially the corners of the square base which are best rounded off, and the point on the cradle base where the oval joins the straight edge.

METHODS

Footing for wood bases

1 Cut the stakes as directed in the individual directions for the basket.
2 Stand the stakes in a tumbler containing water to a depth of approx 1½–2 inches (4–5 cm) for 3 minutes (Plate 19, page 244).
3 Insert the dry ends of the stakes into the holes, pulling them through until only 1½ inches (4 cm) of the damp ends protrude on the other side—the underside of the base.
4 Hold the base with damp ends uppermost, in left hand. * Take any stake (A) and bend it in front of the next (B) to the right, behind the next (C) and let it rest there, on the inside of the circle of stakes** (Fig. 95). Repeat from * to ** with B, C, etc., in turn all the way round, easing up the first few stakes to enable you to insert the last two or three stakes into the right position (Plate 11, page 232). Trim any surplus ends, particularly at corners of the square base.

This footing is also used in some of the baskets as a border, known as a simple trac border.

Randing

This is the simplest of the weaves. The weaver is taken in and out of the stakes, each row coming alternately in front of and behind each stake (Fig. 96). This is achieved by (1) having an uneven number of stakes (as is usual in a wood base), or (2) if an even number has to be used, by using two weavers.

    1 USING ONE WEAVER. Place the tip of the weaver behind a stake with its end pointing to the left. Take it in front of and behind stakes alternately. Use the fingers of the left hand to control the position of the stakes.

        To *join* in another weaver, simply cut off the old end so that it rests behind a stake and points to the right. Lay another piece above it behind the same stake, the end pointing to the left (Fig. 96, page 233).

2　USING TWO WEAVERS. Start one weaver as above, work one round but do not pass the starting point. Add the second weaver behind one stake to the right of the starting point and work one round but do not overtake the first weaver. Work them in turn; do not allow them to pass each other.

To *finish* both methods, leave the weaver/s behind the same stakes from which start was made.

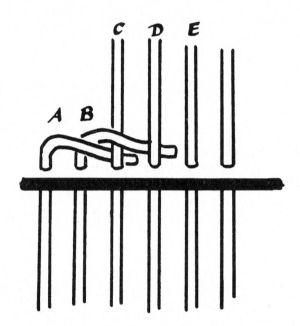

Fig. 95　Footing for wood base

Slewing

This is randing with two or more weavers worked behind the same stakes. It was much used at one time to cheapen the cost of making, since it is quicker to work (Fig. 97, page 233, and Plate 31, page 274).

1　Start as in randing, with one weaver. In front of one, behind one, bring to the front.

Plate 10 (*Facing page*) *Back left to right:* the birdcage, Mrs. Tittlemouse's basket, Mrs. Tiggy-winkle's hassock. *Front left to right:* Cousin Ribby's visiting basket, Hunca Munca's cradle, Mrs. Tiggy-winkle's clothes basket

Plate 9 *Back left to right:* Mopsy's basket, Flopsy's basket (supported by two of the Flopsy Bunnies), Benjamin Bunny's marketing basket. *Front left to right:* Cotton-tail's basket, Mr. Jeremy Fisher's fishing creel.

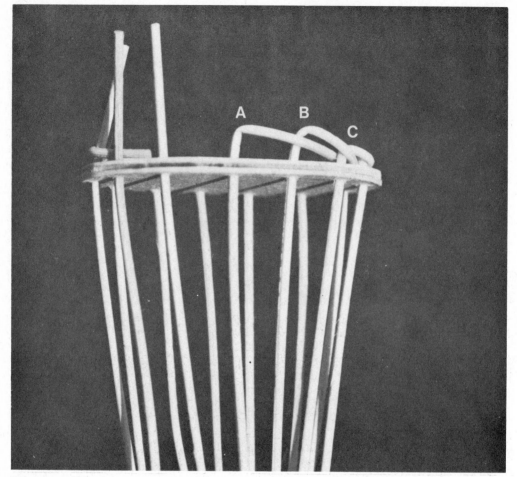

Plate 11 Footing—showing the stroke and the finish

2 Lay a second weaver behind the last stake used, take in front of one, behind one, now using both weavers at once.

3 If more weavers are to be used, lay in another and repeat the above and so on, so that the weavers are laid in in steps.

Care must be taken not to twist the weavers at any stage.

To join, as in randing.

To finish, as in randing, but gradually in steps.

Pairing

This is used mostly in round and oval bases (Fig. 98, page 234).

1 Using two weavers, in consecutive spaces between stakes, take the left-hand weaver, in front of the next stake and bring it out in the next space.

Mrs. Tittlemouse went on her way to a distant storeroom, to fetch cherry-stones and thistle-down seed for dinner.

The Tale of Mrs. Tittlemouse

When they had taken refuge in the coal-cellar he resumed the conversation: "I confess I am a little disappointed . . ."

The Tale of Johnny Town-Mouse

2 Repeat with the left-hand weaver each time, taking only this one stroke at a time.

With practice you will be able to hold both weavers in your fingers at once and, with a twisting movement, work the pairing very quickly.

Fitching
See page 234 and Fig. 99.

Waling
This is a strengthening weave and is invariably used at the foot of a basket, above a wood or woven base, and again at the top of the side weaving to firm the work together before turning down the border.

1 Take three lengths of weaving cane (A, B and C); insert the tips between four consecutive stakes (1, 2, 3 and 4) leaning each tip against the stake to the left and pointing to the left (Fig. 100a, page 235).
2 Tie a piece of string or mark the tip of stake No. 1. This is important.
3 Take the left-hand weaver (A), in front of stakes 2 and 3 and over weavers

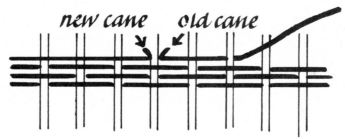

Fig. 96 Randing

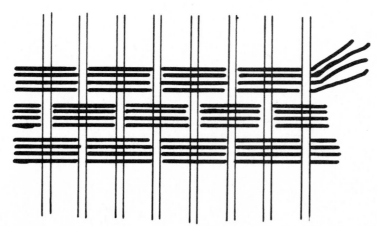

Fig. 97 Slewing

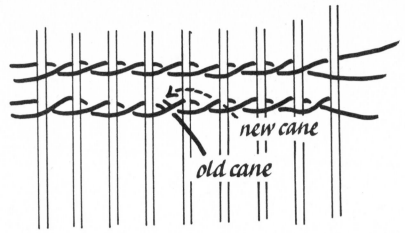

Fig. 98 Pairing

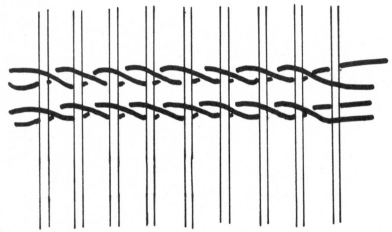

Fig. 99 Fitching

B and C, behind stake 4, and bring it out to the front. You will see that it comes between the next two stakes (Fig. 100b).

4 Repeat with the left-hand weaver which is now B, doing exactly the same movement as before but one stake further on. When completed the weavers will be in C, A, B position (Fig. 100c).

5 Repeat with left-hand weaver which is now C, and when completed, the weavers will be in the A, B, C position again (Fig. 100d).

This triple movement is repeated right round the base, until the *weaver that you are using* reaches the left-hand side of stake 1, the one you marked.

You then work what is known as the step-up or changeover, so that the weaving makes a complete round and does not spiral. (In working very small baskets such as the blackberrying baskets, this really is not very important, but for first-class work, it is always considered a good point if the step-up is worked. It is perfectly simple if you think on the A, B, C basis.)

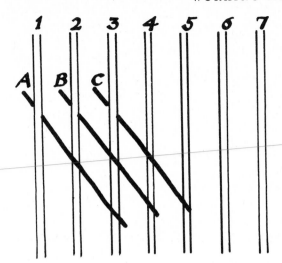

Fig. 100a Waling

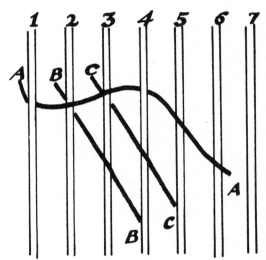

Fig. 100b Waling

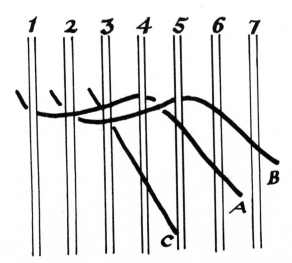

Fig. 100c Waling

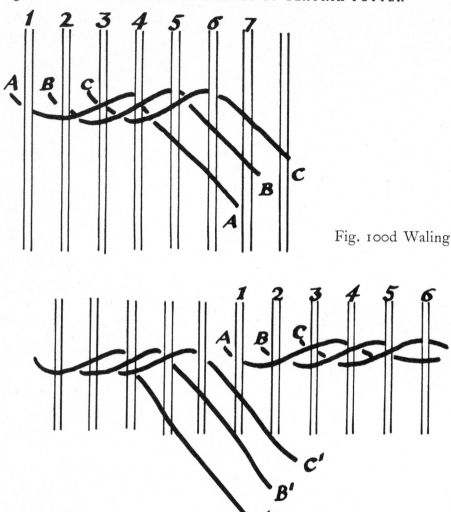

Fig. 100d Waling

Fig. 100e Waling—step-up

6 Call the weaver in your hand C, and continue to use it, taking it in front of
   two more stakes, behind the next and leave it (Fig. 100e). Go back for the
   next weaver to the left, call it B, take it over two stakes and bring to the
   front. Go back for the last one, A, and do the same again. You have simply
   reversed the process—instead of working left to right, you have worked
   right to left. The whole point rests on knowing when you have reached the
   stake marked 1.

7 To finish off waling. Again in a very small basket, you can finish off
   by simply pushing the right-hand weaver through two previous rows of
   waling and bring to the front where the weaver is cut off, allowing it to rest
   against another stake.

   The correct way to finish off can only be achieved if the step-up has been
   worked correctly. On reaching the starting point on the last round, take the

Plate 12 Waling—the position of the weavers

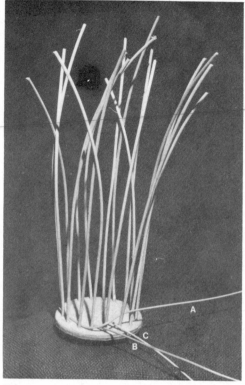

Plate 13
Waling—moving the first weaver

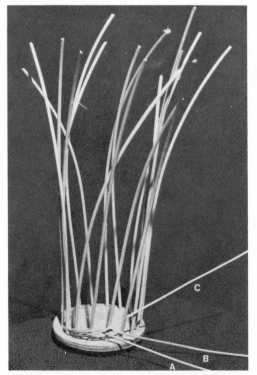

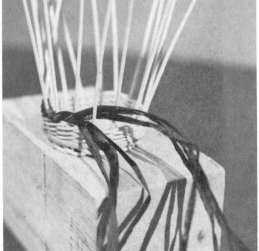

Plate 15 Pairing with twisted Raffene

Plate 14
Waling—the position after the first stroke

usual movement with the left-hand weaver and leave it; take the usual movement with the next weaver and thread it under one row of the previous round,
and leave it in front. Take the last weaver and thread it under two rows of the
previous round. Trim them all off on the outside of basket, letting each
weaver rest against a stake (Plate 16).

Bordering
First see that the weaving is level; if it is not, tap gently with edge of a ruler or a
pair of scissors. Bordering requires very supple stakes or a kinked ugly finish will
result. Stand the work upside down in a bowl of water so that the stakes are
soaked right up to the top of the weaving.

With such small baskets, only very simple borders are possible and the

Plate 16 Waling—three rounds completed

Plate 17
Start of the rope
border

simple trac border (see Footing) is used on several of them. Some of the 'stouter' baskets however call for something bolder and instead of the usual three-rod border, which is not easy to follow from written directions, I am including a version of the rope border which I found in a very old book, published in 1907, which seems to me to be very simple and gives almost the same effect.

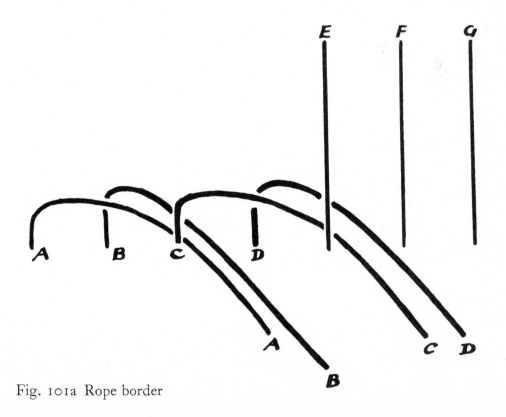

Fig. 101a Rope border

Fig. 101b Rope border

Fig. 101c Rope border

Regard the stakes as A, B, C, D, E, F and G from left to right.

1   Bend A to the right in front of B and behind C. Bend B down on top of A
   (Fig. 101a).

2   Bend C to the right in front of D and behind E. Bend D down on top of C.
   There are now two pairs of bent-over stakes.

3   * Take the upper one of the left-hand pair (B), pass it in front of E, behind F
   and bend E down upon it. Again you have two pairs. Take the upper one of
   the left-hand pair as before (D), in front of F, behind G and bring F down
   upon it (Fig. 101b).

4   Repeat from * until you reach the starting place, when you must pull out the
   first four spokes A, B, C and D, as the beginning is a 'false' start. Pulled out,
   they can now be worked in as the rest of the round.

5   To complete the border, take A and push it in at the opening X; take C and
   so on all round, leaving the stakes on the inside of the basket to be trimmed
   off (Fig. 101c).

HANDLES

These are worked in different ways and instructions are given in the individual
directions.

SHAPING

The experienced basket maker will be able to manipulate the stakes satisfactorily by the pressure of his or her fingers, but the beginner usually welcomes a little assistance. For a round upright basket, a bottle, a cylinder such as the cardboard inside a roll of toilet paper, anything that is the right size, will help to keep the stakes straight, or in the case of a sloping basket, a small orange, or an apple, stood inside the stakes will give the required angle (Plate 18). It is only feasible

Plate 18
An apple helps in shaping the sides

to work a few rounds with such assistance, after which the stakes should be manageable.

FINISHING

You may decide to dye or varnish the basket to match the colour in Beatrix Potter's drawings as nearly as you can, but before doing so, the basket should be 'finished'.

First trim all ends of cane with a slanting cut with the sidecutters, so that each end rests neatly against the stake it is leaning on. Next, sponge the basket over with a damp cloth and then singe off any 'whiskers' the cane may have developed. This is best done over a smokeless flame, such as a little methylated spirits in a tin lid. For safety, stand the tin lid in a saucer of water. Care must be taken to do this operation quickly or singe marks will result. The basket is then ready for any dyeing or varnishing. *Do not singe raffia or Raffene*

Water wood stains are very satisfactory for any slight colouring you want to do. Always try a little on a spare piece of cane.

Some baskets too are improved by a coating of clear varnish or a gloss polyurethane. Mention is made of these in individual directions.

Important

In the directions for making the baskets which follow, it will be assumed that the instructions for preparation of material already mentioned will be followed. Only occasional reminders are given.

Also to avoid unnecessary repetition, methods of working will be referred to by page and figure numbers.

The amount of cane required for each basket is necessarily approximate, since breakages will occur from time to time and some people will weave more tightly than others. The quantities are so small that they have been given in length rather than weight as is more usual. The measurements given in brackets are the nearest convenient metric equivalents.

Using Wood Bases

THE BLACKBERRYING BASKETS

As you will read in *The Tale of Peter Rabbit*, Flopsy, Mopsy and Cotton-tail went gathering blackberries and each had a basket. You can see two of these on pages 11 and 58 of *Peter Rabbit*.

The three baskets I suggest are very simple to make and are shown in Plate 9, page 231. They are an easy way of practising the basic methods before trying the slightly more complicated ones.

FLOPSY'S BASKET

Approximate size: height (excluding handle), $2\frac{1}{2}$ inches (6 cm).
width top, $3\frac{1}{4}$ inches (8 cm).
base, $2\frac{1}{2}$ inches (6 cm) diameter.

Materials

1 wood base, $2\frac{1}{2}$ inches (6 cm) diameter 17 holes (Fig. 102).
17 stakes No. 1 cane, 10 inches (26 cm) long.
3 lengths of No. 0 cane for bottom waling, 30 inches (76 cm) each.
3 lengths of No. 0 cane for top waling, 36 inches (90 cm) each.
A skein of Raffene No. 47 Brown, for sides.
1 piece of No. 12 cane for handle, 12 inches (31 cm) long.
A large-eyed needle.

Method

1 Trace the outline of the base and position of holes (Fig. 102), and cut out (page 229).
2 Prepare stakes (page 226); insert into base leaving $1\frac{1}{4}$ inches (3·2 cm) of the damp end of stakes protruding.
3 Work footing (pages 229 and 230, Fig. 95).

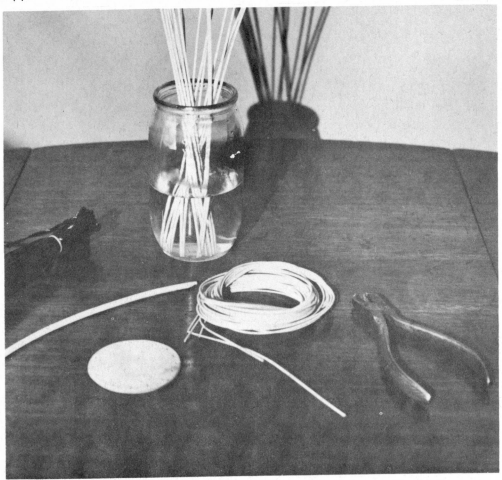

Plate 19 The materials needed for Flopsy's basket

4 Turn base over and work three rounds of waling (page 235, Figs. 100a, b and c). An apple placed between the stakes will help to develop the outward flow (Plate 18).

5 Draw off from the skein of Raffene four lengths, 5 yards (4·5 metres) each. Snip the ends so that the strands are separate.

6 Find the centre of the lengths and loop over any one of the stakes; bring all strands out to the front. Now using each set of four strands alternately, pair (Fig. 98, page 234) with Raffene, lightly twisting the strands between each stroke to form a kind of cord. Keep the stakes splayed out a little (Plate 15, page 237).

7 Stop randing when there is only about 6 inches (15 cm) Raffene left. Work back so that the finishing off is done over the commencing stake. Divide the strands into two or three and thread each in turn through the needle, and weave the ends away neatly and securely. Raffene is very springy and even

TIMMY and Goody Tiptoes stored their
nuts in hollow stumps near the tree
where they had built their nest.

The Tale of Timmy Tiptoes

"A NNA Maria," said the old man rat,
"Anna Maria, make me a kitten dumpling
roly-poly pudding for my dinner."

The Tale of Samuel Whiskers

A nna Maria on the run, with
big bundles on a little wheelbarrow . . .

The Tale of Samuel Whiskers

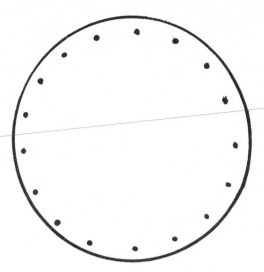

Fig. 102 Base for Flopsy's basket

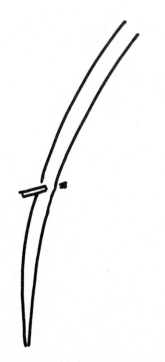

Fig. 103a Handle for Flopsy's basket

after a few stitches, a cut end will work its way out. It is best to tie the ends together firmly on the inside and trim off close.

8 Work three rounds of waling firmly. Finish off.

9 The stakes are now prepared for the working of the rope border. Care must be taken however to keep the Raffene from becoming wet. The basket should be turned upside down and stood in a jug with just sufficient water to

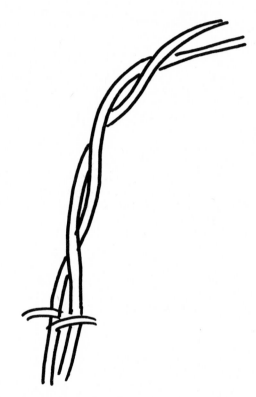

Fig. 103b Handle for Mopsy's basket

reach the border and no more. After 2 or 3 minutes remove and shake surplus water off before turning the basket up the right way. Work rope border (pages 239–40, Fig. 101a, b and c).

10 Sharpen ends of handle to a point. Push the bodkin into a bar of soap (to grease it), and then down through the border and waling, beside one of the stakes. Care must be taken not to split the Raffene, as you push the bodkin down to the bottom waling. Now push the tip of the cane in the soap and slide carefully into the passage you have just made. Repeat on the other side of the basket beside the stake most nearly opposite.

11 No self-respecting basket is complete without the pegging of the handle. Using the bodkin again, pierce the handle cane between the rows of waling, and into the hole made, slide a piece of fine cane (Fig. 103a). Push it through and trim it off close inside and outside the basket. Repeat the other side. This will hold almost any weight and is a good way of mending a broken basket!

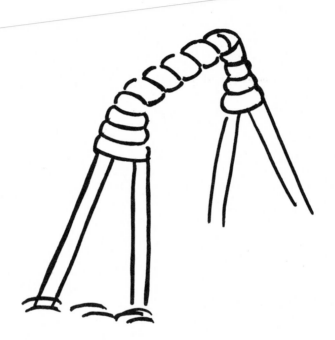

Fig. 103c Handle for Cotton-tail's basket

MOPSY'S BASKET

On page 16 of *Peter Rabbit* you will see that the colour of the 'waisted' basket is not quite consistent; you may wish to use a lighter or darker dye to get the shade you prefer.

Approximate size: height, $3\frac{3}{4}$ inches (9 cm) without handle.
                    width top, 4 inches (10 cm).
                    width base, $2\frac{3}{4} \times 1\frac{1}{2}$ inches (7×4 cm).

Materials
    1 wood base, $2\frac{3}{4} \times 1\frac{1}{2}$ inches (7×4 cm); 15 holes.
    15 stakes No. 1 cane, 7 inches (18 cm) long.

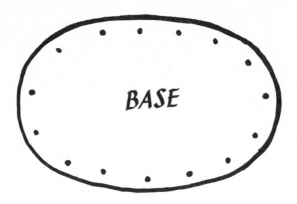

Fig. 104 Base for Mopsy's basket

15 bye-stakes No. 1 cane, 4¾ inches (12 cm) long.
3 lengths of No. 0 cane for bottom wailing, 30 inches (76 cm) each.
900 cm (10 yards) No. 0 cane for randing.
3 lengths of No. 0 cane for top waling, 47 inches (120 cm) each.
2 pieces of No. 8 cane for handle, 11 inches (28 cm) each.
A spot of clear adhesive. Some water dye to stain.

Method

1 Trace the outline of the base and position of holes (Fig. 104) and cut out (page 229).
2 Prepare stakes (page 226); insert into base leaving 1½ inches (4 cm) of the damp end protruding.
3 Work footing (pages 229 and 230, Fig. 95).
4 Turn base over and work three rounds of waling (pages 233 and 235, Figs. 100a, b and c).
5 Take a length of the No. 0 cane and commence randing (page 233, Fig. 96), taking care at the narrow ends of the base where the stakes should be gently manipulated to help them to lean outwards. Continue until the work measures 1½ inches (4 cm) from the base.
6 Now insert the bye-stakes, one beside each stake, pushing the bye-stake well down to reach the bottom waling.
7 Continue randing two more rounds, regarding each stake and bye-stake as one.
8 Now the stakes and bye-stakes are separated, giving an even number of stakes. Insert a second weaver (see page 230). Rand before and behind each stake and bye-stake using the bodkin if necessary to press the randing cane into position. After a round or two the stakes will even out; randing and

the shaping of the ends continue until the basket measures $2\frac{1}{2}$ inches (6·5 cm) from base. Finish the randing over the commencing stake.

9   Work three rounds of waling firmly. Check whether the top of weaving is level; if not, tap gently with edge of ruler.

10 Soak the remaining ends of stakes for 2 or 3 minutes and work a simple trac border. This is the same as the footing (page 229, Fig. 95). Trim, leaving each end leaning against a stake.

11 Soak handle canes for 2 or 3 minutes, then insert both on right of central side stake. Push into weaving for about 1 inch (2·5 cm). Twist one cane round the other about three times, then insert on opposite side of basket (Fig. 103b, page 246).

12 The handle cane is too fine to pierce satisfactorily for pegging. I suggest you use a spot of clear adhesive on the tips of the handle canes on the inside of basket.

13 Try a very little diluted light oak water wood stain on a little spare cane, to match the colour of the basket in the book.

COTTON-TAIL'S BASKET

Approximate size: height (excluding handle), $2\frac{3}{4}$ inches (7 cm).
top, $4\frac{1}{4} \times 3\frac{1}{4}$ inches (11 × 8 cm).
base, $3\frac{1}{4} \times 2\frac{1}{2}$ inches (8 × 6 cm).

Materials

1 wood base, $3\frac{1}{4} \times 2\frac{1}{2}$ inches (8 × 6 cm) with 17 holes (Fig. 105).
17 stakes No. 1 cane, 8 inches (20 cm) long.
6 lengths of No. 0 for top and bottom waling, 40 inches (102 cm) each.
1 length of lapping cane, 80 inches (200 cm).
2 handle canes No. 12 cane, $9\frac{1}{2}$ inches (24 cm) each and a length of raffia, for double handles.

OR

1 length of No. 12, $9\frac{1}{2}$ inches (24 cm) and one length of No. 0, 25 inches (64 cm) for single handle.

Method

1   Prepare stakes as in Flopsy's basket but damp $1\frac{3}{4}$ inches (4·5 cm) of the stakes.

2   Work footing and bottom waling, as in Flopsy's basket (Figs. 100a, b, c and d, pages 235–6). Aim at sloping all stakes slightly outwards.

3 Soak the lapping cane (which is very strong) for 10 minutes, and wrap in damp towel for another 10.

4 Make a slanting cut on one end of lapping cane and starting at the narrow end of base, rand (Fig. 96, page 233) for six rounds. Take care not to pull the stakes inwards. The corners should be bent outwards and a slight slope maintained particularly at the ends. Finish by cutting the cane on a slant over the start.

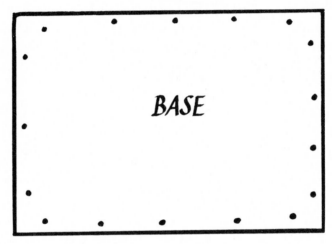

Fig. 105 Base for Cotton-tail's basket

5 Work three rounds of waling (Figs. 100a, b, c and d, pages 235–6). Finish off.

6 Hold basket upside down in water for 3 minutes.

7 Work a trac border, with a slight variation. Take any one stake, * bend it to the right, take it behind the next stake, in front of *two* stakes and behind the third. Taking the next stake to the right, repeat from * until you reach the starting point, when you ease up the first few turned down and fit the last ones into position. Trim off, allowing each stake to rest against another on inside of basket.

8 On page 11 of *The Tale of Peter Rabbit*, it seemed to me that the 'square' basket had only one handle but on page 58 there are definitely two. The colour plate opposite page 52 shows one handle, but I have shown two handles in Plate 9, page 231.

   Single handle. Take one piece of No. 12 cane (well soaked). Shorten one end by 2 inches and cut the ends to a slant; make a passage with a soaped bodkin down the left-hand side of the centre stake, insert the handle so that it reaches the bottom waling. Repeat on the other side of basket. Using a length of No. o cane, damped, thread it through the waling on either side of the handle, so that both ends face the front of basket. Now lace them across the handle, so that you have an open criss-cross (see colour plate opposite page 52). Thread through the waling on other side of basket and weave ends away neatly.

Double handle (Fig. 103c, page 247). Take both pieces of No. 12 cane, make sure they are exactly the same length and slant all four ends. Measure 4¼ inches (11 cm) up from the end, make a very cautious nick with the sharp knife, and measure the same distance up from the other end and make another nick. Do the same with the second handle. Insert handles, one beside 2nd and 4th side stakes (leaving one in the middle). Bend carefully at the nick, and insert the other ends on the other side.

Tie at the top, levelling the cornering of the handles. Bind the handles together with some raffia, threading the end away underneath. Peg the handles.

HUNCA MUNCA'S CRADLE

It wasn't really her cradle, of course, it came from the red brick doll's house. But there on page 48 of *The Tale of Two Bad Mice* sits Hunca Munca, a picture of contentment, her babies warm and snug in the cradle and she herself dressed up very grandly in the clothes she has purloined. Looking perhaps a trifle guilty but none-the-less, very proud.

The cradle is bulging with the large family and I have tried to capture something of this.

Approximate size: to top of hood including rockers, 4½ inches (11 cm).
             length, 6¼ inches (16 cm).
             width, 4 inches (10 cm).

Materials
    1 wood base (Fig. 106), 5½ × 3 inches (14 × 7·5 cm) with 19 holes.
    4 base stakes No. 3 cane, 17 inches (43 cm).
    5 base stakes No. 3 cane, 11 inches (28 cm).
    1 base stake No. 3 cane, 5½ inches (14 cm).
    Bottom waling No. 1 cane, 5 yards (4·5 metres).
    Top and hood waling No. 1 cane, 7 yards (6 metres).
    Randing No. 1 cane, 7 yards (6 metres).
    Trimming—blue and white ribbon about ½ inch (1 cm) wide, 1½ yards
        (138 cm) of each.

Fig. 106 Base for Hunca Munca's cradle

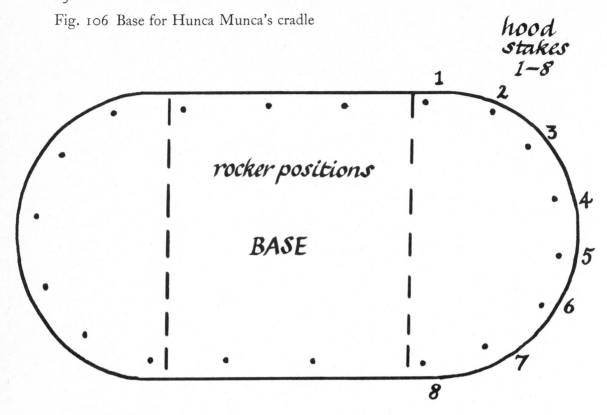

A little white felt to line the base if liked.
Rockers (cut two from Fig. 107). Plywood as for base.

Method

1 FOOTING. This is worked in a different way from the other baskets in order to make the footing less obvious beneath the cradle. Soak the whole of the stakes for a few minutes. Insert the four long ones at the hood end, putting through from the upper side of base, then threading up again through the next hole. Press the loop beneath the base quite flat. Repeat with the other three long stakes. Insert the shorter ones in the same way and the odd single stake is inserted and looped under its neighbour (Plate 20).

2 ROCKERS. I strongly advise the fitting, or at least preparatory fitting of the rockers at this stage. If left till later, you will find the cradle so small that you would need a very small hammer and very small fingers to fix them firmly. The obvious disadvantage of fixing them at this point is that you have to weave with a wobbling base, so you may prefer to simply make the necessary holes for the small nails now and put them in place later.

If you intend to fix the rockers now, then first add the white felt neatening lining. This can be glued on and then trimmed round to fit the edge.

Pierce holes for the nails with the tip of the stabbing awl.

Plate 20 Making the cradle: *left*—the underside of the base; *right*—building up the hood

3 WALING. Work two rounds of waling (Figs. 100a, b, c and d, pages 235–6). Finish off.

4 RANDING. Work fourteen rounds of randing (Fig. 96, page 233). Finish off.

5 TOP WALING. Work two rounds of waling starting at the foot of cradle, and leave the ends of weavers for the next round, which is worked later.

6 BUILDING UP THE HOOD. This is rather like turning the heel of a sock. You work a series of increasings and decreasings. Take a piece of cane, start in the middle of the hood stakes. Number the stakes 1 to 8. Work to Stake 1, * twist the cane in your fingers so that it curls neatly round the stake, turn,

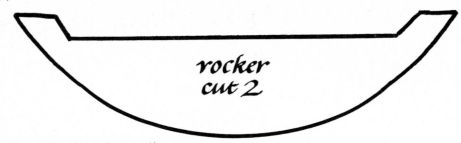

Fig. 107 Rockers for cradle

work to No. 8. Repeat from * working to No. 2 and then to No. 7. Turn and work to No. 3, turn and work to No. 6. You now have four stakes in the middle. Reverse the process, gradually taking in one more stake each row until you reach Nos. 1 and 8 again. Cut off the cane in the centre.

Work another round of waling, taking particular care to press the increasings and decreasings close together. Repeat the operation until the top of the hood is almost at right angles to the sides of the cradle. (The number of rows will depend how closely you are working.) Work a final round of waling and finish off.

7 BORDER. Resoak the remainder of the stakes, then work a border similar to the footing described on page 229 (Fig. 95). Trim.

8 FINISHING. Thread the white ribbon into a darning needle and wrap over and under the border, taking it through the waling. Sew the ends together on inside of cradle. Then wrap the blue ribbon so that some white shows between each wrapping.

You may prefer to leave the cradle unvarnished. It rather depends on the shade of cane you are using. Some of it is so very white that it hardly matches the cradle on page 48 of *The Tale of Two Bad Mice*, and I prefer a slightly creamier look. I think, too, the cradle looks better for a lining of white felt on the wood base.

HUNCA MUNCA'S BIRDCAGE

The birdcage would of course have been a brass one, but you may like to make this one to complete the picture.

Approximate size: height, $5\frac{1}{2}$ inches (14 cm).
            base, $2\frac{1}{2}$ inches (6 cm).

Materials
    1 wood base, $2\frac{1}{2}$ inches (6 cm) diameter with 17 holes (same as Flopsy's) (Fig. 102, page 245).

17 stakes No. 1 cane, 10 inches (26 cm) each.

3 lengths of No. 0 cane, 30 inches (76 cm) each for bottom waling.

1 length of No. 0 cane, 40 inches (102 cm) for fitching.

1 length of No. 0 cane, 90 inches (230 cm) for top pairing.

1 strand of raffia.

1 brass curtain ring about ¾ inch (2 cm) diameter.

A piece of gilt chain (off a broken necklace?) or gold thread 4 inches (10 cm) long.

A little adhesive tape.

Method

1 Prepare stakes (page 226).

2 Work footing (page 229, Fig. 95).

3 Turn base over and work three rounds of waling (pages 233 and 235, Fig. 100a, b, c and d). The stakes are to be kept upright.

4 Fitching (or fetching as it is sometimes referred to in very old basketry books) is worked ¾ inch (2 cm) above the waling. Well-damped cane is necessary. Take a length and making a loop in its centre by twisting the cane, hold it between the finger and thumb of both hands. Slip the loop over one of the stakes and work carefully and firmly (page 234, Fig. 99). Fitching is simply pairing in reverse, the left-hand weaver being taken under instead of over the next. On reaching the starting point, it is necessary to secure the loop. Take one length of cane up through the loop, and the other down, and continue for another round. To finish, keeping the pattern, thread each cane down into the weaving beside two consecutive stakes.

5 Pairing (Fig. 98) is now worked ¾ inch (2 cm) above the last row of fitch. Commence in the same way as for fitching and secure the loop as before. Work firmly but do not draw the stakes in. Work five rows and finish off as before.

6 The stakes are now firmly upright and you need them to bend inwards to form the neck of the cage. It is best to damp the stakes for a minute or two and then tie them together with string and allow to dry in position.

7 While they are drying, prepare the swinging ring. If you have a piece of old necklace chain, undo one of the links and slip the chain through the ring, linking it to the chain again to secure. If you have no chain, a piece of gold thread will do.

8 When the stakes are dry, remove the string and position the stakes so that they lie in a neat circle and do not overlap. Hang the chain in the centre and secure all together with a little adhesive tape. Trim off the ends of the stakes flat except for one which is bent over to form a handle. The adhesive tape is now bound over with raffia, the end of which is threaded into itself to secure.

I personally think the birdcage is best given a coat of clear varnish or polyurethane but this is of course optional.

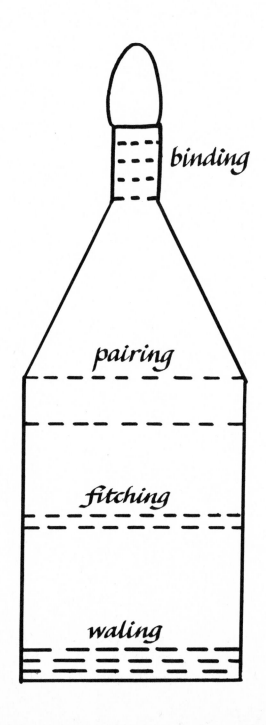

Fig. 108
Outline of
birdcage

Woven Round Bases

COUSIN RIBBY'S VISITING BASKET

I have called this her 'visiting' basket as to me it seems to go so well with her elegant garments, obviously put on to visit her neighbour even though she was only going on the pretext of borrowing some yeast. No doubt she was looking forward to a good gossip. The basket is just the sort one would use to take a specially-made cake, or some tarts or jellies.

On page 15 of *The Tale of Samuel Whiskers* you will see Cousin Ribby at the open door.

The basket perhaps looks difficult. In fact, once the base is made, it is a very easy one. If you follow the plates for the border you should have no trouble at all.

Approximate size: height including handle, 5 inches (13 cm).
base, 4 inch (10 cm) diameter.

Materials
6 base stakes No. 5 cane, 6 inches (15 cm) each.
Approx. 16 yards (14 m) No. 0 for weaving.
Border stakes No 3 cane
6 'A' stakes, 4 inches (10 cm).
6 'B' stakes, $6\frac{3}{4}$ inches (17 cm).
6 'C' stakes, 9 inches (23 cm).
6 'D' stakes, $10\frac{1}{2}$ inches (27 cm).
Handles: 2 pieces of No. 12 cane, 15 inches (38 cm) each. A strand of raffia. A little clear adhesive.

Method
1 Soak the base stakes for 3 minutes. Shake the water off them. Soak the weaving cane for 1 minute and wrap in a damp towel.
2 Use a piece of old board to work on. Hold one stake firmly on the board with

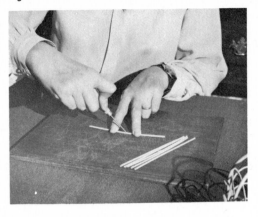

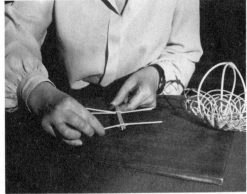

Plate 21 Starting a round base —Cousin Ribby's visiting basket

Plate 22 Sliding the stakes on to form a cross

two fingers (Plate 21). With the point of the bodkin, pierce the centre of the stake, halfway along, push the bodkin through, thus making a small slit.

3 Slide one stake through the slit thus made, then two more beside it.

4 Now pierce the remaining two stakes and slip them on to the others to form a cross (Plate 22 and Fig 109a).

Fig. 109a Cousin Ribby's basket—The cross

Fig. 109b Opening out

5 Take a piece of damped weaving cane and form a loop by twisting it between the fingers to make it pliable. Do this at a point that will give you one length about 6 inches (15 cm) longer than the other, thus avoiding two joins in the same place later on. Pass this loop over one arm of the cross, holding both ends of cane in front of the cross with your left thumb.

6 The base is worked in pairing (Fig. 98), that is, using two weavers alternately, always working with the left hand weaver a stroke at a time. For the first round, the 'pair' is worked over the three stakes of each arm as one, then on the next round, the arms are opened out and paired singly. You may need at first to use the bodkin to press the weaving well down so that the work is neat and closely woven (Plate 23). Continue until the work measures about 1½ inches (3.5 cm) across.

7 Border stakes are now inserted. This is a very small basket and there is quite a strain on the inserted end of the border stakes when the sides are

23

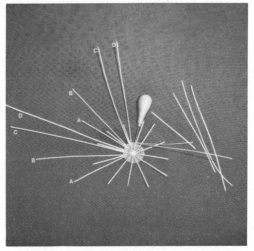

24

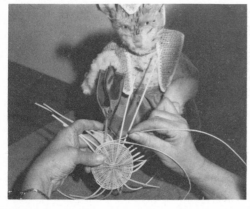

25

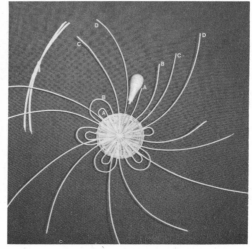

26

27

Plate 23 Opening out—pressing down the weaving with the stabbing awl

Plate 24 Inserting the border stakes —note position

Plate 25 Working the basket on its side to develop the shape

Plate 26 Starting the border—the As and Bs in position

Plate 27 The Bs and Ds in position

drawn up. They are therefore inserted early and a little clear adhesive is a help.

It is important that the 24 border stakes are inserted in the correct order. Sharpen the ends to a slant then dip in the adhesive.

Insert one A stake on the left of a base stake, then one B on the right of the same stake; insert one C and one D on either side of the next stake to the right and so round the base.

Now continue pairing but over the two border stakes and one base stake as one. Work two rounds in this way.

By now the spaces between the sets of stakes will be getting too wide for firmness, therefore the stakes are now separated, working the As and the Cs together with their respective base stakes, and the Bs and Ds singly. Work until the base measures $3\frac{1}{4}$ inches (8 cm).

Add a third weaver in the space beyond the second pairing weaver and work two rounds of waling, resting the base on its side on a table and working in this position. This will help the shape to develop.

8   The border: hold the basket in a bowl of water so that the stakes are well damped. Wrap up for a few minutes in a damp towel. Then 'mould' the stakes over to the left in an arc so that when they are put into position they do not crack. Again slant the ends with a sharp knife and use a little adhesive as each stake is inserted.

Follow Plates 24, 25, 26 and 27 carefully. Damp the border stakes before bending over.

(a) All the As are bent over to the left and the tip inserted on the right of the Ds.

(b) All the Bs are bent over to the left, passed in front of the Ds and inserted on the right of the Cs.

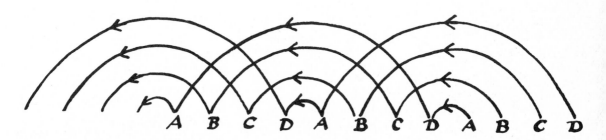

Fig. 110 Diagram of border

    (c) All the Cs are bent over to the left, behind the Ds, in front of next Cs, and beside the Bs.

    (d) All the Ds are bent over to the left, behind the Cs in front of the Bs and beside the As.

9 Handles: make a slanting cut on the ends of the handles and insert one end into the space beside one of the As. The second handle goes in a similar place beside the next A. The other ends of the handles are positioned similarly on the other side of the basket. Tie together at top of arc with a piece of raffia and, making sure the two handles are of even length, wrap the raffia firmly for about 1 inch (2·5 cm) and with the raffia threaded into a needle, run the end back on itself and secure.

    The handle should be pegged as described on page 246 for Flopsy's basket.

10 Finishing: this basket not only looks more 'finished' with a coat of polyurethane, but the coating helps to firm the border and keep it in position. Singe carefully to remove surplus whiskers, then coat.

MRS. TITTLEMOUSE'S BASKET

Study page 24 of *The Tale of Mrs. Tittlemouse* and I think you will agree that her basket is very important to her, and to her character. She is using it as a protective weapon, for I am sure she is as frightened of Mr. Bumble Bee as I am of mice. You will see too why her basket is in the woven base group, for no wood base would satisfy Mrs. Tittlemouse.

But Mrs. Tittlemouse is very small and her basket must be in proportion. This means working with very fine cane and trying to achieve a strong-looking basket at the same time. The picture on page 28 of *The Tale of Mrs. Tittlemouse* shows the basket to have sloping 'shoulders', a very popular shape at one time, often used on egg baskets. There used to be a basket known as the Banbury cake basket of this shape.

Approximate size: height (excluding handle), $1\frac{3}{4}$ inches (4·5 cm).
                    base, $1\frac{1}{2}$ inches (4 cm) diameter.

Materials
    5 base stakes No. 3 cane, $2\frac{1}{2}$ inches (6 cm) each.
    1 length of No. 000 cane for base weaving, 5 feet (1·50 m).
    17 side stakes No. 1 cane, 5 inches (13 cm).
    1 No. 000 cane for side weaving, 10 feet (3·10 m).
    3 lengths of No. 000 cane, 33 inches (84 cm) each for top waling.

Fig. 111a Mrs. Tittlemouse's basket—The cross

cut off

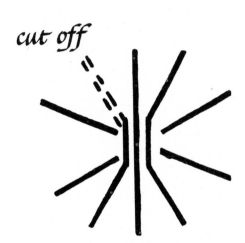

Fig. 111b Removal of one stake

3 lengths of No. 000 cane, 25 inches (64 cm) each for bottom waling.
3 lengths No. 0 cane for handle, 20 inches (51 cm).

Lid
4 stakes No. 0 cane, 2½ inches (6 cm).
1 length of No. 000, 55 inches (140 cm).
16 border stakes No. 000, 4 inches (10 cm).
3 lengths No. 000, 24 inches (61 cm) each for waling.

Plate 28 Mrs. Tittlemouse and her very small basket (note the slope of the shoulders and the plaited handle)

Method

1 Prepare cane for base as described in Cousin Ribby's basket and make the cross in the same way, but putting two stakes through three (Fig. 111a).

2 This base is worked in randing throughout; take the length of base weaving cane, insert one tip in the slit at the side of one arm of cross, take in front of and behind each arm alternately for one round.

3 On the second round open out all the stakes except two which are worked as one for a few rounds, then cut off one stake close to the weaving from this pair (see Fig. 111b), thus making an uneven number of stakes. Continue randing until the work measures $1\frac{1}{2}$ inches (3.5 cm) across, then add a second weaver and work one row of pairing (Fig. 98). Trim off any remaining ends of stakes, close to the weaving.

4 Sides: make a slanting cut on one end of the side stakes and insert into base using a little clear adhesive, insert one stake on either side of every base stake, except one, which will only have one stake in order to make an uneven number of stakes.

5 Insert the three 25-inch weavers between three consecutive stakes and work a round of waling (Fig. 100a, b, c, d, page 235). Soak the stakes right up to the weaving, then with your thumb turn the stakes up sharply to form the edge of the base. Work two more rounds of waling fairly tightly so as to straighten the side stakes. Finish off.

6 With a length of weaving cane work 12 rounds of randing, keeping the sides slightly flowing outwards. Trim off any surplus cane.

   To achieve the 'shoulder' effect, now add the 33-inch weavers and work a round of waling firmly. Then push the stakes inwards and work two more rounds of waling very closely.

7 Border: soak the stakes right up to the waling, then work a simple border in the same manner as a footing, in front of one and behind one.

8 Handle: soak three lengths of No. 0 cane and wrap in damp towel. When really soft, insert each piece from the front of the basket between the 1st and 2nd row of waling, round a stake and out to the front, so that you have six ends in two groups of three. Divide these into three twos and plait, keeping the canes flat. The plait should be 5 inches (13 cm) long and then the canes are inserted into waling on other side of basket and woven away to match.

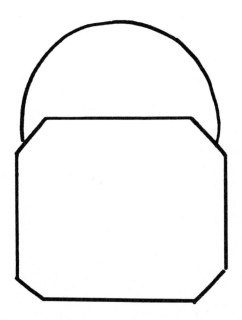

Fig. 112 Outline of basket

9 The lid: this is made similarly to the base except that only a 2 × 2 cross is made. The lid is then paired until it measures ½ inch (1 cm) less than the top of the basket.

10 The border stakes are then inserted, one on either side of the base stakes (a little adhesive is helpful). Now work two rounds of waling. Then the rope border is worked. The lid is then fastened to the basket with a piece of raffia to form a hinge.

Woven Oval Bases

BENJAMIN BUNNY'S MARKETING BASKET

Benjamin Bunny is striding off to his cousin's market garden with his strong-looking basket on his arm, obviously hoping to stock up his larder. (See *The Tale of the Flopsy Bunnies*, page 12.) Nearly all country baskets were made of white or brown willow, but as with the other baskets in this book, we have suggested using cane as it is not easy to obtain small quantities of fine willow.

By using comparatively thick cane, and some willow working methods, one can achieve a 'willow' effect, and a coat of clear varnish will give the basket that mellow sun-burnt look of a much-used basket.

This is an oval basket, with a woven base.

Approximate size: height (excluding handle), about $2\frac{1}{2}$ inches (6 cm)

top, 6×4 inches (15×10 cm).

base, $3\frac{1}{2} \times 2\frac{1}{2}$ inches (9×6 cm).

Materials

3 base stakes No. 5 cane, 5 inches (13 cm) long.

3 base stakes No. 5 cane, 4 inches (10 cm) long.

2 lengths of No. 1 cane for base weaving, approx. 50 inches (125 cm) each.

22 side stakes No. 3 cane, 8 inches (20 cm) long.

22 side weavers No. 1 cane, 12 inches (31 cm) long.

6 lengths of No. 1 cane for top and bottom waling about 48 inches (120 cm) each.

1 piece of No. 12 cane, 12 inches (31 cm) for handle.

10 lengths of No. 1 cane, $15\frac{1}{2}$ inches (40 cm) each for handle.

Method

1 Soak base stakes for 3 minutes; soak weaving cane for 1 minute and wrap in damp towel.

2 Slit the three short base stakes (see Ribby's basket 2 and 3, pages 257–8) and

slip the three long pieces through them. Position the short stakes as shown in Fig. 113.

3 Using No. 1 cane, insert end in space on left-hand side of one end 'arm' of the base, and push down until held by the middle cross stakes.

4 Take the cane over the end arm, in and out of the side stakes, over the other end arm and the other side stakes. Repeat once.

5 Now work another round but this time separating the end arm stakes into singles.

6 Add a second piece of weaving cane so that it comes 'over' where the previous piece has gone 'under'. Let one cane follow the other but never overtake. This second weaver is necessary as in this basket there is an even number of base stakes, and therefore, to achieve the randing effect (Fig. 96) two weavers must be used alternately (page 230). Continue until the weaving measures $3\frac{1}{2} \times 2\frac{1}{2}$ inches (9×6 cm).

7 Trim off remaining ends of base stakes close to edge of weaving.

8 Staking: stand the side stakes in sufficient water to soak to a depth of $1\frac{1}{2}$ inches ($3 \cdot 5$ cm). Soak the waling cane and side weavers for 3 minutes and wrap in damp towel.

9 Insert the damped ends of side stakes beside the base stakes but noting carefully the number of stakes to be inserted as indicated in Fig. 113. Make

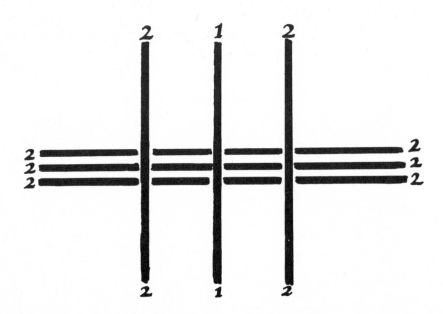

Fig. 113 Benjamin Bunny's basket—number of stakes

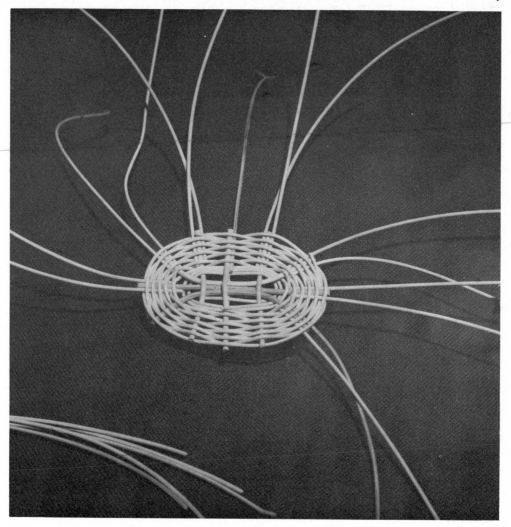

Plate 29 Staking up Benjamin Bunny's basket

a slanting cut on the side stakes in order to make a neat fit when inserted into the base. If there is any difficulty do not force them in but use a soaped bodkin to grease the passage first.

10 Bottom waling: insert the ends of three of the weavers on left-hand side of three of the side stakes, well into the base weaving and work one round of waling (Fig. 100a, b, c, d and e, pages 235–6) with the stakes kept flat. Pin base to block of wood with bodkin.

11 Squeeze the stakes (which should still be damp) with the round-nosed pliers, bend the stakes upwards and work three rounds of waling, at the same time establishing the shape of the basket which should be slightly flowing out at the ends and straight at the sides. Finish off and trim.

12 French weaving: this is introduced for the sides, (a) because it gives a slightly more 'willow' effect, (b) as an added interest to you, and (c) for those who may be able to obtain some willow.

(For the latter you will want 22 'rods' of white willow, as thin as you can get them. And you will commence with the butts (the thick end) which are best cut to a slant.)

French weaving is difficult to illustrate clearly either by photographs or diagrams but Fig. 114 shows you the starting position.

All 22 weavers are inserted round the basket. Then one stroke is made with each weaver in turn to make a complete round. Further rounds are worked until the tips of the weavers are reached:

(a) Take a weaver, lay it between two stakes, with tip inside basket and pointing to the left. * Pass it in front of the stake on the right, behind the next and leave in front.
(b) ** Take a second weaver, lay it between the next stakes to the *left* and repeat from *.
(c) and so on from **, always placing the next weaver to the left of the previous one.
(d) On reaching the starting point, you will appear to have two weavers left over. Look inside the basket and you will see that at the start there are two spaces with no tips of weavers showing. Ease up the first two weavers and you will see the spaces for the last two weavers to enter.

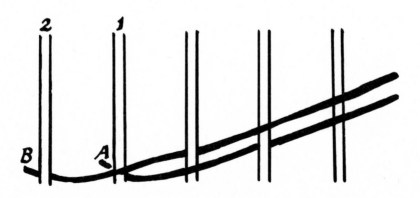

Fig. 114 French weave

You now proceed in a series of rounds. It is as well to mark two stakes where you start the round—you can begin anywhere—so that you will recognise the place. Thus:

(e) Take the first weaver * in front of the next stake behind the next and to the front, thus making a pair of weavers in one space. Clip together with a small clothes peg **.

(f) Take the next weaver to the left and repeat from * to ** making a second pair of weavers. These two pairs are your starting point.

(g) Now continue as before until you reach the starting point, then work the bottom weaver of each pair, thus completing the round. Continue round by round until you reach the tip of any one stake. You then complete that round and trim off any others that may be slightly longer.

N.B. While weaving you also have to keep a watch on the shape of the basket—sloping slightly outward at the ends and upright at the sides.

13 Top waling: with the remaining three lengths of damped cane, work the three rounds of waling (Fig. 100a, b, c, d and e, pages 235–6). Finish off. Make sure the top is level. If not, tap the weaving gently with the edge of a ruler to straighten it.

14 Stand the stakes upside down in water right up to the top waling for 5 minutes.

15 Work a rope border as in Fig. 101a, b and c, pages 239–40.

16 Soak the handle for 15 minutes. Slant the ends.

Using the soaped bodkin, make a passage for the handle cane through the waling and side weaving to the bottom waling on the right-hand side of the centre side stake. Repeat the other side. Insert the handle cane and gently bend it over into an arc and insert on the other side.

Soak the handle wrapping canes for a minute and wrap in damp towel for 5 minutes, while you trim the basket closely inside and out.

Insert four of the canes on the right-hand side of one handle end and four similarly on the other side of the basket. Make sure these weavers all lie flat.

Take one set of four, keeping them flat with thumb and finger, take them behind the basket, up and over the handle (Plate 30) twice, once over the 'bow' of the handle, twice more on the other side and they will spring into place, leaning to the left of the handle in front of basket.

This wrapping will have left a 'lane' for the four from the other side of basket. Repeat the above with these four. You will now probably have a slight gap left. It is not essential to close this 'grinning' gap but it is considered better workmanship if you do. Take one of the spare pieces, insert into base of handle in a place convenient for the empty lane, follow the lane closely and fasten the cane into position beside the others. If necessary add the second spare piece starting from the opposite side.

Plate 30 Twisting the handle canes on Benjamin Bunny's basket

The ends of the wrapping cane are now inserted back through the weaving and woven away into the waling.

17 Finishing: trim and singe (see page 242) carefully. A coating of clear polyurethane will give the basket that sun-baked look that white willow acquires, and a slight shine. All willow baskets get a 'polished' look from constant use.

MRS. TIGGY-WINKLE'S CLOTHES BASKET

A delightful basket to make. And when you have made it you can put it on the corner of your kitchen table and knock it about a little. For the basket on page 39 of *The Tale of Mrs. Tiggy-winkle* looks much-used, often probably overfilled with damp washing, an ample, capacious basket, that a little—just a little—bending out of shape would make much more realistic, though I fear some true craftworkers may find it difficult to bring themselves to take such action.

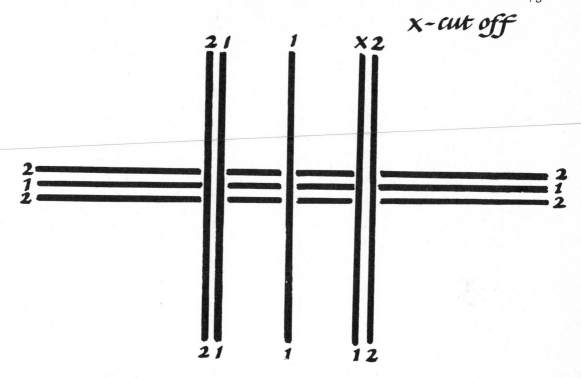

Fig. 115 Mrs. Tiggy-winkle's basket—number of stakes

A clothes basket should, properly, be made of willow, for cane repeatedly damped by wet washing would soon mould, but as for other baskets in this book where we have tried to simulate the realism of Beatrix Potter's drawings, we have had to accept cane for the purpose. I think you will be pleased enough with the effect of this one.

Approximate size: height, $3\frac{1}{4}$ inches (8 cm) including handles.
top, $5\frac{1}{4} \times 4$ inches (13 cm × 10 cm).

Materials

3 base stakes No. 5 cane, 6 inches (15 cm) each.
5 base stakes No. 5 cane, 4 inches (10 cm) each.
2 lengths No. 1 cane for base weaving, approx. 65 inches (165 cm).
23 side stakes No. 1 cane, 9 inches (23 cm) each.
6 lengths No. 1 cane for top and bottom waling, approx. 60 inches (150 cm)
    each.
4 lengths No. 0 cane for slewing, approx. 90 inches (2 metres).
2 pieces No. 5 cane, 7 inches (18 cm) for handles and 2 lengths of No. 1 for
    wrapping, 10 inches (25 cm) each.

Method

1 Prepare base stakes and weaving cane. Slit short stakes and insert long ones as for Benjamin Bunny's basket but positioned as in Fig. 115.

2 This base is randed but as it has no handle across the basket, it is not so necessary to have an even number of base and side stakes. Therefore an uneven number of base stakes is used and only one randing cane will be necessary.

Take a length of No. 1 cane, insert into the slit at the left of one set of three stakes, rand round twice, weaving the two sets of three and the four pairs as one stake each. On the third round, open out the threes and three of the four pairs, but continue working the pair marked x (Fig. 115) as one for another three rounds, then cut one of them away level with the weaving. Continue to rand until the base measures $2\frac{1}{2}$ inches (6 cm) across.

3 Staking: insert the base stakes, following the numbers of stakes to be inserted shown by the numbers on Fig. 115. Slant the stakes to be inserted, at the ends of the basket. Push all down as far as they will go, using soaped bodkin to make a passage if necessary. Work one more round of randing, then trim off the *base* stakes close to edge of weaving.

Plate 31 Slewing the sides of Mrs. Tiggy-winkle's clothes basket

4 Re-damp the stakes and squeezing with round-nosed pliers close to the edge of base, bend them up sharply.

5 Take three lengths of No. 1 cane and insert into base between four stakes. Wale one round. Work now holding the basket on its side and wale more tightly to pull the stakes upright, allowing the end stakes to flow slightly outwards. Work three rounds. Finish off. Pin the base to the block for easier working.

6 The sides are slewed (page 233 and Plate 31). Use four weavers. Watch that the weavers do not get out of position, nor leave gaps between the rows. Work seven rounds and finish off in steps.

7 Lay in three lengths of No. 1 cane and work two rounds of waling firmly.

8 Border: re-damp the stakes and work rope border (page 239, Fig. 101a, b and c).

9 Handles: sharpen both ends of the handle canes. Insert centrally at each end of basket, beside two stakes, leaving two stakes in between. Push down to base.

Take a length of No. 1 cane, insert down the waling beside the right-hand side of the handle, twist over the handle, through waling on other side, twist back again. Repeat once. It is not necessary in this basket to work a tight twist as was done in Benjamin Bunny's basket. Work second handle in similar manner.

10 Finishing: this basket improves with a little 'moulding'. Thoroughly damp the whole basket, then mould it as one might a piece of clay, giving the sides a nice rounded 'bent-out' look, and letting the handles bend in a little as though with much use.

A clothes basket is invariably left in the garden or in Mrs. Tiggy-winkle's case, probably by the hedges and consequently gets sun-baked. A touch of diluted light oak water stain will add to the effect of this basket, or a coating of polyurethane will give it a warm creamy look.

Using Raffia

MRS. TIGGY-WINKLE'S HASSOCK (or footstool)

On page 23 of *The Tale of Mrs. Tiggy-winkle*, you will see that that plump busy little person is standing on a little hassock or footstool, that probably was once a square-cornered shape but through much use, has become rounded. It is likely it was made of soft meadow rushes, found in many districts. You can still find some rush hassocks in country churches. One of these is Brookland Church down on Romney Marsh in Kent, where there are not only rush hassocks, but rush seating in the horse-box pews.

For Mrs. Tiggy-winkle's hassock, however, I suggest that garden raffia is a very good substitute for rushes and rather easier to plait. The treated garden raffia is very pleasant to use and needs no damping.

Approximate size: $4 \times 3\frac{1}{4} \times 1\frac{1}{2}$ inches ($10 \times 8 \times 3 \cdot 5$ cm).

Materials
> About $\frac{1}{4}$ lb (113 grammes) of garden raffia.
> A large-eyed darning needle.
> A piece of foam rubber $3\frac{1}{2} \times 3 \times 1\frac{1}{4}$ inches ($9 \times 7 \cdot 5 \times 3$ cm).

Method
Shake out the bundle of raffia and if it is very creased, hang it or hold it for two or three minutes in the steam of a boiling kettle. This will straighten it and the strands will gradually uncurl. Alternatively, if you have a damp shed or greenhouse, hang it there for a day or so and the raffia will be more usable.

1 Plaiting: take enough strands of raffia (probably about 12) that will make a plait about $\frac{3}{8}$ inch (1 cm) across. Plait firmly and *fatly*, rather than elongated. You will need about 36 inches (90 cm) of plait which is roughly the usual length of raffia. If necessary, add in more strands, leaving the ends sticking out, to be cut off neatly later.

> You will need a second length for the base of the hassock about 27 inches (68 cm) long.

PIGLING Bland and Pig-wig
sitting by the fire on their
coppy stools.

The Tale of Pigling Bland

THIS is a Tale about a tail – a tail
that belonged to a little red squirrel,
and his name was Nutkin.

The Tale of Squirrel Nutkin

2 Sewing: thread a fine piece of raffia into the needle. Unravel about 3 inches (7 cm) of one end of the longer plait and thin to tapered point with scissors. Replait.

Wind the end of the threaded piece of raffia round the tapered end for about $\frac{1}{2}$ inch (1 cm), secure by pushing needle through the plait and trim end of plait close.

Fig. 116 Mrs. Tiggy-winkle's hassock—stitching the plait

Fold back the plait for about $1\frac{1}{4}$ inches (3·5 cm), still using the same thread, and keeping the plait flat, stitch the folded edges together; work the needle back to the starting position and continue to stitch the plait together in an oval (Fig. 116). As you progress, aim at slightly 'squaring' the 'corners' of the oval. When the work measures 3 inches (8 cm) across, it is time to shape the sides. This is done by pulling the plait tightly as you stitch and by stitching the plait on edge. Gradually the sides will stand upright.

Stitch two rounds or until the sides reach the top of the foam rubber cushion when placed inside. You have now worked the top and the sides.

Cut the remainder of the plait, leaving about 1¼ inches (3·5 cm) unstitched. Unravel, taper as before and stitch so that the edge is level.

The base is now started as before, with the shorter plait; stitch until the work fits the under side of the hassock. Taper again and stitch to the sides.

3 Finishing: trim off any stray ends of raffia and very lightly press with a warm iron and damp cloth. A very light coating of polyurethane or clear varnish I think improves and prevents the raffia from becoming tatty.

SQUIRREL NUTKIN'S RUSH BASKET

Nothing could be simpler than the making of Squirrel Nutkin's little egg basket. If you are lucky you may be able to find, in July or August, some soft meadow rushes. Otherwise you can use some coloured Raffene, judiciously mixed to give the greeny-browny look of natural rush.

Approximate size: top, 4 × 2¾ inches (10 × 7 cm).
               depth, 2 inches (5 cm).

Materials

    Soft meadow rushes—very roughly as many as you could span in your two hands.
    Some green button thread or linen thread; needle.
                   or
    Raffene: 1 skein of No. 54 moss green.
            1 skein of No. 47 brown.
            1 skein of No. 33 fawn.
    A large darning needle.

Method

1 Preparations for rushes, see Materials, Tools and Preparation (page 227). Raffene requires no preparation other than cutting into lengths about 60 inches (160 cm) long.
2 Plaiting: this is done as for Mrs. Tiggy-winkle's hassock (page 276).
3 Sewing: this is the same as for the hassock, except that since Raffene is so very springy, it is not easy to taper satisfactorily. Instead, simply wrap the ends together very tightly with a piece of Raffene, thread the end through the needle, and secure before starting to stitch the plait together.

Start tightening up the pull on the plait when the base measures about 2¼ inches (5 cm) across. The sides are then worked to a depth of three plaits.

Again it is not so simple to taper the ends, and these are best woven in pattern into the plait below, keeping the top as level as possible. A little gentle pressing with a warm iron and damp cloth on the nose of the ironing board and then levelling the top with the fingers while the plait is still damp, is all the finishing that is necessary.

MR. JEREMY FISHER'S FISHING CREEL

You have only to look at the curious shape of a traditional fishing creel, with its sloping back and swelling sides, to realise that here is a really difficult basket for any amateur to make, and to try to make one small enough for Mr. Jeremy Fisher is frankly beyond most of us. (See page 19 *The Tale of Mr. Jeremy Fisher*.) Instead I have suggested a very simple way of making this basket. It is a raffia-cum-cardboard model, which if made with care can look very realistic, as you will see in the colour plate opposite page 125.

Materials

Some firm cardboard about 10 × 4 inches (25 × 10 cm).
(Shoe box cardboard or the backing sheet of a writing pad will do, or if thin, two pieces can be cut and glued together to make a firmer foundation.)
Garden raffia or treated garden raffia. One small hank (approx. $\frac{1}{4}$ lb or 113 grammes).
A large-eyed long needle.
A length of thonging leather, or strip of leather cut to about $\frac{1}{8}$ × 18 inches (3 mm × 46 cm).
A ruler, pencil, tracing paper, a very sharp knife (such as a Stanley Knife No. 199), some clear adhesive (Uhu, Bostik clear, Elmer's Glue All, etc.) transparent adhesive tape.
A fine sewing needle and some invisible nylon sewing thread. A few pins.

Method

1 Cutting out: trace the outline of the pattern very carefully (Fig. 117), marking the hinge and strap spots. Transfer the tracing to the cardboard. Cut the cardboard with accuracy, using a ruler and very sharp knife.

2 Wrapping: the pieces are now wrapped with raffia. Take a strand of fairly wide raffia, cut off any rough end, lay it in position (Plate 32) and fasten it to the cardboard with a small piece of adhesive tape. Wind round and round, keeping the raffia flat, adjusting the width to cover the angled sides. Cover with a good thickness of raffia. Thread the end through needle and weave away on wrong side of section.

3 Weaving: each piece is now woven in chequer-board or basket weave

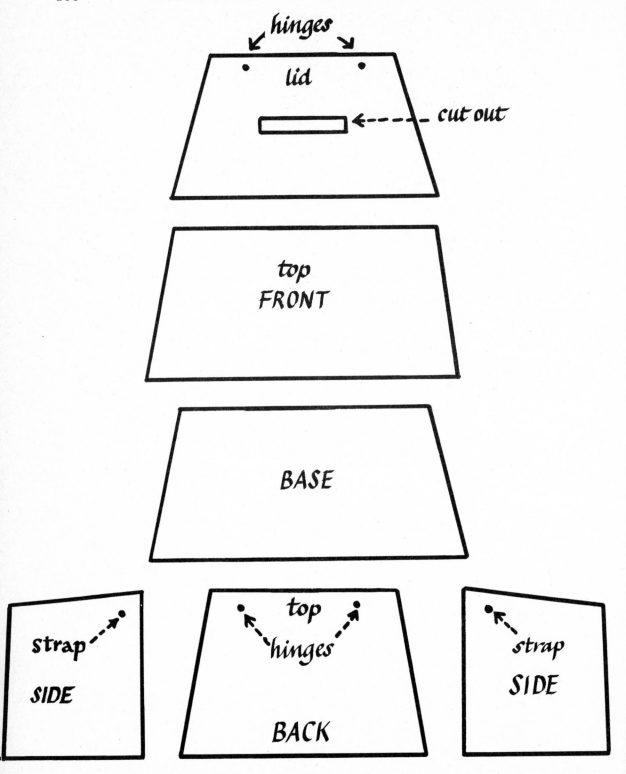

Fig. 117 Pattern for Mr. Jeremy Fisher's fishing creel

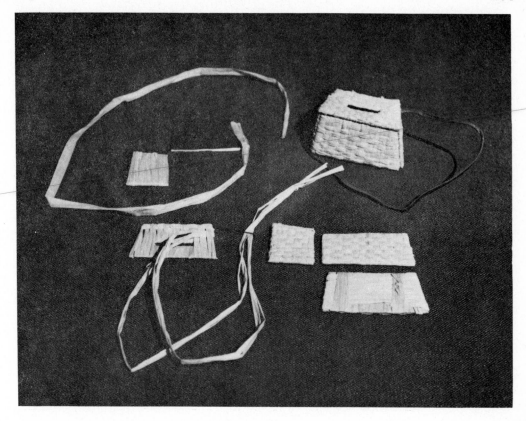

Plate 32 Making Mr. Jeremy Fisher's fishing creel
        Top left to right: one side piece wrapped; the start of the wrapping; the
        finished basket
        Bottom left to right: the weaving of the lid; one side piece and front
        covered showing chequer-board weaving; inside of the front piece

(Plate 32). Take a good piece of raffia, or two pieces if it is rather thin, thread
into needle and start by taking the needle in and out of the back of the work.
Bring to front at top (shorter edge) and pick up small stitches (about $\frac{1}{4}$ inch
(5 mm) each stitch). Make the first and last stitch rather smaller so that as
the work increases the stitches balance out. The raffia has a tendency to twist;
it is better to take one stitch at a time. Keep the amount of raffia picked up as
even as possible. To join in another piece of raffia it is best to tie the old and
new ends together with a reef knot at the back of the work. Finish off by
threading through the back again.

4 The lid: few people can resist opening a lid, so it is as well to neaten this by
   weaving the chequer-board stitch on both sides.

5 Making up: trim off any stray ends or wisps of raffia. Press the weave lightly with a slightly damp cloth and warm iron. Using the sewing needle and invisible thread, the sections are now oversewn together. Commence by holding the back and one side section together and start sewing at the top, making sure they are both level. Oversew to the bottom, then back again and fasten off.

Sew the other side section to the back; then the front section is sewn to the other two sides.

The base can be fixed in with the clear adhesive, but if you should decide to take Mr. Jeremy Fisher to the nearest lake as Margaret Hutchings and I did to take the photographs, he is sure to get his basket wet, when the bottom will probably come out. So I suggest you stick it in with adhesive first, pinning it in position until hard. Then, to make sure, oversew with the invisible thread.

6 Hinges and strap: pierce the holes indicated with the bodkin and thread the thonging through the strap holes. Knot the thonging on the inside of the basket and trim.

For the hinges, thread a piece of raffia and work a loose hinge through both pairs of holes and tie on the inside, or thread away in the weaving.

7 Finishing: a pleasant finish to the basket is a coat of clear gloss polyurethane.

PART THREE
THE FURNITURE
AND ACCESSORIES

General Instructions

All the models have been designed using only the simplest of joints, enabling even the most unskilled to carry out a fair piece of work. Likewise only the simplest of materials are recommended in the texts owing to the difficulty in obtaining authentic woods. It would of course be great fun if, for example, Pig-wig's chair were to be made from solid oak and Appley Dapply's chair from beech. Why not try it!

All the pieces have been designed to be as near to scale as possible with the animals in Part One of the book. When making a model, please note the following:

1 Read right through the instructions, referring to the plans as necessary and make sure you understand them and that you have everything you need before starting work.

2 The small sizes of spruce are all obtainable from any good local model shop and this is easy to carve.

   If you cannot buy this locally, cut down these sizes from small stock sizes of deal or obechi, both being very easy to obtain and easily carved.

3 Substitute any sheet parts of plywood, with solid sheet material wherever possible, as this is much more authentic.

4 Small mortises are simplest made by drilling two holes the width of the tenon in diameter and cutting out the material between the holes with a lino tool or a very sharp penknife.

5 Sand each individual piece of the models with glass-paper before gluing in place.

6 Always use Five Minute Epoxy glue on all the models. There are many brands on the market now which enable you to use a small quantity. It is necessary to hold each piece in place for only a few minutes while the glue sets and you carry on with another piece. It is also remarkably strong.

7 In the text, staining with shoe polish is advised. This is easily applied with a soft rag to all flat areas and with a cocktail stick to reach into small joints and cavities. The whole model can then be brushed carefully but firmly with a

Plate 33 *Left to right:* Pig-wig's and Pigling Bland's coppy stool; Pig-wig's chair; chair for the Old Woman who Lived in a Shoe and Hunca Munca's nursing chair

    shoe brush to give a polish. This is also an excellent, simple method of staining.

8 Instead of tracing the individual pieces from the plan, it is simple to use carbon paper underneath the page and trace with a cocktail stick, if you prefer this method.

PIGLING BLAND'S SIGNPOST

'Pigling Bland went on alone dejectedly; he came to a sign-post...'

Refer to the cover of *The Tale of Pigling Bland*, as well as to the colour plate opposite page 85 of this book.

Materials

    13 inches (33 cm) of $\frac{1}{2}$-inch (13-mm) square spruce.
    12 inches (31 cm) of $\frac{3}{4} \times \frac{1}{8}$-inch (19 × 3-mm) spruce.
    3 inches (8 cm) square of $\frac{1}{4}$-inch (6-mm) plywood.

Method

  1 See plans on pages 298–9 and prepare a 13-inch (33-cm) length of $\frac{1}{2}$-inch

(13-mm) square material and sand all over to a very smooth finish. Mortise three sides of this post where indicated to take $\frac{3}{4} \times \frac{1}{8}$-inch (19 × 3-mm) spruce arms on plan.

2 Cut three pieces of $\frac{3}{4} \times \frac{1}{8}$-inch (19 × 3-mm) material, 4 inches (10 cm) long and sand very smooth. These should be a snug fit in the mortises of the post. Glue these three arms in place, making sure that they make a right angle with both the post and each other.

3 Prepare a 3-inch (8-cm) square of $\frac{1}{4}$-inch (6-mm) material and, as plan, cut out a $\frac{1}{2}$-inch (13-mm) square to take the post. Glue the post in place, making sure that when in place and on a level surface, the post is absolutely vertical.

4 When dry, lightly sand all over and paint all (with the exception of the base) with two coats of white eggshell finish paint. Paint the base with two coats of grassy green paint.

5 Finally, with an oil-based felt tip pen, write on the directions, one on each arm, back and front:
To Market Town 5 miles—Over the Hills 4 miles
To Pettitoes Farm 3 miles

COPPY STOOL FOR PIG-WIG AND PIGLING BLAND

'...*Pigling...sitting on the edge of his coppy stool.*'

Refer to the many pictures in *The Tale of Pigling Bland*, as well as to the colour plate opposite page 276 of this book.

Materials
12 inches (31 cm) of $\frac{1}{2}$-inch (13-mm) square spruce.
At least 3 inches (8 cm) square of $\frac{1}{4}$-inch (6-mm) plywood or spruce sheet.

Method
1 Look at plans on page 300 and draw a 3-inch (8-cm) circle on the piece of sheet wood but do not cut out yet.

2 Trace the position of the three legs within the circle as per plan and then drill out carefully so that the legs will make approximately an 80° angle with the seat, once again as per plan.

3 Cut out and sand smooth the circular seat.

4 Carve the three legs to a very rough circular cross-section as a very old stool would be. Ensure, however, that the section is as near round as possible where the legs enter the seat and then slightly dome their tops as they protrude through the seat approximately $\frac{1}{16}$ inch (2 mm).

5 Glue the three legs in place, manipulating them to be at equal angles to the seat.

6 When dry, polish the whole stool with furniture polish.

PIG-WIG'S CHAIR

Refer to the picture on page 67 of *The Tale of Pigling Bland*, page 28 of *Appley Dapply's Nursery Rhymes*, as well as to the colour plate opposite page 276 of this book.

Materials

> 3 ft (92 cm) of $\frac{1}{2}$-inch (13-mm) square spruce.
> 3 ft (92 cm) of $\frac{3}{8} \times \frac{1}{8}$-inch (10 × 3-mm) spruce.
> 3 ft 10 inches (117 cm) of $\frac{1}{2} \times \frac{1}{8}$-inch (13 × 3-mm) spruce.
> 6 inches (16 cm) of $\frac{3}{8}$-inch (10-mm) square spruce.
> 6 inches (16 cm) square of $\frac{1}{4}$-inch (6-mm) plywood.
> 5 × $1\frac{1}{4}$ inches (13 cm × 32 mm) of $\frac{1}{8}$-inch (3-mm) spruce.

Method

1 Cut out the two back uprights and carve to shape as per plan, pages 302–5. All parts are easily carved with a very sharp penknife and smoothed down with fine glass-paper. Similarly cut out and carve both front legs and the central front stretcher from the appropriate sized woods, leaving an $\frac{1}{8}$-inch (3-mm) square tenon on the ends of the front stretcher as shown on plan.

2 Cut all side, back and the remaining front stretchers remembering the tenons on all pieces. The bottom two side members will now be planed to only $\frac{3}{8}$ inch (10 mm) depth.

3 Trace the top-rail direct from the plan on to the small piece of $\frac{1}{8}$-inch (3-mm) sheet. Cut out and sand smooth.

4 Cut all mortises in both the back and front uprights to receive the tenons of the stretchers. This is done with either an $\frac{1}{8}$-inch (3-mm) drill sunk to the correct depth or may be carved out with a narrow V-shaped lino tool.

5 Place the back uprights on a flat surface, offer up the top-rail and two back stretchers to ensure a snug fit. When satisfied, glue all five pieces in place, make sure all is absolutely square and leave to dry. Repeat this with the front legs and stretchers.

6 When both are dry, remove from building board and offer up three side stretchers to one back upright and glue in place. Repeat this with the other side. Immediately manipulate and glue the front frame in place, make sure all angles are square and leave in place to set, the chair lying on its back.

7 Cut the seat from $\frac{1}{4}$-inch (6-mm) plywood approximately $\frac{1}{16}$ inch (2 mm) oversize and trim to exact size with plane and chisel, taking special care of the fit between the two back uprights. Sand side and front edges to a smooth

round section. Finally, glue in place with a two-pound weight holding the seat firmly in place.

8 The remaining construction consists of cutting the back slats *exactly* to size and gluing in place in their correct alignment.

9 To finish off Pig-wig's chair, stain to simulate 'that old oak look'. If using a proprietary stain, follow the makers' instructions. The original models were stained with shoe polish applied fairly generously with a smooth rag and brushed down with the brown shoe polish brush to that patina, reminiscent of this type of chair. 'Tuxan Oakwood' polish is recommended.

SQUIRREL NUTKIN'S RAFT

'They made little rafts out of twigs . . .'

Refer to the pictures on pages 15 and 31 of *The Tale of Squirrel Nutkin*, as well as to the colour plate opposite page 277 of this book.

Materials
14 pieces of sapling twig approximately $\frac{3}{4}$ inch (19 mm) diameter and 12 inches (31 cm) long.
One small skein of raffia.

Method
1 Look at plan on page 301, place two pieces of twig parallel on a flat surface, lay one other piece on top of these at right angles close to one end and bind in place with raffia on one side only. Repeat this right down one fore and aft member with repeated bindings until twelve pieces are bound tightly. Tie off.

2 Repeat this with another fore and aft member, tying off very tight.

3 The distance between these two fore and aft members should be approximately 9 inches (23 cm).

ANNA MARIA'S WHEELBARROW

'I am sure I never gave her leave to borrow my wheel-barrow!'

Refer to the picture on page 67 of *The Tale of Samuel Whiskers*, as well as to the colour plate opposite page 245 of this book.

Materials
5 × 4 inches (13 × 10 cm) of $\frac{1}{8}$-inch (3-mm) plywood or spruce sheet.
18 × 3 inches (46 × 8 cm) of $\frac{1}{8}$-inch (3-mm) plywood or spruce sheet.

26 inches (66 cm) of $\frac{1}{4}$-inch (6-mm) square spruce.

1 inch (25 mm) of $\frac{1}{4}$-inch (6-mm) hardwood dowel.

3 inches (8 cm) square of $\frac{1}{4}$-inch (6-mm) plywood.

3 inches (8 cm) of 14-gauge piano-wire.

Method

1 Cut out base and four sides of the bin of the wheelbarrow as plan, pages 306–7. Note the slight angles that the sides make with the front, base and back and sand the edges of the latter three to make a good join.

2 Glue the sides and then the back and front to the base with the base on a flat surface and allow to dry.

3 Cut the two chassis members and two legs from $\frac{1}{4}$-inch (6-mm) spruce and make a half lap-joint where the legs join the chassis members.

4 Place the two chassis members on a flat surface, toed in towards their front as plan and glue the now dry completed bin directly on top in line with the bottom sides, the half lap-joints facing inwards.

5 Trace the outline of the wheel on to the small piece of $\frac{1}{4}$-inch (6-mm) plywood, cut out all material between the spokes and finally cut out round the perimeter. Sand to a smooth finish. Cut two discs $\frac{1}{2}$ inch (13 mm) diameter of $\frac{1}{8}$-inch (3-mm) plywood, sand smooth and glue one either side in the centre of the wheel. For the axle, drill a $\frac{1}{16}$-inch (2-mm) hole through the centre of this assembly.

6 Mount a short length of $\frac{1}{4}$-inch (6-mm) hardwood dowelling in the vice and drill a $\frac{1}{16}$-inch (2-mm) hole down grain-wise at least 1 inch (25 mm). Cut two pieces from the end of the dowel $\frac{1}{2}$ inch (13 mm) long.

7 Take the complete chassis and bin, mount the handles in the vice and drill another $\frac{1}{16}$-inch (2-mm) hole through the front to take the axle, noting as drilling, the angle made with the chassis members.

8 Thread a $1\frac{7}{8}$-inch (47-mm) length of 14-gauge wire through first one side chassis member then one piece of dowel, the wheel assembly, the other dowel and finally through the other chassis side. A small blob of epoxy glue on its ends will hold the axle in place.

9 Offer up and glue the legs at their half lap-joint, allowing them to splay slightly out at the bottom.

10 Leave overnight to thoroughly dry and stain the whole wheelbarrow with Tuxan Avocado Shoe polish with the exception of the wheel rim, which is stained black.

A CHAIR FOR THE OLD WOMAN WHO LIVED IN A SHOE

Refer to the picture on page 24 of *Appley Dapply's Nursery Rhymes*, as well as to the colour plate opposite page 224 of this book.

Materials

24 inches (61 cm) of $\frac{1}{8}$-inch (3-mm) hardwood dowel.

8 inches (21 cm) of $\frac{1}{4}$-inch (6-mm) hardwood dowel.

3 inches (8 cm) of $\frac{1}{4}$-inch (6-mm) birch or spruce.

$3\frac{1}{2}$ inches (9 cm) of $\frac{1}{2}$-inch (13-mm) square spruce.

Method

1 Look at plan on page 308 and cut out seat from $\frac{1}{4}$-inch (6-mm) sheet material, drill four $\frac{1}{8}$-inch (3-mm) holes in back, $\frac{1}{8}$ inch (3 mm) deep as plan, to take the uprights.

2 Carve top from $\frac{1}{2}$-inch (13-mm) square spruce with a very sharp penknife and also drill four $\frac{1}{8}$-inch (3-mm) holes in the bottom, once again $\frac{1}{8}$ inch (3 mm) deep to take the uprights. When drilling, note the slight angle the uprights make with both the seat and the top.

3 Cut the four legs to the length shown on plan and note the angles at which the ends must be cut.

4 Mark on all the legs the positions of the entry of the stretchers and very carefully noting the angle they make with the legs, drill $\frac{1}{8}$-inch (3-mm) holes $\frac{1}{8}$ inch (3 mm) deep in the legs to take these stretchers.

5 Cut out all stretchers from $\frac{1}{8}$-inch (3-mm) dowel.

6 Cut out all uprights from $\frac{1}{8}$-inch (3-mm) dowel.

7 Drill out, as plan, the $\frac{1}{4}$-inch (6-mm) holes to take the legs in the underneath of the seat, $\frac{1}{8}$ inch (3 mm) deep.

8 Attempt to assemble the whole chair without glue and adjust any piece as necessary.

9 When satisfied, sand all pieces with fine sandpaper to a very smooth finish and glue in place with quick epoxy glue, holding in place until set.

10 Leave overnight for glue to harden completely and after a final very light sanding with flour paper, polish with furniture polish.

HUNCA MUNCA'S NURSING CHAIR

'... *Hunca Munca went back and fetched a chair* ...'

Refer to the illustration on page 48 of *The Tale of Two Bad Mice*, as well as to the colour plate opposite page 225 of this book.

Materials

6 × 3 inches (15 × 8 cm) of $\frac{1}{8}$-inch (3-mm) spruce sheet or plywood.

9 × 1 inch (23 cm × 25 mm) of $\frac{1}{4}$-inch (6-mm) spruce sheet.

12 inches (31 cm) of $\frac{1}{4}$-inch (6-mm) square spruce.

Method

1 Trace two back legs from plan (page 310) onto sheet of ¼-inch (6-mm) spruce and cut out. Cut out the two seat bearers and the two front legs and make a middle lap-joint between the back legs and the seat bearers and an end lap-joint between the front legs and seat bearers as plan.

2 Glue the three pieces for one side in place (flat over plan) and allow to dry. Repeat this for the other side and allow to dry.

3 Cut the seat exactly as pattern, sand to a very smooth finish and glue in place on the two seat bearers to fit exactly between the two back legs, making sure that these are absolutely vertical.

4 Cut the back very slightly oversize horizontally: with a fret saw cut out a small heart as indicated: with a sheet of medium glass-paper placed on a flat surface, sand the edges of the back to and fro until a tight fit is reached between the back legs. Sand the back to a smooth finish and glue exactly in place.

5 Cut both front and back top-rails exactly to size and glue in place.

6 Sand the whole chair lightly with fine glass-paper and then flour paper and finally polish with furniture polish.

COUSIN RIBBY'S UMBRELLA HANDLE

'. . . *they poked under the beds with Ribby's umbrella* . . .'

Refer to the picture on page 15 of *The Tale of Samuel Whiskers*, as well as to the colour plate opposite page 124 of this book.

Materials

7½ inches (19 cm) of ¼-inch (6-mm) hardwood dowel.
2 inches (5 cm) of ½-inch (13-mm) square spruce.

Method

1 Look at plan on page 300, cut a 7½-inch (19-cm) length of ¼-inch (6-mm) diameter hardwood dowel and sharpen one end with a pencil sharpener.

2 Take a short length of ½-inch (13-mm) square spruce, mount in the vice and drill a ¼-inch (6-mm) hole grain-wise through the core to a depth of ½ inch (13 mm).

3 Remove from vice and carve a knobbly pattern on the same end as the hole, approximately 1 inch (25 mm) long. Sand smooth and finally cut off at this length of approximately 1 inch (25 mm).

4 Insert the blunt end of the handle into the ¼-inch hole in the knob and glue in place.

5 Sand all to a very smooth finish and polish with furniture polish.

MRS. TIGGY-WINKLE'S IRONING TABLE

'...*at the table, with an iron in her hand stood a very short, stout person* ...'

Refer to page 23 of *The Tale of Mrs. Tiggy-winkle*, as well as to the colour plate on the back cover and jacket of this book.

Materials

> 8 × 4 inches (21 × 10 cm) of $\frac{1}{8}$-inch (3-mm) birch plywood.
> 12 inches (31 cm) of $\frac{1}{2}$-inch (13-mm) square spruce.
> 19 inches (48 cm) of $\frac{1}{2}$ × $\frac{1}{8}$-inch (13 × 3-mm) spruce.

Method

1 Look at plan on page 309 and prepare a perfect 8 × 4 inch (203 × 101 mm) rectangle of $\frac{1}{8}$-inch (3-mm) birch plywood for the table top by sanding very smooth.
2 Cut four legs exactly $2\frac{7}{8}$ inches (73 mm) long from $\frac{1}{2}$-inch (13-mm) square spruce. Mortise the top of the legs $\frac{1}{4}$ inch (6 mm) deep to take $\frac{1}{2}$ × $\frac{1}{8}$-inch (13 × 3-mm) longitudinal members on only one side.
3 Build two end frames over plan using these mortises and allow to dry.
4 On underside of table top, mark out where these end frames will be fitted and glue both perpendicularly in place.
5 Cut the two longitudinal members from $\frac{1}{8}$ × $\frac{1}{2}$-inch (3 × 13-mm) spruce to be a snug fit between legs and glue in place.
6 Sand smooth and polish with furniture polish.

MRS. TIGGY-WINKLE'S CLOTHES-HORSE

'*Then she took something else off a clothes-horse* ...'

Refer to the picture on page 28 of *The Tale of Mrs. Tiggy-winkle*, as well as the colour plate on the back cover and jacket of this book.

Materials

> 54 inches (137 cm) of $\frac{3}{8}$-inch (10-mm) square spruce.
> 54 inches (137 cm) of $\frac{3}{8}$ × $\frac{1}{8}$-inch (10 × 3-mm) spruce.
> 12 inches (31 cm) of $\frac{5}{16}$-inch (8-mm) tape or webbing.
> 64 × $\frac{1}{4}$-inch (6-mm) brass pins.
> Balsa cement.

Method

1 Cut six pieces of $\frac{3}{8}$-inch (10-mm) square spruce exactly 8 inches (203 mm) long and sand smooth.

2 Mortise one side of each of the above uprights as per plan (page 311) to take the $\frac{3}{8} \times \frac{1}{8}$-inch (10 × 3-mm) cross members to a depth of $\frac{1}{8}$ inch (3 mm).

3 Cut nine pieces of $\frac{3}{8} \times \frac{1}{8}$-inch (10 × 3-mm) spruce exactly $5\frac{1}{2}$ inches (140 mm) long and ensure that their ends are a snug fit in the uprights and that the total width of the clothes-horse is exactly 6 inches (152 mm).

4 On a piece of scrap paper, draw an exact rectangle 8 × 6 inches (203 × 152 mm) and over this, construct three frames from two uprights and three cross members each, simply by gluing and placing a heavy weight on top, to ensure all is flat. When dry, remove from paper.

5 The three frames must now be joined with $\frac{5}{16}$-inch (8-mm) tape or webbing. Take the middle frame only and as shown on plan, cement four strips of tape or webbing $1\frac{1}{2}$ inches (37 mm) long to the front of the frame and then, immediately below but on the reverse side, a further four strips of material.

6 Using balsa cement these will soon be dry. Take one of the other frames and lay flat beside the centre frame. Take the two lower pieces of hinge, draw them up between the join of the two uprights on to the top of the bare frame and cement in place. Similarly, when dry, turn over and draw the two remaining pieces through the join and cement in place on the opposite top side. Take care that no cement reaches any of the material directly between the uprights when laid on flat surface.

7 Repeat with the third frame.

8 For authenticity, put four $\frac{1}{4}$-inch (6-mm) pins with fairly large heads through the hinges on front and back, it being assumed that these are holding the hinges in place. If made correctly, the clothes-horse will hinge in any way.

MRS. TIGGY-WINKLE'S IRON

'. . . she fetched another hot iron from the fire.'

Refer to the pictures on pages 27 and 31 of *The Tale of Mrs. Tiggy-winkle*, as well as to the colour plate on the back cover and jacket of this book.

Materials

2-inch (5-cm) square of $\frac{1}{8}$-inch (3-mm) spruce or plywood.
2-inch (5-cm) square of $\frac{1}{4}$-inch (6-mm) spruce or plywood.
4 inches (10 cm) of 14-gauge piano-wire.

Method

1 Carve the bottom half of the iron from $\frac{1}{8}$-inch (3-mm) material and sand to a very smooth finish (see plan on page 309).

2 Carve the top half of the iron from $\frac{1}{4}$-inch (6-mm) material and sand to a

very smooth finish. This will be approximately $\frac{1}{16}$ inch (2 mm) less in dimensions than the lower half.

3 Glue these two pieces together and allow to dry.

4 From 14-gauge piano-wire, bend the handle to shape as plan, allowing approximately $\frac{1}{4}$ inch (6 mm) extra to enter the iron body. Drill the complete iron to accept the handle with two $\frac{1}{16}$-inch (2-mm) holes as plan, $\frac{1}{4}$ inch (6 mm) deep.

5 Introduce a small amount of glue to these holes and press the handle in place.

6 Paint the whole iron with matt black paint and finally glue a sliver of silver-foil to the base, trimming off with a razor blade, or paint with aluminium paint.

'We must send for John Joiner at once, with a saw.' (*The Tale of Samuel Whiskers*)

THE PLANS

total length 13"

PIGLING BLAND'S SIGNPOST

base

300

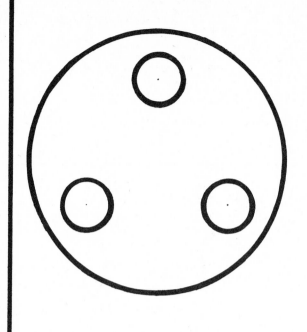

COUSIN RIBBY'S UMBRELLA HANDLE

COPPY STOOL
for PIG-WIG and PIGLING BLAND

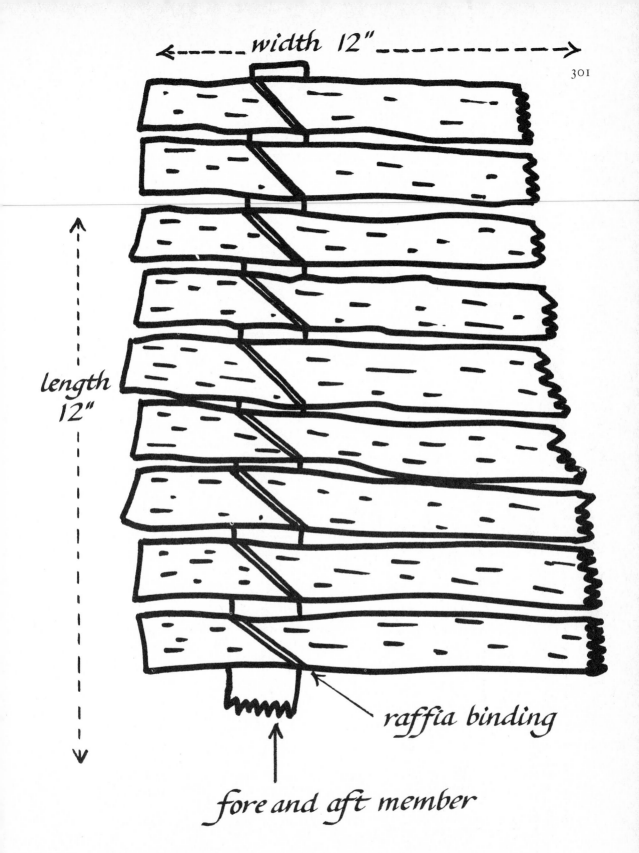

width 12"

length 12"

raffia binding

fore and aft member

SQUIRREL NUTKIN'S RAFT

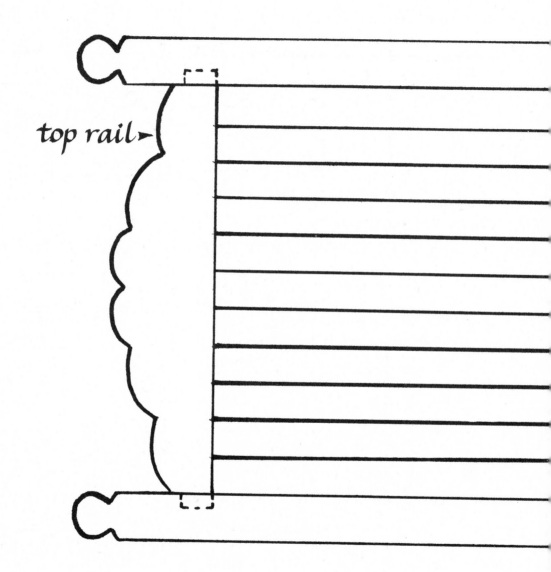

top rail ►

PIG-WIG'S CHAIR

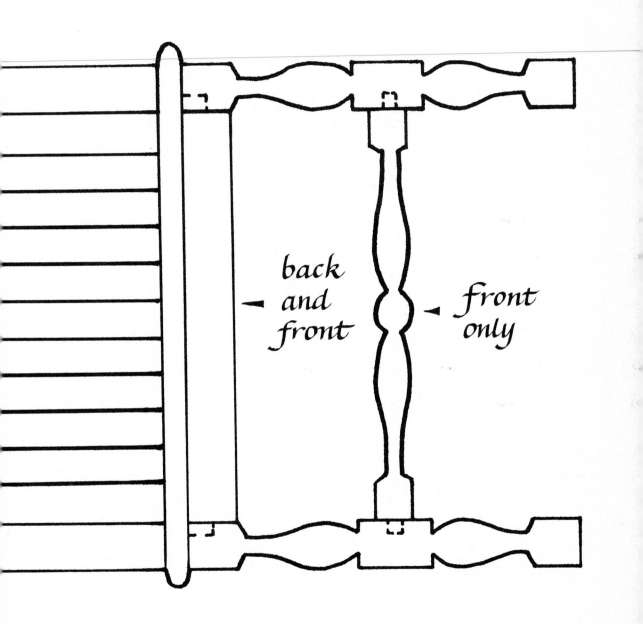

back
and
front

front
only

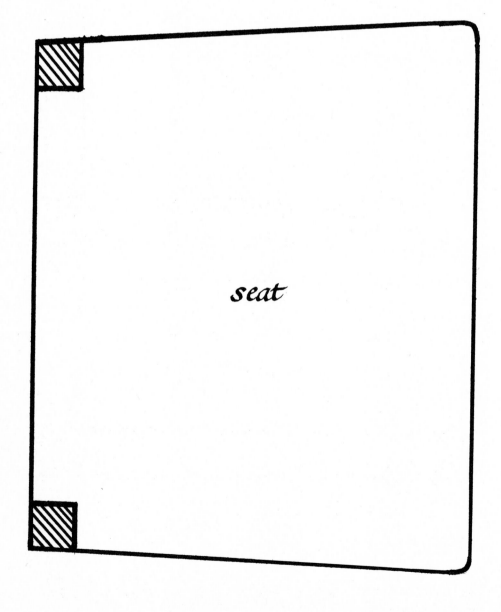

seat

305

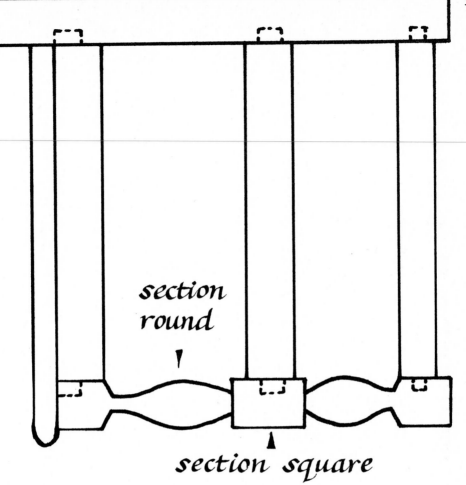

section
round

section square

back central stretcher

PIG-WIG'S CHAIR

front

back

307

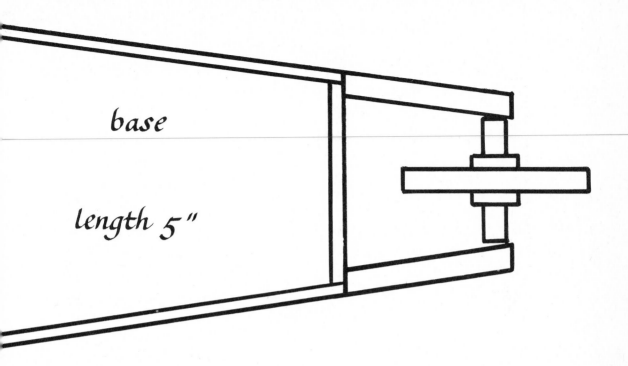

base

length 5"

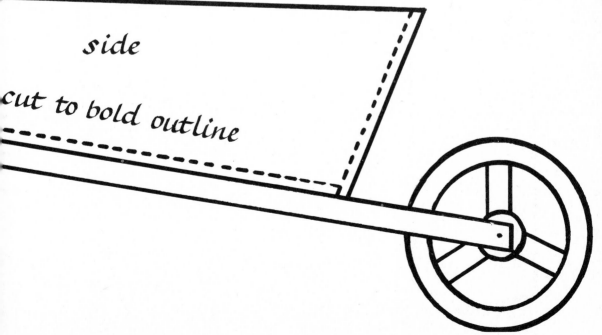

side

cut to bold outline

ANNA-MARIA'S WHEELBARROW

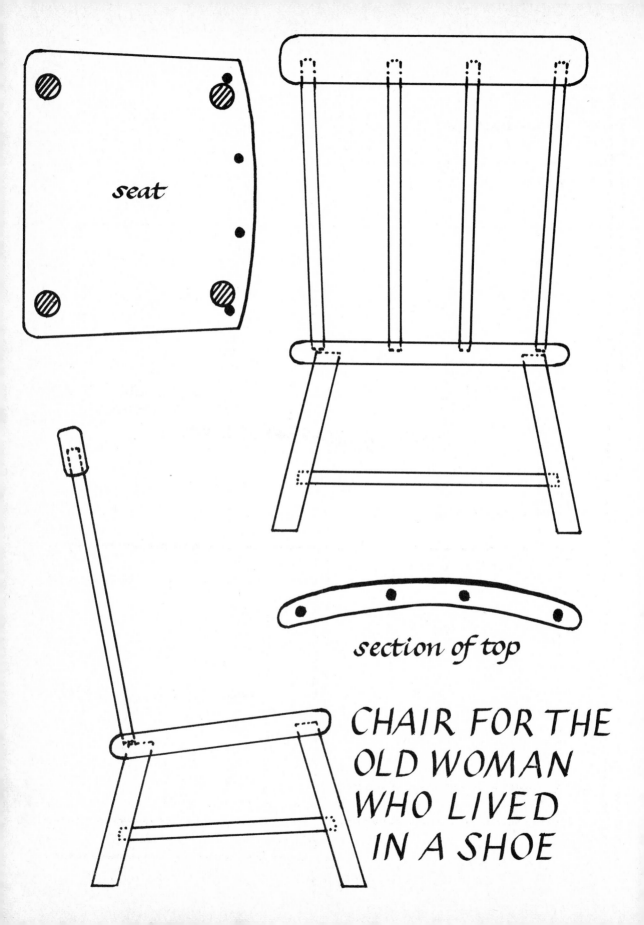

seat

section of top

CHAIR FOR THE
OLD WOMAN
WHO LIVED
IN A SHOE

MRS TIGGY-WINKLE'S IRONING TABLE

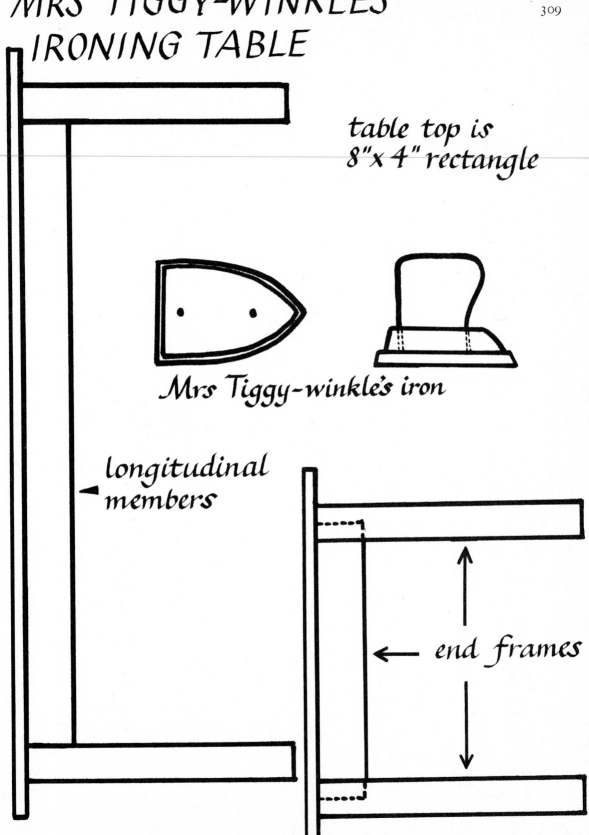

table top is
8"x 4" rectangle

Mrs Tiggy-winkle's iron

longitudinal
members

end frames

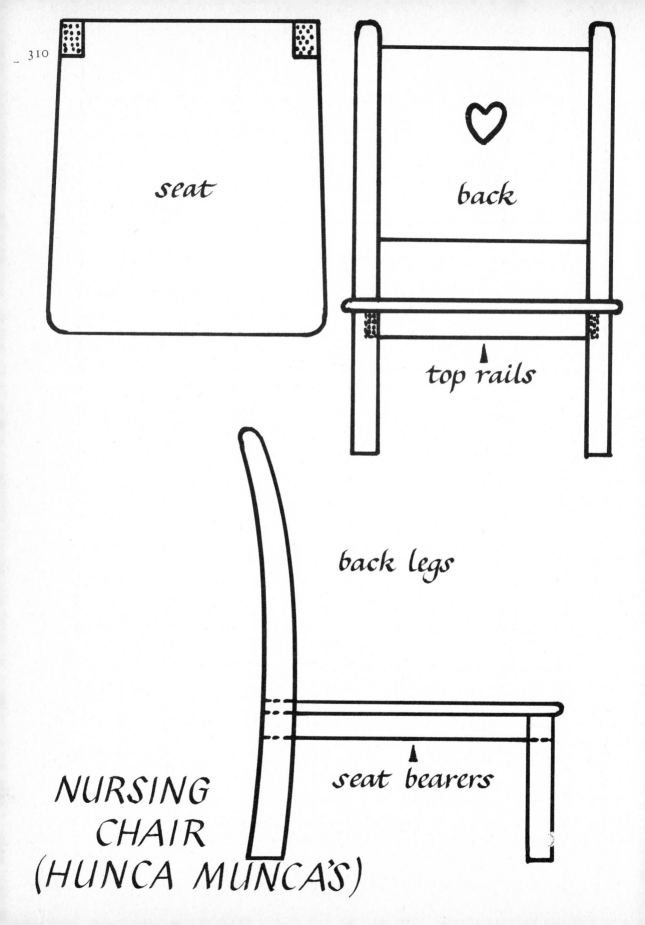

310

seat

back

top rails

back legs

seat bearers

NURSING
CHAIR
(HUNCA MUNCA'S)

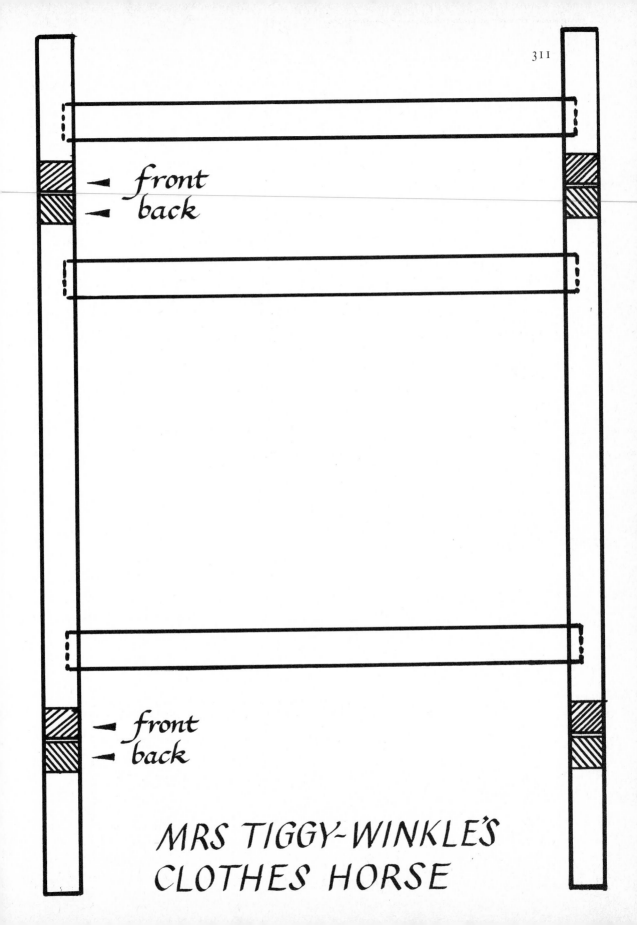

front
back

front
back

MRS TIGGY~WINKLE'S
CLOTHES HORSE

List of Plates

314

TALE PIECE

What fun we've had doing this and now it's all over we laugh and remember:

The petrified face of the milkman as he plodded up the garden path to find a woman flat on her stomach roaring 'Stay where you are', (her camera looking like a machine gun) as his shadow threatened to engulf her picture of Ribby in the doorway.

The way his face lit up when we tried to explain and it dawned on him that he had unknowingly been bringing milk to Beatrix Potter herself (he's very deaf, bless him).

The embarrassed sidelong glances of passers-by as they tried not to notice Anna Maria pushing her wheelbarrow up our village street. (They might just as well have joined in the fun.)

Anne's face when she stumbled upon me making Tom Kitten into a roly-poly pudding with a real suet crust—her hasty retreat and her decision not to stay to lunch.

The couple I disturbed in the fields whilst picking up feathers to use as an experiment for Mrs. Tiggy-winkle's quills—*He:* 'Are you going to stuff your own pillows?' *Me:* 'Yes.' *She:* 'Take no notice of her, she's queer—always round here picking things up, probably out on parole.'

Eve, with one eye on a Flopsy Bunny, dreamily remarking how delicious the lettuce jelly was—Never again do I slave to make her a refreshing concoction of lime and fresh grapefruit.

The face of the little girl who on learning that Jeremy Fisher was actually staying in London with Eve, enquired if he made the house very wet and whether she gave him butterfly sandwiches for tea.

It had to end *sometime*—more's the pity. Miss Potter created so many animals, carrying so many baskets, sitting on so many chairs that we could have kept on and on and ON. When we thought the book was large enough we just had to *stop* and here we are at

The End